RECENT ECONOMIC THOUGHT SERIES

Editors:

Warren J. Samuels
Michigan State University
East Lansing, Michigan, USA

William Darity, Jr.
University of North Carolina
Chapel Hill, North Carolina, USA

Other books in the series:

Magnusson, Lars: MERCANTILIST ECONOMICS
Garston, Neil: BUREAUCRACY: THREE PARADIGMS
Friedman, James W.: PROBLEMS OF COORDINATION IN
 ECONOMIC ACTIVITY
Magnusson, Lars: EVOLUTIONARY AND NEO-SCHUMPETERIAN
 APPROACHES TO ECONOMICS
Reisman, D.: ECONOMIC THOUGHT AND POLITICAL THEORY
Burley, P. and Foster, J.: ECONOMICS AND THERMODYNAMICS:
 NEW PERSPECTIVES ON ECONOMIC ANALYSIS
Brennan, H.G. and Waterman, A.C.: ECONOMICS AND RELIGION:
 ARE THEY DISTINCT?
Klein, Philip A.: THE ROLE OF ECONOMIC THEORY
Semmler, Willi.: BUSINESS CYCLES: THEORY AND EMPIRICS
Little, Daniel: ON THE RELIABILITY OF ECOONOMIC MODELS:
 ESSAYS IN THE PHILOSOPHY OF ECONOMICS
Weimer, David L.: INSTITUTIONAL DESIGN
Davis, John B.: THE STATE OF THE INTERPRETATION OF KEYNES
Wells, Paul: POST-KEYNESIAN ECONOMIC THEORY
Hoover, Kevin D.: MACROECONOMETRICS:
 DEVELOPMENTS, TENSIONS AND PROSPECTS
Kendrick, John W.: THE NEW SYSTEMS OF NATURAL ACCOUNTS
Groenewegen, John: TRANSACTION COST ECONOMICS AND BEYOND
King, J.E.: AN ALTERNATIVE MACROECONOMIC THEORY
Schofield, Norman: COLLECTIVE DECISION-MAKING: SOCIAL CHOICE
 AND POLITICAL ECONOMY
Menchik, Paul L.: HOUSEHOLD AND FAMILY ECONOMICS
Gupta, Kanhaya L.: EXPERIENCES WITH FINANCIAL LIBERALIZATION

Race, Markets, and Social Outcomes

Edited by

Patrick L. Mason
Associate Professor of Economics
University of Notre Dame

and

Rhonda Williams
Associate Professor of Afro-American Studies
University of Maryland at College Park

Kluwer Academic Publishers
Boston / Dordrecht / London

Distributors for North America:
Kluwer Academic Publishers
101 Philip Drive
Assinippi Park
Norwell, Massachusetts 02061 USA

Distributors for all other countries:
Kluwer Academic Publishers Group
Distribution Centre
Post Office Box 322
3300 AH Dordrecht, THE NETHERLANDS

Library of Congress Cataloging-in-Publication Data

Race, markets, and social outcomes / edited by Patrick L. Mason and
   Rhonda Williams.
      p.   cm. -- (Recent economic thought series ; 54)
      Includes bibliographical references and index.
      ISBN 0-7923-9893-9 (alk. paper)
      1. Race relations--Economic aspects. 2. Afro-Americans--Economic
conditions. 3. Afro-American businesspeople. 4. Entrepreneurship--
United States. 5. Wages--United States. 6. Discrimination in
employment--United States. 7. Crime--Economic aspects--United
States. 8. Medical care--United States. I. Mason, Patrick L.
II. Williams, Rhonda Michèle. III. Series.
HT1531.R33   1997
305.8'00973--dc21   97-7145
                                                                   CIP

Printed on acid-free paper

Printed in the United States of America

CONTENTS

CONTRIBUTING AUTHORS

Timothy Bates is professor of labor and urban affairs at Wayne State University. His most recent book, *Banking on Black Enterprise*, was published by the Joint Center for Political and Economic Studies in 1993. His next book, *Illusive American Dream: Self-Employment Among African Americans and Asian Immigrant Americans*, is forthcoming from Johns Hopkins University Press in 1997. Professor Bates is a consultant to various government agencies, including the Civil Rights Division of the U.S. Department of Justice and the U.S. General Accounting Office.

Gary A. Dymski is associate professor of economics at the University of California, Riverside. He has also taught at the University of Southern California. He was a Research Fellow in Economic Studies at the Brookings Institutions in 1985–86 and taught at the Bangladesh Institute for Development Studies in summer 1992. He has written numerous articles on banking and monetary theory, financial and urban policy, Post Keynesian economics, racial inequality and discrimination, and exploitation. He is a co-author of the 1991 study, *Taking it to the Bank: Poverty, Race, and Credit in Los Angeles*. He co-edited the 1993 book, *Transforming the U.S. Financial System: Equity and Efficiency for the 21st Century* (M.E. Sharpe), with Gerry Epstein and Robert Pollin, and was co-editor with Robert Pollin of the 1994 book, *New Directions in Monetary Macroeconomics: Essays in the Tradition of Hyman P. Minsky* (University of Michigan Press). Professor Dymski is a Research Associate of the Economic Policy Institute, and a member of the editorial boards of the *International Review of Applied Economics* and *Geoforum*.

Kwabena Gyimah-Brempong is Professor of Economics at the University of South Florida, Tampa. Prior to coming to USF, he was Professor of Economics at Wright State University, Dayton, OH. Professor Gyimah-Brempong has published numerous articles in a wide variety of refereed professional journals. His most recent publications include "Explaining the Wage Gaps Between White and Minority Males: Human Capital Versus Race," *Applied*

Economics (forthcoming); "Political Instability and Savings in Less Developed Countries: Evidence from Sub-Saharan Africa," *Journal of Development Studies* (1996), and "The Effects of Race on the Utilization of Physicians' Services," *International Journal of Health Services Research* (1996). Professor Gyimah-Brempong's research interests include the economics of crime, labor market discrimination, production of public services, and economic development of Sub-Saharan Africa.

David R. Howell is associate professor and chair, urban policy analysis and management, New School for Social Research. Professor Howell's research focuses on labor markets and urban economic development. His recent publications have explored the implications of labor market segmentation and the adoption of advanced production techniques for employment, skills, and earnings. He is currently studying the effects of employment restructuring and immigration on the economic status of African-American and native-born Hispanic workers in large metropolitan areas.

Wilhelmina Leigh is senior research associate at the Joint Center for Political and Economic Studies in Washington, D.C.. She specializes in policy research in the areas of health and housing. Prior to her employment at the Joint Center in 1991, she was a principal analyst at the U.S. Congressional Budget Office and had worked for the Bureau of Labor Statistics (U.S. Department of Labor), the U.S. Department of Housing and Urban Development, the Urban Institute, and the National Urban League Research Department. Dr. Leigh also has taught at Harvard University, Howard University, the University of Virginia, and Georgetown University. Her most recent publications include: a report on "The Health Status of Women of Color," which also appears as a chapter in *The American Woman (1994–1995) Where We Stand: Women and Health* (1994), a chapter on "The Health of African American Women" in the book *Health Issues for Women of Color: A Cultural Diversity Perspective* (1995), and a chapter in the 1996 issue of *The State of Black America* on "U.S. Housing Policy in 1996: The Outlook for Black Americans."

Patrick L. Mason is associate professor of economics at the University of Notre Dame. His research and teachings interests include labor market discrimination and inequality, the economics of family formation and transitions, globalization and labor, labor law reform, unemployment, and African American studies. His publications have appeared in the *Cambridge Journal of Economics*, *Review of Black Political Economy*, *Journal of Quantitative Economics*, and other refereed journals. His current research focuses on race, skill, and intertemporal wage changes since 1968.

Samuel L. Myers, Jr. is the Roy Wilkins Professor of Human Relations and Social Justice at the Hubert H. Humphrey Institute of Public Affairs, University of Minnesota. Professor Myers is a specialist in the impacts of social policies on the poor. He has pioneered in the use of applied econometric techniques to examine racial disparities in crime, to detect illegal discrimination in credit markets, to assess the impacts of welfare on family stability, and to evaluate the effectiveness of government transfers in reducing poverty. His most recent publications include: "The Effect of Commute Time on Racial Earnings' Inequality" (with Lisa Saunders), *Applied Economics* (1996), "Racial Differences in Home Ownership and Home Equity Among Pre-Retirement-Aged Households" (with Chanjin Chung), *The Gerontologist* (1996), *The Black Underclass: Critical Essays on Race and Unwantedness* (with William A. Darity, Jr., William Sabol, and Emmett Carson), Garland Press, 1994; "Who Benefits from Minority-Business Set-Asides? The Case of New Jersey," Journal of Policy Analysis and Management (1996); "Racial Discrimination in Housing Markets: Accounting for Credit Risk," with Tsze Chan, *Social Science Quarterly* (1995); "Family Structure and the Marginalization of Black Men: Policy Implications," in M. Belinda Tucker and Claudia Mitchell-Kernan, editors, *The Decline in Marriage Among African Americans*, Russell Sage/UCLA Press, 1995.

William M. Rodgers, III is assistant professor of economics, The College of William and Mary. His primary research is in labor economics; however, he has written in public finance and development. Professor Rodgers has published articles in *World Development, Public Finance Quarterly, The American Economic Review Papers and Proceedings*, and has work forthcoming in the *Review of Black Political Economy* and *Industrial and Labor Relations Review*. Professor Rodgers has also testified before the Joint Economic Committee of the United States Congress on raising the federal minimum wage. During the 1995–96 academic year, he worked as a Consultant to Labor Secretary Reich's Chief Economist.

William Spriggs is a senior economist for the Minority Staff of the Joint Economic Committee for the U.S. Congress. There he performs research on the likely effects of policy on the wages and hours of American workers, and assists in preparing background material and offering expert advice to Democrats in Congress. Dr. Spriggs was brought onto the JEC by Kweisi Mfume in October 1994. Previously, from October 1993, Dr. Spriggs served as the Director for the National Commission for Employment Policy. The Commission was established to advise the President and Congress on employment and training policy. While at the Commission, Dr. Spriggs served on a task force for the National Economic Council that was aimed at anti-discrimination enforcement. Dr. Spriggs came to Washington in the summer of 1990, working as an economist at the Economic Policy Institute, where he did research on labor relations and labor market regulations. He did important work on the minimum wage and international labor standards. While at EPI, Spriggs was often quoted by the press on economic issues, and made several appearances on television and radio, including the McNeil Lehrer NewsHour, C-SPAN, the CBS Evening News, and National Public Radio. Before coming to Washington, Dr. Spriggs taught for six years at Norfolk State University in Virginia, where he also directed the Honors Program, and for two years at North Carolina A & T State University in Greensboro. Spriggs has numerous publications, has presented at several international conferences, and has done consulting work for various state, local and international agencies. Dr. Spriggs married Jennifer Dover in August 1985, and they are the parents of a handsome son, William born in April 1995.

Shelley I. White-Means is professor of Economics and a research professor in the Center for Research on Women at the University of Memphis. She is President of the National Economic Association, a Post-Doctoral Fellow of the Gerontological Society of America, and a member of the steering committee for the National Academy on Aging. Prior to employment at the University of Memphis, Dr. White-Means taught at Cornell University, Department of Consumer Economics. Professor White-Means' research emphasizes long term care for ethnic elderly; labor market implications of caregiving; and access and utilization of medical services by blacks and Hispanics. Grants from the Milbank Memorial Fund, US Department of Agriculture, and the Retirement Research Foundation funded this research. Her most recent publications include: "Opportunity Wages and Workforce Adjustments: Understanding the Costs of In-Home Elder Care," *Journal of Gerontology* (1996);"What Cost Savings Could Be Realized by Shifting Patterns of Use from Hospital Emergency Rooms to Primary Care Sites?" *American Economic Review* (1995); "Labor Supply of Informal Caregivers," *International Review of Applied Economics* (1995); and "Conceptualizing Race in Economic Models of Medical Utilization: A Case Study of Community-Based Elders and the Emergency Room," Health Services Research (1995).

Rhonda Williams is a political economist and associate professor of Afro-American Studies at the University of Maryland at College Park. Her research interests include the race-gender dimensions of economic restructuring, the nexus of cultural studies and economic policy, race ideology, discrimination theory and anti-discrimination policy. Williams' work has appeared in the *Review of Economics and Statistics*, *The Review of Black Political Economy*, *Review of Radical Political Economics*, *The American Economic Review*, *Feminist Studies*, and numerous edited volumes.

Introduction

THE JANUS-FACE OF RACE: REFLEC-
TIONS ON ECONOMIC THEORY

Patrick L. Mason and Rhonda Williams

Many economists are willing to accept that race is a significant factor in US economic and social affairs. Yet the professional literature displays a peculiar schizophrenia when faced with the task of actually formulating what race means and how race works in our political economy. On the one hand, race matters when the discussion is focused on anti-social behavior, social choices, and undesired market outcomes. Inexplicably, African Americans are more likely to prefer welfare, lower labor force participation, and unemployment. On the other hand, race does not matter when the subject of discussion is economically productive or socially acceptable activities and legal market choices (for example, wages and employment).

This Janus-faced construction of race is maintained by economists' stubborn adherence to the market power hypothesis. The market power hypothesis asserts that racial discrimination and market competition are inversely correlated. Discriminatory behavior will persist only in those sectors of society where the competitive forces of the market are least operative. When applied to the labor market, the market power hypothesis suggests that pre- and post-labor market decisions represent disjoint sets. On average, members of a disadvantaged social group may accumulate a lower amount of or a lower quality of productive attributes because of discrimination in marital, residential, or school choice, or because of substantial animosity in day-to-day interpersonal relations with members of a privileged group. These markets and social customs are imperfectly competitive or operate with substantial information problems. However, within the labor market the rate of return to productive attributes is invariant across social groups. On average, individuals are paid in proportion to their contribution to output, though discrimination may occur in the process of augmenting individual productive capacity. Agents who discriminate in pre-labor market behavior may also prefer to do so in the labor market as well, but competitive market forces effectively neutralize individual discriminatory preferences.

The collection of papers in this volume challenge the market power hypothesis. Along the way, these essays assess a series of interrelated questions. Is racism a significant variable in the competitive allocation of market goods and services? What are the limitations of conventional modes of analysis to explain variations in interracial economic outcomes? Finally, are there any policy or political strategies that we can derive from recent theoretical and empirical research? The authors address the role of race and racism in several markets: labor (wages and unemployment), health, crime, self-employment, and housing and credit.

Equation (1) presents a naive version of the market power hypothesis. In this model X is vector of characteristics, R (race) assumes a value of 1 if the individual is an African American and 0 if the individual is white, and ε is a random error term. The dependent variable (y) represents the natural logarithm of the wage rate or hours of work in the labor market, health status or medical treatment in the health care market, the supply of offenses in the crime market, the probability of receiving a loan or the amount of the loan in the mortgage market, and earnings or business participation probabilities among the self-employed.

$$y = X\beta + R\delta + \varepsilon. \tag{1}$$

In the naive version of the market power hypothesis, the variation in X fully explains the variation in y. Interracial variations in market outcomes are the result of interracial variations in individual attributes. Hence, race does not matter, i.e., $\delta = 0$.

Among others, heterodox economists take issue with the market power hypothesis as represented by equation (1). Regardless of the product or factor markets considered — labor, crime, health, housing, or entrepreneurship — the alternative research finds that race is a statistically significant and substantive variable. Routinely, empirical researchers have found that $\delta \neq 0$. After adjusting for observable and individual-specific characteristics, such as education, age, region of the country, metropolitan location, parent's socioeconomic status, and other appropriate variables, researchers have consistently found the following outcomes: African American workers earn less than white workers ($\delta < 0$) and have less access to stable employment ($\delta < 0$); African Americans have poorer health status and receive lower quality of treatment than whites ($\delta < 0$); African Americans are less likely to be granted a housing loan than whites and if they do receive a housing loan it is more likely to be a lower amount and have a higher interest rate than a loan made to an otherwise identical white person ($\delta < 0$); and, African Americans have a lower entrepreneurship rate than whites ($\delta < 0$) and among those who are self-employed African Americans obtain lower earnings ($\delta < 0$). Finally, analysis of aggregate data has shown that African Americans have a greater probability of criminal participation than whites ($\delta > 0$), while analysis of microdata has found no significant race effect ($\delta = 0$).

This pattern of outcomes is certainly consistent with the notion that racism is a strong determinant of the life-chances of African Americans. Indeed, during the periods of the civil rights (1954–1965) and black power (1965–1973) movements most economists and other social scientists interpreted the empirical results in precisely this fashion. In the post-black power era, a new common sense has emerged among economists which asserts that although race is an important variable, racism (discrimination), *per se*, is not an important factor in market outcomes.

An important intellectual origin of this reversal of interpretive perspectives can be traced to how neoclassical economists think about competition. For the neoclassical economist, competition levels the playing field. All goods and services of a given type and quality receive an identical price. If identical goods and services are treated differently an opportunity for arbitrage exists and, in the long run, resource mobility will eliminate this irrational price differential. For most market transactions, neither the race of the buyer nor the race of the seller has economic meaning. Therefore, neoclassical theory suggests that competition will insure that racism does not exert a systematic and sustained impact on competitive market outcomes.

Statistically, this argument yields a more sophisticated version of the market power hypothesis. It suggests that equation (1) has omitted some important explanatory variable (v), which is highly correlated with race and with the observed outcome. If we include v in the statistical model, such as in equation (2), then neoclassical competitive analysis suggests that race will be statistically insignificant or, if significant, substantively small and decreasing in importance over time.

$$y = X\beta + R\delta + v + \varepsilon. \tag{2}$$

The introductory chapter by Timothy Bates and David Howell challenges even the most sophisticated presentation of the market power hypothesis. They discredit the argument that spatial and skills mismatches may explain why $\delta < 0$. So-called mismatch theories explain that inner city African Americans tend to earn less than otherwise identical whites because "they possess the wrong skills and live in the wrong places." Assuming that these mismatches are captured by the vector v, then $\delta = 0$ in equation (2).

Skill and spatial mismatches represent temporary competitive imperfections or information problems. If true, the mismatch hypothesis has rather straightforward policy suggestions — encourage greater skill acquisition by African Americans and greater access to jobs in the suburbs. The approach then diverts economists' attention away from the issue of persistent labor market discrimination.

Bates and Howell cast doubt on mismatch hypotheses by emphasizing the role of "personal contracts and informal networks that bar most minorities from the skilled construction trades...."[1] Within the construction industry, they find that this source

---

[1] For jobs which do not require a college degree, Holzer (1996) finds that 35–40 percent of new hires obtained their jobs through informal referral mechanisms, e.g., referrals from current employees, acquaintances of employer. Cocoran, Datcher, and Duncan (1980) found that over half of employees obtain their jobs through informal referees. Yet, in Holzer's sample 50–60 percent of employers claimed to follow affirmative action procedures in their recruitment process.

of social capital (job networks and informal contacts) simultaneously governs entry, occupational mobility from unskilled to skilled positions among the employed, and the opportunity to find work among the self-employed. In short, access to work can be a great barrier for African Americans even when employment is growing, spatial and skills mismatches are not relevant, and African Americans have more years of education than their white competitors (as is the case in the Bates and Howell sample). Differential access to persons embedded into positions of power, authority, and control over resources is an element of competitive advantage in the construction industry. Since African Americans have less of this important source of social capital, discrimination can and will persist because of the very nature of the competitive process. Competition is rivalry and winners can and do seek to preserve and consolidate their winnings. (Darity and Williams, 1985; Darity, 1989; Mason, 1995; Williams and Kenison, 1996. These essays more fully develop an alternative analysis of competition, race, and discrimination).

In their case study of New Jersey, Samuel Myers and William Spriggs also confirm the importance of competitive rivalry and interracial differences in social capital as major explanatory variables for determining the probability of entry into and the likely success of entrepreneurship. Further, Myers and Spriggs combine an economic historical approach with econometric analysis to demonstrate the inter-market links among crime, self-employment, housing, and labor markets.

Specifically, the Myers and Spriggs chapter shows that employment discrimination and occupational segregation block African American entry into professional/managerial employment. Additionally, for those African Americans able to obtain professional/managerial employment in the private sector, these same forces limit access to entrepreneurial skills and opportunity. In the public sector, African Americans professional/managerial workers find block opportunities with regard to state contracting and procurement.

For those African Americans able to get beyond the blocked opportunities in the labor market, residential discrimination confines their entrepreneurial activity to the provision of professional services (such as funeral homes) and small basic services shops (such as barbers and beauty salons).

Myers and Spriggs also argue that block labor market opportunities contribute to the development of criminal enterprise within African American communities. Entrepreneurial talent that might otherwise have been utilized for legitimate pursuits is used for illegitimate activity. Additionally, crime becomes a disproportionate source for raising venture capital for otherwise legal enterprises.

For Myers and Rodgers, v represents a vector of variables designed to capture blocked opportunities. Because these block opportunities are systematically greater among African Americans (than whites), including v in the regression should lower δ. In this instance however the lower value of δ does not represent the absence of discrimination; instead, including the variables related to opportunities might provide us with specific knowledge of how race interacts with market competition.

Rather than blocked opportunities or spatial and skills mismatches, some human capital theorists have stated that v represents either unobserved productive attributes or observed proxies for labor quality such as standardized test scores.[2] Murray and Herrnstein (1994) also believe that v captures genetically endowed productive attributes that are differentially distributed by race. In either case, interracial differences in labor quality provide the major explanation for remaining interracial differences in labor market outcomes.

Using cross-sectional data, Rodgers and Spriggs (1995) have successfully challenged the notion that interracial differences in test scores are a major cause of interracial differences in wages. In this volume, William Rodgers discusses changes in the inter- and intraracial distribution of wages between 1963 and 1992. His analysis of changes in the wage distribution (rather than the mean wage rate) shows that unobserved productive attributes cannot explain the slowdown in interracial wage convergence since 1979. Specifically, human capital theorists have argued that the slowdown in interracial wage convergence from at least 1979 onward is not due to rising discrimination but is due to an increase in the rate of return to skill. They also assert that standard human capital models (equation 1) do not adequately control for labor quality. Because the median wage for African Americans is at the 31st percentile of the white wage distribution, an increase in the rate of return to skill will raise the relative wages of the most skilled workers, regardless of race, and thereby generate greater inequality among whites and between whites and African Americans. However, Rodgers finds that among men it is only better skilled African Americans who have lost ground relative to white counterparts because of the increase in the rate of return to skill. His results are diametrically opposed to those of Juhn et al. (1991). Hence, neither cross-sectional nor longitudinal data rules out the possibility of racial discrimination as an important source of interracial earnings differentials.

Gary Dymski's chapter alerts us that theories of housing and credit discrimination are very underdeveloped and that the status of empirical research in this area is quite contentious. As such, policy recommendations in this area are also subject to substantial dissension. Having forewarned the reader, the content of Dymski's chapter contests the analytical separation of pre- and post-labor market outcomes. He also shows that competitive rivalry in the credit and housing market is not necessarily efficient. Competitive behaviors will not on their own eliminate discrimination because spillover effects, externalities, and search costs present monopsony power to lenders in the housing market.

Housing segregation (redlining) and credit discrimination means that African American workers are less likely to live in neighborhoods that are populated by people with significant control over resources and decision-making. And, as we know from Bates and Howell, this form of social capital is crucial to gaining access to more desirable employment opportunities. Neighborhood and other affiliational clusters are not solely pre-labor market institutions. On the contrary, they are cru-

---

[2] Unobserved attributes are those productive attributes which may be observable to the employer but which are unobservable to the econometrician. Juhn, Murphy, and Pierce (1991) interpret v as unobserved productive attributes. Ferguson (1995), Maxwell (1995), Neal and Johnson (1995), and O'Neill (1990) argue that standardized test scores are a proxy for n.

cial institutions for gaining access to resources and decision-makers within the labor market.

Dymski's chapter gives further concrete meaning to the notion of institutional racism. Race does not matter when African Americans are the decision-makers, but it does matter when they are not. Once again we find that for equation (2) $\delta < 0$, but the decision-unit is a real estate company, bank, or some other agent unaccountable to African American communities.

Just as there are intermarket links between housing and credit markets and labor markets, there are also intermarket links between labor and health care markets. Health status is both an independent variable with respect to labor market outcomes and a dependent variable which is at least partly determined by labor market outcomes. Thus, racial discrimination in the labor market has a potential to lower health status which in turn may lower earnings.

Beyond these direct intermarket links, it has been argued that $\delta < 0$ in health status equations because African Americans are less likely to have insurance than whites. African Americans are relatively more uninsured than whites because African Americans are disproportionately employed in jobs which do not provide health insurance. Job-based private health insurance is the dominant source of health insurance for Americans. African Americans are also disproportionately out of the workforce and unemployed than whites, thereby providing an additional disconnection from the primary source of health insurance. If African Americans had the same insurance status as whites there would be no interracial differentials in medical utilization patters or health status. In short, if we allow v to represent insurance status then $\delta = 0$ in equation (2).

Shelley White-Means demonstrates that this argument is false. Health status (y) is a function of health prevention measures, insurance status, and race. Race is a direct determinant of health status because of interracial differences in such factors as

cigarette and alcohol targeting, the supply of fresh fruits and vegetables due to residential segregation and quality of housing, education and employment opportunities, community violence and environmental toxins, as well as the stressful impact of racism on physical and mental health... In sum, racial disparities in health status are due to differences in vulnerability to behavioral, psychosocial, economic, and environmental risk factors and resources.

Additionally, race is a direct determinant of health status because medical treatment varies by race, even after accounting for differences in income and insurance status.

White-Mean's findings have important labor market implications. The discrimination coefficient (δ) from the traditional wage equation underestimates the impact of discrimination on well-being and intergenerational wealth accumulation — it is a single market estimate. Racial segregation in the occupational structure places African Americans in jobs with lower or no insurance benefits, which reduces current health status and thereby lowers future earnings. These future earnings in turn reduce future health status relative to the health status that African Americans might reasonably expect in a non-discriminatory environment. Also, reduced life chances during one's youth are very much related to later life opportunities for senior citizens. Labor market discrimination during youth lowers resources to meet the health needs that increase as one ages. Ultimately, this gap between the elderly's needs and resources must be partially offset by family resources. But heavy time commitments to elderly family members reduce the current earnings of the young, and also have costs in terms of life satisfaction and physical well-being of the young. Given that African American women also face gender-based occupational segregation and are the most likely providers of family care, White-Means' results suggest that African American women will disproportionately suffer the aforementioned reduction in health status and the resulting earnings losses and reduction in life satisfaction.

White-Means suggests both race-neutral and race-specific policies for narrowing the interracial gap in health status. The health status of low income persons will be improved if they are able to purchase either a higher quality or a higher level of health services. This can be achieved by increasing the progressivity of the income tax system, which will raise the take-home-pay of the lowest earners, and by allowing premiums, deductibles and co-payments to vary with the income level of the insured. She also argues that health care planners address the issue of racial differences in physical proximity to health care facilities and racial inequity in health care for elderly.

Wilhelmina Leigh examines the relationship between health status, race, and competition in the health care industry. In terms of our econometric analysis, she finds $\delta < 0$ but does not seek "v." Instead, Leigh argues for greater competition — by which she means an increase in the number of health care providers — as an avenue for reducing racial disparities in the quality of physician services, hospital services, and in insurance coverage. However, she points out that increased competition in the health care industry may *lower* overall efficiency in the provision of health care. Greater market efficiency and a reduction in racial inequality *are not* mutually supportive as in standard neoclassical analysis.

To date, neither federal nor state policy makers have acted to close the interracial gap in health care status. This absence of sustained action lends credibility to the Darity, et al. (1994) thesis that low income African Americans, the so-called underclass, are "unwanted and unneeded" by social managers. Contemporary research on race and crime also suggests the economic expendability of African Americans. Specifically, "the well known fact" that African Americans are more likely to be incarcerated than whites has inspired many researchers to hypothesize that African Americans have a greater taste for crimes than whites. In this context $v = 0$ and $\delta > 0$ because of greater criminal propensities among African Americans.

Certainly, African Americans are overrepresented as victims and perpetrators of crime (Maguire and Patore, 1995). They are also a disproportionate share of the prison population. It is rather straightforward to inquire then, "Why are African Americans over-represented in the criminal justice system?" The range of responses to this question have been numerous. African Americans may be over-represented in the criminal justice system due to discriminatory behavior by decision-makers within the criminal justice system (Myers, 1987; Dubois, 1987). On the other hand, Murray and Herrnstein (1994) represent the long tradition which asserts that African Americans are relatively more disposed towards criminal behavior because of bio-genetic differences, i.e., lower intelligence quotients than whites. Still, a third camp argues that the so-called African American underclass has a more criminal culture (Loury, 1984; Wilson, 1987). Finally, some scholars have examined the connection between the socioeconomic conditions faced by African Americans and criminal behaviors (Gyimah-Brempong, 1986; Myers and Sabol, 1987).

Kwabena Gyimah-Brempong's chapter follows the latter strategy. He uses aggregate data to examine the relationship between race, the supply of criminal offenses, and economic opportunity. In contrast to many analysts, he finds no relationship between property crimes and race after adjusting for differences in economic opportunities. Gyimah-Brempong argues that there is a missing variables problem (v) in crime rate models that use aggregate data. Although these studies frequently find $\delta > 0$, the researchers rarely provide a causal explanation. Gyimah-Brempong's results with aggregate data however are in agreement with the results generally obtained with the use of microdata, which control for differences in economic advantage. The policy implication is straightforward: improving economic opportunities is a form of crime prevention.

BEYOND THIS VOLUME

The chapters in this volume collectively illuminate the limitations manifest in neoclassical economists' analysis of race, markets, and social outcomes. We believe that these limitations are deeply rooted in two mainstream theoretical commitments: the market power hypothesis and an asocial, nonhistorical conceptualization of race and racism. Much of the discussion in the preceding pages has focused on the inability to reconcile the market power hypothesis with actually observed market outcomes. In these closing pages we address alternative paradigms for theorizing race and competition in capitalist economies, which also utilize a rich historical understanding of race and racism.

We take Neo-Marxian and Marxian efforts to reconstruct the economics of discrimination as an entry point. Unlike neoclassical theorists, today's Marxists begin theorizing with the historically based proposition that Western capitalist societies are racialized class (and gender) formations (Williams, 1964; Marable, 1983; Reich, 1981).[3]

By racialization we mean the processes by which individuals learn to 'read' specific phenotypes as indicative of discrete and naturally occurring breeding populations, or 'races.' Each market actor learns to analyze her/his personal and social environment (family life, neighborhoods, religious institutions and concepts, schools, workplaces, sources of entertainment, etc.) through historically specific "racial projects." These projects are the pre- and supra-market processes through which market actors construct what race means, how it is culturally represented, and how race organizes and explains social structures and relations of power (Omi

---

[3] Bob Gooding-Williams, 1994 conversation; populations subsume gender differentiation.

and Winant, 1994; Winant, 1994). For example, we might periodize US racial eras of accumulation as follows: slavery (1619–1865), Reconstruction (1865–1877), Jim Crow (1877–1965), the Second Reconstruction (1954–1973), and the White Backlash (1969–present). Historically-specific and racialized economic projects define each era. A fuller elaboration would identify the specific relations through which market actors learn to interpret and produce race-specific socioeconomic outcomes. In turn, in each era the creation and transformation of racial projects is intimately related to the secular processes of capital accumulation and capitalist competition.

If indeed racialization is a hegemonic force, then race is deeply constitutive of (and constituted by) class and gender relations and subjectivities. Market actors do not blindly engage capitalists, creditors, workers and clients as asocial abstractions. Rather, they interpret the ascriptive (racial and gender) characteristics of each agent as sources of economic information. Market participants then use (or attempt to use) this information to define and pursue their own self-interest. Economic theories seeking to address 'race' must therefore envision market actors as subjects creating and created by a multiplicity of racialized projects that simultaneously interpret racial dynamics and organize racialized market outcomes (Omi and Winant, 1994:56).

In this context, discrimination is not simply a matter of 'tastes;' rather, discrimination is a racialized economic project that furthers racial domination. It is this notion of discrimination that informs a generation of Marxist theories (Baron, 1972; Harris, 1972; Mason, 1993, 1995, and 1996; Darity, 1989; Darity and Williams, 1985; Williams, 1994; Williams and Kenison, 1996; Shulman, 1990; Reich, 1981). Although differing in detail, Marxists and Neo-Marxists alike argue that capitalism's social relations of production and exchange are racialized; alternatively put, the production and distribution of the conditions necessary for a life-enhancing existence — wealth, income, health, housing, work, etc. — are racialized projects with discernible class and gender outcomes.[4] Unlike neoclassical formulations these theories suggest (1) that race will almost always matter in the reproduction of capitalist economics and the determination of market outcomes, and (2) that discrimination is no mere aberration. Rather, discrimination is endogenous to capital accumulation and emanates from the competitive struggle for material advantage. When successful, discriminators secure more wealth, higher incomes, more and better jobs, superior access to health care, and privileged access to state protection and resources.

Discrimination is certainly a reasonable factor to consider in explaining interracial differences in incarceration rates. Consider the number and nature of decisions involved between the time a crime is committed and jail time is allocated for the crime. Given that an individual has decided to commit a crime, (s)he may or may not be arrested. If arrested, (s)he may be severely or only minimally charged. And, given the extent of the charges, a conviction may or may not follow. Given that a conviction is obtained, the sentence may be maximal or minimal. Finally, given the sentence, the individual may be paroled or may be forced to serve the entire sentence. So, after controlling for a specific crime, there are 11 possible jail times asso-

---

[4] Similarly, class projects yield race-gender outcomes and gender projects yield race-class outcomes.

ciated with an offense which are determined by 5 separate decisions — each one of which may be affected by racial discrimination, an inability to afford competent legal council, public policy, etc. But, all of these decisions are outside the hand of individual African Americans — except the choice of committing a crime — and largely outside the control of the African American community.

Thus racial domination and the interracial distribution of power are major determinants of economic and social outcomes. Economic analysis can only be enriched by systemic incorporation of both social phenomena. However, the taking of this analytic step necessitates a substantive departure from neoclassical theories of competition, according to which race matters only in imperfectly competitive markets. The chapters in this volume challenge the adequacy of the market power paradigm and point to the need for a more robust theoretical framework.

Recent developments in Marxian analyses of competition and discrimination provide a more hospitable home for the theorizing of discrimination as a social relation of domination practiced by and constitutive of racialized market actors. Marxists theories explicitly engage racialized subjects, communities, and market behavior. Moreover, they do so in a competitive analysis which normalizes the differentiation of market outcomes for comparable entrepreneurs and workers (Botwinick, 1993; Mason, 1995; Williams and Kenison, 1996).

As a case in point, we return to the Bates and Howell chapter. White women's success in the New York construction industry highlights the importance of racialized community in the creation and employment of social capital. Unlike their African American counterparts, these women are the wives, friends, and daughters of white men in the industry, and apparently draw upon these relationships to generate business opportunities. The New York case dramatizes the economic import of social capital and the competitive advantage it confers. Insofar as the production and use of social capital is a racialized project, the continuation of the social relations from which this capital originates will enhance the reproduction of racial inequality in the construction trades, whatever the racial distribution of productive abilities.

Patrick L. Mason
South Bend, Indiana

Rhonda Williams
College Park, Maryland

REFERENCES

Baron, H. (1971). "The Demand for Black Labor: Historical Notes on the Political Economy of Racism." *Radical America* (March-April):1–46.

Botwinick, H. 1993. *Persistent Inequalities: Wage Disparity Under Capitalist Competition.* New York: Princeton University Press.

Cocoran, M, L. Datcher, and G. Duncan. 1980. "Most Workers Find Jobs Through Word of Mouth." *Monthly Labor Review*, 103:33–55.

Darity, Jr., W. 1989. "What's Left of the Economic Theory of Discrimination." In *The Question of Discrimination: Racial Inequality in the U. S. Labor Market*, S. Schulman and W. Darity, eds., 335–374. Middletown, CT: Wesleyan University Press.

_____, S. Myers, Jr., E. Carson, W. Sabol. 1994. *The Black Underclass: Critical Essays on Race and Unwantedness*. New York: Garland Publishing, Inc.

_____ and R. Williams. 1985. "Peddlers Forever?: Culture, Competition, and Discrimination." *Papers and Proceedings of the American Economic Review* 75 (2) (May):256–261.

Dubois, W. E. B. 1987. "The Negro Criminal." Review of Black Political Economy 16 (1–2) (Summer-Fall): 17–32.

Ferguson, R. 1995. "Shifting Challenges: Fifty Years of Economic Change Toward Black-White Earnings Equality." *Daedalus* Winter:37–76.

Gyimah-Brempong, K. 1986. "Empirical Models of Criminal Behavior: How Significant a Factor is Race?" *Review of Black Political Economy* 15 (Summer): 27–43.

Harris, D. (1972). "The Black Ghetto as 'Internal Colony': A Theoretical Critique and Alternative Formulation." *Review of Black Political Economy* (Summer): 3–33.

Holzer, H. 1996. *What Employers Want: Job Prospects for Less Educated Workers*. New York: Russell Sage Foundation.

Juhn, C., K. Murphy, and B. Pierce. 1991. "Accounting for the Slowdown in Black-White Wage Convergence." In *Workers and Their Wages*, M. Kosters, eds., 107–143. Washington, D.C.: The AEI Press.

Loury, G. 1984. "Internally Directed Action for Black Community Development: The Next Frontier for 'The Movement.'" *Review of Black Political Economy* 13 (1–2) (Summer-Fall): 31–46.

Maguire, K. and A. Patore, eds. 1995. *Sourcebook of Criminal Justices Statistics 1994*. US Department of Justice, Bureau of Justice Programs 1995. Washington, DC: USGPO.

Marable, M. 1983. *How Capitalism Underdeveloped Black America: Problems in Race, Political Economy and Society*. Boston: South End Press.

Mason, P. 1996. "Race and Egalitarian Democracy: The Distributional Consequences of Racial Conflict." In *The Impact of Racism on White Americans*, Benjamin Bowser, ed., 68–87. Newbury Park, CA: Sage Publications, Inc.

_____. 1995. "Race, Competition and Differential Wages." *Cambridge Journal of Economics* 19 (4) (August): 545–568.

_____. 1993. "Accumulation, The Segmentation of Labor, and Racial Discrimination in Employment." *Review of Radical Political Economics* 25 (2) (June): 1–25.

Maxwell, N. 1994. "The Effect on Black-White Wage Differentials of Differences in the Quantity and Quality of Education." *Industrial and Labor Relations Review* 47 (2) (January):249–264.

Murray, C. and R. Herrnstein. 1994. *The Bell Curve: Intelligence and Class Structure in American Life*. New York: The Free Press.

Myers, Jr., S. 1987. "Introduction." Review of Black Political Economy 16 (1–2) (Summer-Fall): 5–16.

Myers, Jr., S. and W. Sabol. 1987. "Unemployment and Racial Differences in Imprisonment." Review of Black Political Economy 16 (1–2) (Summer-Fall): 189–210.

Neal, D. and W. Johnson. 1994. "The Role of Pre-Market Factors in Black-White Wage Differences." Unpublished mimeo.

Omi, M. and H. Winant. 1994. *Racial Formation in the United States: From the 1960s to the 1990s, 2nd edition*. New York: Routledge.

O'neill, J. 1990. "The Role of Human Capital and Earnings Differences Between Black and White Men." *Journal of Economic Perspectives* 44:25–45.

Reich, M. 1981. *Racial Inequality*. Princeton NJ: Princeton University Press.

Rodgers, III W. and W. Spriggs. 1995. "What Does the AFQT Really Measure: Race, Wages and Schooling and the AFQT Score." Unpublished Paper, The College of William and Mary and the Joint Economic Committee, US Congress.

Shulman, S. 1990. "Racial Inequality and White Employment: An Interpretation and Test of the Bargaining Power Hypothesis." *Review of Black Political Economics* 18 (3) (Winter): 5–20.

Williams, E. 1964. *Capitalism and Slavery*. London: Andre Deutsch Limited.

Williams, R. 1991. "Competition, Discrimination and Differential Wage Rates: On the Continued Relevance of Marxian Theory to the Analysis of Earnings and Employment Inequality." In *New Approaches to the*

Economic and Social Analysis of Discrimination, R. Cornwall and P. Wunnava, eds., 65–92. New York: Praeger.

Williams, R. 1987. "Capital, Competition, and Discrimination: A Reconsideration of Racial Earnings Inequality." *Review of Radical Political Economics* 19 (2):1–15.

_____ and R. E. Kenison. 1996. "The Way We Were?: Discrimination, Competition, and Inter-Industry Wage Differentials in 1970." *Review of Radical Political Economics* 28 (2) (June):1–32.

Wilson, W. J. 1987. *The Truly Disadvantaged: The Inner City, The Underclass, and Public Policy*. Chicago: University of Chicago Press.

Winant, H. 1994. *Racial Conditions: Politics, Theory, Comparisons*. Minneapolis: University of Minnesota Press.

Part I

Self-Employment: Escape from Racism?

1

THE STATUS OF AFRICAN AMERICAN MEN IN THE NEW YORK CITY CONSTRUCTION INDUSTRY

Timothy Bates and David Howell

INTRODUCTION

In the competition among social scientists to explain the eroding labor market status of African Americans over the past two decades, mismatch theories have become particularly influential. Typifying skill mismatch scholarship, John Kasarda marshals extensive evidence that job growth — especially in large central cities — is increasingly dominated by white-collar industries seeking college-educated employees (1990). Spatial mismatch analyses proceed in a fundamentally different, but complementary manner, demonstrating that job growth in urban areas is increasingly concentrated in suburbs (Ihlanfeld and Young, 1996; Wilson, 1987). Central city black residents in these scenarios suffer because they possess the wrong skills and live in the wrong places. Policy recommendations follow readily from both mismatch stories: labor market gains require that black workers raise their skill levels; greater access to jobs in suburbia is also necessary.

The popularity of mismatch explanations has diverted attention from racial discrimination as a determinant of labor market outcomes. Attacking skill deficiencies is fundamentally different than combating discrimination in hiring and wage determination considerations. This study analyzes the performance of black male workers in the New York City construction labor market during the 1980's. This particular market was chosen because of the minimal relevance of mismatch theories: few construction jobs require college credentials and job growth in the 1980's was heavily concentrated in the central city, particularly in Manhattan, Queens and Brooklyn (US Department of Commerce, various years). Construction in the 1980's boomed in New York City and most of the workers filling these jobs were male blue-collar employees.

With its extensive mass transit system and the concentration of construction jobs in the most accessible parts of the city, it is unlikely that physical access to construction jobs was a problem for African Americans in New York City. Given the general irrelevance of skill and spatial mismatches to this particular labor market, how did African Americans fare? Did this instance of blue-collar job growth in the central city generate progress towards income parity in the construction labor market? Did black workers gain a share of the new jobs proportionate somehow to their share in the general population of the region? In fact, they did not.

Our findings demonstrate that black/white earnings ratios widened considerably over the 1979–1989 time period among workers employed in New York City area construction. Furthermore, the share of construction jobs held by African Americans declined, and this decline was most pronounced in the skilled construction occupations. Contemporary explanations for black/white employment and earnings inequality constitute a multifaceted, increasingly cumbersome literature; causal relationships tend to become blurred. Findings of this study, while not ruling out the relevance of mismatch explanations of growing inequality, do clearly suggest that employment discrimination is a powerful and enduring source of labor market disadvantage for African American male workers.

According to Moore, the presence of employer discrimination in a labor market niche such as construction should cause blacks to be relatively overrepresented among the self-employed (1983). Self-employment is increasingly widespread among construction workers, accounting for over 20 percent of total employment in construction nationwide (Devine and Mlaker, 1992). In fact, blacks are underrepresented among the self-employed in the New York City area construction industry. Pursuing Moore's logic, the inference to be drawn from the low level of black self-employment in New York construction is that employer discrimination is absent. A powerful thread in American culture holds that discriminatory barriers in the labor market do *not* block the aspirations of those who are willing to work hard and live frugally. If the labor market does not adequately reward one's skills and effort, one can open up his/her own business. Ivan Light argues that Asian immigrants have traditionally pursued self-employment with great frequency because they were subjected to discrimination in the labor market: "Asian immigrants were poor and visibly non-European and were subject to discrimination on that account. These very qualities tended to force Chinese and Japanese into the classic small business occupations..." (1972, P. 5). Because self-employment is seen as a method of avoiding racist employment practices, this line of analysis is consistent with the view that blacks should be overrepresented among the self-employed: "the extra disadvantages of blacks ought, strictly speaking, to have stimulated them to more extensive self-employment..." (Light, 1972, p. 5).

The (unstated) premise of the Moore-Light analysis is that the barriers handicapping black employment prospects are not relevant to shaping the prospects facing black entrepreneurs. The experience of minorities pursuing self-employment in New York City construction is examined in detail in this study. Findings of this investigation indicate that the same barriers undermining employment in New York construction also create an inhospitable environment for minorities trying to operate small construction firms. The terms "black" and "minority" are sometimes used interchangeably in our analysis of construction self-employment. In fact, blacks are the dominant minority group among the construction self-employed in New York, Latinos are a close second; Asians are not a factor.[1]

THE STATUS OF BLACK MALES IN NEW YORK CITY CONSTRUCTION

There are many ways to slice the data on minority involvement in the New York City construction industry. Our initial analysis, including New York City and surrounding counties in 1980 (including Nassau and Westchester counties), reveals that 4.3 percent of all nonminority males and 2.6 percent of all African American males 19–39 years old worked in construction. Importantly, well over half of black male employment was in the skilled construction occupations in 1980, but their presence was also pronounced in the unskilled laborer occupation, which employed 22.8 percent of young black male (and 15.7 percent of white male) New York area construction workers.[2]

The focus of our construction employment analysis (Table 1.1) is out-of-school males 19–39 years old who reside in New York City proper, Westchester, or Nassau counties. African American males in these age brackets are the ones who have experienced the most pronounced deterioration in employment status in recent years (Peterson and Vroman, 1992; Moss and Tilly, 1992). The narrow geographic focus confines our analysis to an area possessing a dense enough mass transit web to minimize the relevance of spatial mismatch considerations.[3] Among this male group, "significant labor force attachment" was defined as existing when 1989 earnings exceeded $3420 (or $2000 for 1979) *and* weeks worked in 1979 (1989) was at least 20. Such workers are "active" by definition. Defined in this way, significant labor force attachment characterized 75.5 percent of the non-Hispanic white males in 1979 and 77.0 percent in 1989; corresponding figures for young non-Hispanic black males were 59.9 percent in 1979 and 59.9 percent in 1989. Percentages of active workers were relatively stable for the relevant groups of black and

---

[1] This approach is expedient because it alleviates sample size constraints that would otherwise complicate the analysis of self-employed black New York area residents working in construction. A detailed discussion of this is presented in Timothy Bates (1993a).

[2] These figures are drawn from Census Bureau population public use microdata samples for 1980.

[3] Data on employment status were drawn from the 5 percent public use microdata samples (PUMS) of the 1980 and 1990 Census Bureau population census files for New York City, Nasssau, and Westchester counties.

white young males over the 1979–1989 period. In this labor market situation, construction was clearly a bright spot: construction was employing a rising share of the young male active workforce; the share of active workers in construction was:

	1980	1990
White	5.7%	8.8%
Black	4.3%	6.6%

The figures measuring job growth coexist with a declining relative black share of jobs at the skilled end of the construction employment spectrum. The ratio of skilled to unskilled workers was:

	1980	1990
White	5.38	5.65
Black	3.38	3.04

New York area black construction workers were more overrepresented in unskilled labor jobs in 1990 than they had been in 1980; the exact opposite trend typified whites.

In light of this evidence of declining black employment quality, it is not surprising that, compared to white workers, relative earnings of black construction workers dropped sharply from 1979 to 1989. Table 1.1 indicates that for active young white construction workers, 1979 average earnings were $14,159 and 1989 earnings (not inflation adjusted) were $30,921; corresponding black worker earnings were $11,121 and $21,604, producing the following black/white earnings ratios for New York area construction employees:

1979 black/white earnings ratio = .785

1989 black/white earnings ratio = .699

Relative earnings of young, active black male workers in all fields were 69.1 percent of white earnings in 1979, indicating that the earnings gap in construction (78.5 percent) was less than in the broader New York City labor market. By 1989, the corresponding figures had dropped to 57.5 percent and 69.9 percent respectively for active young workers. These results demonstrate that in a sector responsible for a growing share of New York City's blue-collar employment — in which neither skill nor spatial mismatches appear to be relevant — the employment status of young black male workers sharply declined in the 1980's.

Table 1.1. The Employment Status of New York City Area Out-of-School Males
19–39 Years Old

	White, Non-Hispanic		Black, Non-Hispanic	
	1979	1989	1979	1989
1. *Active Workers all fields*				
a. Average earnings	$16,876	$37,783	$11,663	$21,721
b. Average weeks worked	47.9	48.6	47.2	47.2
2. *Active workers employed in construction*				
a. Average earnings	$14,159	$30,921	$11,121	$21,604
b. Average weeks worked	44.8	46.7	43.6	44.9
3. *Active workers in construction by occupation group*				
a. *Skilled blue collar*				
1. Average earnings	$13,995	$29,320	$11,553	$20,712
2. Average weeks worked	44.6	46.5	45.0	45.0
b. *Unskilled*				
1. Average earnings	$11,109	$24,449	$9,221	$20,271
2. Average weeks worked	42.1	44.6	38.9	43.2
4. *Black/White earnings ratios %*	1979		1989	
a. *All active*	69.1%		57.5%	
b. *All active construction* *including white collar*	78.5%		69.9%	
c. *Construction skilled blue collar*	82.6%		70.6%	
d. *Construction unskilled*	83.0%		82.9%	

Source: Census Population public use microdata samples, 1980 and 1990.

    The purpose of this study is not to refute mismatch theories but to question the
wisdom of focusing too heavily upon educational deficiencies and physical access to
jobs. Quite irrespective of mismatches, blacks face numerous labor market barriers
that are fundamentally rooted in the fact that they are black. Consistent with these
findings, Waldinger and Bailey argue that attempts to eradicate racist practices in
New York construction, never highly effective, actually atrophied during the 1980's
(1991). This change in political climate may explain the relative decline of black
worker status in the New York City construction industry during the 1980's. The
policy implications of the Waldinger/Bailey thesis are that economic opportunities

are accessible through routes other than higher levels of educational credentials or improved mass transit to suburbia: they are accessible through political struggle.

Neither the spatial nor the educational mismatch approaches have obvious applicability to explaining why blacks experienced declining relative wages in New York construction, nor why their share of jobs lagged most in the skilled labor occupations. Well over three quarters of the New York City construction labor force possess no education beyond high school. The most obvious educational gap present is between minority and nonminority self-employed in construction: minorities, on average, are more educated. New York area nonminorities self-employed in construction are more likely to be high school dropouts and less likely to be college graduates than African American construction firm owners. Our point here is not to analyze group educational credentials exhaustively, but to illustrate that popular analyses of labor market disadvantage lack explanatory power when they seek to explain relative wages and employment patterns in New York City construction.

POLITICAL STRUGGLE

Ed Koch, New York City mayor from 1978 to 1990, is perhaps best remembered for his declaration that, in an environment of funding constraints, he would prefer to build prisons rather than schools. Mayor Koch, with his active opposition to programs designed to reduce racial inequality, was somewhat ahead of his time. New York City, by 1978, was one of only two of the twenty largest cities in the United States that had no program promoting preferential procurement access for minority vendors; Memphis was the other (Bates 1993b). With his active opposition to affirmative action, Koch represented a public policy turning point in New York.

The 1960's and 1970's had been noteworthy in New York because the public sector had clearly succeeded in forcing open somewhat greater access to construction jobs (Waldinger and Bailey, 1991). Most of New York's construction unions, finding it impossible to practice business as usual in this era, pragmatically gave ground when the anti-discrimination forces were strongest, but nothing approaching non-discriminatory job access was established. Consider, for example, the New York Plan, adopted with great fanfare in 1970. Initially, the Plan sought to enroll 800 minority trainees to work on government-sponsored or subsidized projects. In March 1971, four unions, including the electrical workers, sheet metal workers, and plumbers union, announced that they would not accept trainees. Although all but the sheet metal workers eventually agreed to cooperate with the New York Plan, the process was always contentious. The New York Plan placed 5,000 trainees on jobs between 1971 and 1988: only 800 of those trainees were ever accepted into unions in the construction trades.

In 1978, the year Koch was elected mayor, the New York State Department of Labor set the minority population percentage as the target for the minority share of apprenticeships. Since the Department never pursued enforcement remedies, these goals were ignored; "the Department has never moved to deregister an apprenticeship program on grounds of discrimination" (Waldinger and Bailey, 1991, p. 305).

Exact measurement of the decline in concern about racial equality upon minority construction employment in the New York City area is beyond the scope of this study. The fact that we cannot measure it, however, does not justify relegating this particular phenomenon to obscurity. Political pressure helped to open up construction jobs to black workers in the 1960's and 1970's; the decline of the share and quality of construction jobs held by blacks in the 1980's is consistent with the hypothesis that prevailing political climate shapes job access in this sector. Furthermore, the pattern of declining relative share — concentrated in the skilled construction occupations — is consistent with the fact that the traditional barriers in construction have included the restricted access to skilled trades propagated by union-run apprenticeship programs. This pattern of restricted access to skills acquisition is not linked to educational background considerations; rather, it is rooted in the reality of powerful old-boy networks that protect their own (Tweedie, McDonald, and Sterrett, 1992; Bates 1992).

SELF-EMPLOYMENT AS A RESPONSE TO DISCRIMINATION IN THE LABOR MARKET

Faced with declining relative wages and declining government pressure to open up the construction industry to minorities, one option facing black construction workers is to create their own firms. Many blacks had moved into skilled occupations during the previous era of reduced discriminatory barriers: the majority of the male African Americans working in New York construction in 1980 were in skilled occupations, most commonly working as craftsmen (Bates 1992). These workers could have had shifted into self-employment during the 1980's in order to escape the discriminatory barriers in the construction labor market.

This section explores the success of New York area minorities pursuing self-employment in construction. Experiences of self-employed blacks and Hispanics are found to be quite similar, with Hispanics doing somewhat worse than blacks in construction. They are pooled into the broader "minority" category in the following analyses of construction self-employment; Asians were rare in this grouping. "Minority," refers to self-employed persons in construction, who are roughly half African American and nearly half Hispanic. Movement into self-employment had indeed been pronounced among minority construction workers. Of all minorities self-employed in New York area construction as of 1987, 78.6 percent had entered self-employed since 1979. Coexisting with high entry was high exit: by late 1991, 36.9 percent of the minority business enterprises (MBEs) in New York construction that were operating in 1987 had gone out of business; the corresponding figure among the self-employed nonminorities was 16.4 percent. New York MBEs in construction failed at over twice the rate of nonminorities over the 1987–1991 period. In fact, MBE closure rates were highest in construction's special trades; only 58.4 percent of the MBEs operating in 1987 were still in business by the end of 1991, versus a nonminority survival rate of 79.7 percent.[4] Not only are their failure rates twice as high; mean sales of MBEs in the special trades ($93,324) are barely half of the nonminority annual sales figure of $177,462 (Table 1.2). Note that the data on small businesses analyzed in this section are drawn from the U.S. Bureau of the Census Characteristics of Business Owners data base (Bates, 1990). Why did the New York area minority construction firms perform so poorly?

Table 1.2. Traits of New York Area Minority and Nonminority Construction Firms in Operation During 1987.

A. All Construction	MBE	Nonminority
1987 total sales (mean)	$113,430	$320,423
Number of employees (mean)	1.0	2.1
Total financial capital* (mean)	$8,853	$19,775
Percent of firms still in business, 1991	63.1%	83.4%
Owners: Percent college graduates	16.3%	13.5%
Owners: Percent high school dropouts	34.3%	30.1%
Owners: years of work experience (mean)	10.5	12.4
Annual owner labor input hours (mean)	1,524	2,058
B. Special Trades Only		
1987 total sales (mean)	$93,324	$177,462
Number of employees (mean)	1.0	1.7
Total financial capital* (mean)	$7,091	$6,934
Percent of firms still in business, 1991	58.4%	79.7%
Owners: Percent college graduates	13.8%	12.4%
Owners: Percent high school dropouts	36.9%	41.5%
Owners: years of work experience (mean)	11.2	12.0
Annual owner labor input hours (mean)	1,407	2,029

* at the point of self-employment entry
Source: U.S. Bureau of the Census Characteristics of Business Owners Database

Past studies of small business survival patterns indicate that poorly capitalized firms headed by owners whose educational backgrounds are weak are leading candidates for business failure (Bates, 1993c). Indeed, 36.9 percent of minorities who operated firms in the special trades in 1987 had not completed high school, and the average firm in this group started out with a capitalization of only $7,091 (Table

---

[4] These statistics are based upon samples of firms put together by the enterprise statistics division of the U.S. Bureau of the Census. The geographic area covered by this firm sample is expanded to encompass the New York City metropolitan area broadly defined (including New York City, three adjoining New York counties, and eight New Jersey counties). This expanded area helped to expand the underlining sample size of minority-owned construction firms; full details appear in Bates (1993a).

1.2). Possessing little education or capital, such firms are obvious candidates for marginality and dissolution. Yet, nonminority firms in special trades in the New York area, were *more* likely to be headed by high school dropouts in 1987 — 41.5 percent of the owners had not finished high school — and the average firm had been established with a financial investment of only $6,934. Finally, MBEs in the special trades are only marginally profitable as a group, while their nonminority cohorts operate profitably.

A comparison of MBE construction firms still operating in 1991, versus those closed down, revealed stark differences, which are particularly pronounced in five areas. First, failed MBEs in construction generated very little revenue: 1987 sales among the survivors ($156,433) were over four times higher than sales among the closed firms ($37,785) (Table 1.3). Second, and closely related, owners of failed firms worked far fewer hours, suggesting a limited ability to find work. Owners of surviving MBEs spent 1,810 hours, on average, working while the owners of closed down construction firms averaged only 999 hours. Third, most of the failures were firms in operation for two or fewer years. Fourth, MBEs in the special trades were heavily overrepresented in the failure column in Table 1.3. Fifth, surviving MBEs in construction started out with nearly twice the financial capitalization of discontinued operations. The portrait of the firm most likely to fail —very small, young, little access to work, undercapitalized, and working in special trades — reflects the fact that it is hard for minority construction firms to get started and underway in the New York market. Most fail during their first few years of operation.

Table 1.3. Comparison of Surviving and Discontinued New York Area Minority Construction Firms.

	Surviving Firms*	Discontinued Firms
1987 total sales (mean)	$156,433	$37,785
Number of employees (mean)	1.3	0.3
Total financial capital (mean)	$10,393	$5,942
Percent in the special trades	76.4%	90.9%
Owners: percent college graduates	16.9%	14.4%
Annual owner labor input hours (mean)	1,809.6	999.2
Tenure in this small business (as of 1987)		
Two years or less	27.2%	71.3%
Five plus years	48.9%	15.5%

Source: U.S. Bureau of the Census Characteristics of Business Owners Database.
*All of the firms analyzed in this table were operating in 1987. Survival and discontinuance were measured by surveying owners in late 1991 to find out which firms were still in operation.

While MBEs in all lines of small business lag behind their nonminority cohorts in the New York City area, it is noteworthy that MBE construction firms lag *much further behind* than MBEs in other industries. MBEs accounted for 11.2 percent of all New York area small businesses in 1987, but only 5.6 percent of the construction firms (Bates, 1993a). MBEs tend to have higher firm closure rates than nonminority firms, but closure in construction is much higher than in other fields: 24.2 of the area MBE firms operating in 1987 had closed down by late 1991, versus a construction industry closure rate of 36.9 percent among MBEs.

When the MBEs in construction are analyzed from a traditional paradigm (stressing human capital and financial capital) a question arises: Why do New York area minorities in the special trades do *far* worse than nonminorities? Particularly in the special trades — which dominate the small business construction sector — MBE owners are better educated and begin operations with no financial capital disadvantage. In fact, such human capital and financial capital factors simply are *not* the crux of MBE disadvantage in construction. The crux of the matter appears to be discriminatory access to skills training, and to work. Even skills acquisition, when possible, does not solve the problem of old-boy networks, where work is parceled out to in-group members, few of whom are minorities.

Beneath the laws and the regulation and the collective bargaining agreements lies a reality of personal contracts and informal networks that bars most minorities from the skilled construction trades in the 1980's and 1990's, just as it did back in the 1950's. "A high proportion of skilled workers report having fathers or relatives in the trades." (Waldinger and Bailey, 1991, p.299). The skilled construction trades represent an extreme example of why minorities cannot get their fair share of jobs when educational barriers do not stand in their way. Construction is dominated by small firms that hire and promote through informal mechanisms. This structure has proven to be quite effective at frustrating anti-discrimination enforcement efforts. During the booming 1980's, black relative share in New York City skilled trades declined. "By the end of the 1980's, blacks were even more underrepresented in the industry and in its skilled trades that they had been in 1970" (Waldinger and Bailey 1991, p. 296). This explains why minorities in construction's special trades do worse than minorities in other lines of self-employment: Construction has been more resistant to nondiscriminatory practices than other sectors of society.

Discrimination in construction, as portrayed above, is not something that minorities can escape by switching their labor force status from "employee" to "self-employed." The same sorts of barriers are handicapping minorities when they make the leap from construction employee to construction self-employment. The resulting disadvantage manifests itself in two ways: *first*, lack of relevant skills and access to networks simply depresses the number of MBE construction firms. "We find 22.7 percent fewer minority-owned firms in the New York City market than we would expect absent discrimination in the construction industry" (Tweedie, McDonald and Sterett, 1992). *Second*, the firms that are formed by minorities are much smaller, less profitable, and more failure-prone than cohort nonminority firms, particularly in the special trades.

Many of the attractive types of work are closed off to the MBEs in construction. Access to the larger and more complex jobs, in particular, is limited because the only hope of access for small MBEs is through the route of subcontracts. The large general contractors naturally pick and choose the firms working as subcontractors on major projects. A knowledgeable official in New York State government clarifies why large jobs do not go to MBEs: "Are there any minority contractors who could take on a $20 or $30 million contract? In my experience, no there are not" (Regional Alliance for Small Contractors, 1992, p.1). Government procurement regulations often dictate "shotgun weddings" on public sector construction projects: prime contractors may be required to utilize minority subs. Such regulations often fail to protect the minority sub from abusive practices of prime contractors that resent being forced to work with MBEs. Simply not paying small, poorly capitalized MBE subcontractors on a timely basis is one effective way of undermining these firms. A detailed study of over 4,000 MBEs selling goods, and services to state and local governments has shown the MBE construction firms active in this market are *more* likely to go out of business than cohort firms sticking to the private sector (Bates and Williams, 1995).

New York State, like most state governments, often does require participation of Disadvantaged Business Enterprises (DBEs) in public sector construction. DBEs in New York can be either minority or women-owned businesses. A comparison of MBE and women-owned construction firm[5] performance in New York is highly instructive. Nonminority women working in construction are concentrated in the clerical occupations; their representation in the skilled occupations is much lower than that of blacks (Bates 1992). Yet nonminority women self-employed in construction reported mean 1987 sales of $429,591, far higher than mean sales for cohort nonminority males ($300,878) in the New York area (Bates 1993a).

In the New York area, women begin their construction firms with financial capital investments averaging over 50 percent above those of nonminority male owners in the industry. Women have achieved their firm size advantage over men despite the fact that

over half of them have owned their construction firms for two or fewer years! Per hour of labor input, women owners generate much higher firm revenues than white male and minority construction firm owners; sales in 1987 per hour of owner labor input averaged:

Female Owners	$264 per hour
Male Owners	$145 per hour
Minority Owners	$74 per hour

In contrast, minority owners of area construction companies generated a puny $74 in firm revenues during 1987 for each hour of owner labor input.

How do women owners — most of whom are recent entrants into construction self-employment — generate such high revenue volumes? Table 1.2 indicated that firms in the special trades generated much lower average sales in 1987 than other lines of contracting. Nonminority women are *overrepresented* in the special trades,

---

[5] Women-owned firms refers to those owned by nonminorities. MBEs owned by women are included in the minority business grouping.

where they account for 19.8 percent of the area nonminority firms (they account for 8.4 percent of the other nonminority contractors). Lacking access to skills acquisition and work experience in the special trades, nonminority women nonetheless attract much more work than their male cohorts in construction. How do they do it?

The answer, of course, has nothing to do with access to apprenticeship programs or other human capital factors. *Women achieve such success in construction only when they are well attached to the appropriate industry networks.* Their situation is exactly the opposite of that facing MBEs in construction: although they lack the skill, they have entry to the networks that control access to work. They are the in-group. They achieve success because their husbands and, or fathers work in the industry. In fact, 64.5 percent of the total revenues of women-owned construction firms operating in 1987 in the New York area went to multi-owner firms, and many of those other owners were male family members and relatives (Bates 1993a). The relative frequency of multi-owner male-owned construction firms was a small fraction of the female total.

Nonminority women owning New York area construction firms are commonly members of the applicable industry networks that block minority progress in all aspects of construction — skills acquisition, employment, and access to work for MBEs. These firms, in turn, compete with MBEs when preferential procurement programs call for greater DBE participation in public sector procurement.

The success experienced by nonminority women in building construction firms illustrates the importance of "social capital" to one's performance in the self-employment realm. Glenn Loury (1989, 1981, 1977) has asserted the importance of social capital, defined as cultural attributes or values derived from one's family and community background, for determining socioeconomic status. Loury (1989) understands that there are externalities to social capital: one may benefit (or be harmed) from the existence of a particular type of social capital without being a direct contributor.

Typically, economists have accepted a rather "narrow interpretation" of Loury's concept of social capital, implying that social capital includes only "values" obtained from one's family and community backgrounds. These cultural attributes increase the quality and quantity of observed individual productive attributes (such as education) and thereby indirectly increase earnings. The case of nonminority women owners of construction firms suggests that a "broad interpretation" of Loury's social capital hypothesis is possible. Individual economic well-being is related to the extent of one's connections to individuals embedded into positions of power and authority in the marketplace. Presumably, persons from high socioeconomic status backgrounds (white women in the construction industry) are likely to have more accessible and more varied connections to the set of individuals embedded into positions of power and authority than observationally equal or more educated persons from lower socioeconomic status backgrounds (African Americans). Differences in earnings within this broad interpretation of the social capital thesis are not the result of differences in productive attributes, as implied by the conventional approaches to racial inequality.[6]

CONCLUDING REMARKS

One theme raised in Mr. Gulianni's successful campaign for mayor was the unfair advantage enjoyed by MBE vendors in the competition for New York City's procurement business. Mayor Dinkins had established preferential procurement program for minority vendors in 1992. Gulianni eliminated bid preferences allowed to MBEs in the awarding of city contracts. Challenging the discriminatory environment in New York City construction is not high on the political agenda.

In the favorable political environment of the 1960's, minorities generally, and blacks specifically, increased their access to jobs in New York's construction industry (Waldinger and Bailey, 1991). By 1980, most blacks working in construction were in the skilled occupations. This pattern was altered in the 1980's: while new construction boomed in New York, blacks' share of the resultant skilled jobs and earnings declined. Among those seeking to go out on their own, access to work was a major stumbling block and successful small business creation was often aborted. Particularly in the special trades, minority self-employed were often out of business after several years. Nonminority firms in the special trades enjoyed no financial capital or owner education advantages over minorities. Nonminority startups in construction faced less of a lag than minorities in generating substantial revenues; firms in business for a year or two show a particular advantage over minority firms of the same age (Bates, 1993a). Once again, nonminorities entering construction self-employment often have immediate access to networks that provide them work, while minority firms must try to build up these contracts with networks gradually during their early years of operation. Many MBEs never survived the slow startup phase. *Access to work is the key to understanding differences in the performance of minority and nonminority-owned construction firms operating the New York area special trades.* The average minority owner worked 1,524 hours in 1987, versus 2,058 hours for nonminorities. Among MBE construction firms operating in 1987 that had shut down by late 1991, most were able to generate only negligible annual revenues. The hypothesis that labor market discrimination can be circumvented by pursuing self-employment appears to have little applicability: the same discriminatory processes that typify the labor market appear to have their counterparts in the small business construction sector.

Is construction an atypical line of self-employment or do similar discriminatory processes operate in other sectors of the economy? It is atypical in the sense that very large jobs are widespread, and access to work often entails acceptance of subcontractor status by small firms. Industries where markets are more widely accessible to young small businesses may be more amenable to MBE growth. However,

---

[6] See Mason (forthcoming) for an extended discussion of the narrow versus the broad interpretation of social capital.

construction (in the absence of discriminatory practices) offers huge advantages to MBEs that are lacking in many other fields. Advanced educational credentials are *not* a barrier to entry in construction; large financial capital investment is *not* a barrier to entry in construction.

Construction is unique in that the conventional barriers do not apply. Construction offers a direct test of how blacks fare when job and self-employment access into a predominantly nonminority industry is *not* blocked by gaps in educational attainment. The findings suggest that political activism must be high on the agenda if economic parity is ever going to be attained.

The discriminatory barriers prevalent in construction reflect, in part, the dominance of this industry by small firms. Hiring practices in small businesses are generally network-based: jobs are most accessible to family members, relatives, friends, and friends of friends. Most small businesses operating in large metropolitan areas have no minority employees: minorities commonly are not members of the relevant networks. Even among nonminority-owned small firms operating in minority communities, most of the employees are white (Bates 1994). In an era when African American job seekers in many cities are increasingly reliant upon the small business sector for jobs (Bates, 1994), their employment prospects may increasingly resemble those prevailing in New York's construction market.

REFERENCES

Bates, T. 1990. "New Data Bases in the Social Sciences: The Characteristics of Business Owners Data Base." *Journal of Human Resources* 25 (4) (Fall):752–756.

_____. 1992. "Appendix D: Expected Representation of Minority and Women-Owned Businesses and Barriers Related to their Underrepresentation," In *Opportunity Denied: A Study of Racial and Sexual Discrimination Related to Government Contracting in New York State*, Division of Minority and Women's Business Development, editors, pages 1–207. Albany: New York State Department of Economic Development.

_____. 1993a. "Assessment of the New Jersey, New York City Area Small Business Construction Sector." Report to the Port Authority of New York and New Jersey, and the Regional Alliance of Small Contractors (October).

_____. 1993b. *Assessment of State and Local Government Minority Business Development Programs*." Contract #50–SABE-2–00086, final report. Washington, D.C.: U.S. Department of Commerce Minority Business Development Agency.

_____. 1993c. *Banking on Black Enterprise*. Washington, D.C.: Joint Center for Political and Economic Studies.

_____. 1994. "Utilization of Minority Employees in Small Business," *The Review of Black Political Economy* 23 (1) (Summer):113–21.

_____. and D. Williams. 1995. "Preferential Procurement Programs Do Not Necessarily Help Minority-Owned Businesses." *Journal of Urban Affairs* 17 (1) (February):1–17.

Devine, T. and J. Mlaker. 1992. "Inter-Industry Variation in the Determinants of Self-Employment." unpublished manuscript. University Park, PA.: Pennsylvannia State University.

Ihlanfeld, K. and M. Young. forthcoming. "Housing Segregation and the Wages and Commutes of Urban Blacks," *Review of Economics and Statistics*.

Kasarda, J. 1990. "City Jobs and Residents on a Collision Course: The Urban Underclass Dilemma," *Economic Development Quarterly* 4 (4) (November):313–19.

Light, I. 1972. *Ethnic Enterprise in America*. Berkeley: University of California Press.

Loury, G. 1989. "Why Should We Care About Inequality?" In *The Question of Discrimination: Racial Inequality in the U.S. Labor Market*, S. Schulman and W. Darity, eds., 268–290. Middletown, CT: Wesleyan University Press.

———. 1981. "Intergenerational Transfers and the Distribution of Earnings," *Econometrica* 49 (4):843–867.

———. 1977. "A Dynamic Theory of Racial Income Differences," In *Women, Minorities, and Employment Discrimination*, A. Lemond and P. Wallace, eds., 153–186. Lexington, MA: Lexington Books.

Mason, P. (forthcoming). "Competing Explanations of Male Interracial Wage Differentials: Missing Variable Models Versus Job Competition." *Cambridge Journal of Economics*.

Moore, R. 1983. "Employer Discrimination: Evidence from Self-Employed Workers," *Review of Economics and Statistics* 65 (3) (August):496–500.

Moss, P. and C. Tilly. 1992. *Why are Black Men Doing Worse in the Labor Market?* Report to the Social Science Research Council. Washington: D.C.

Peterson, G. and W. Vroman, eds. 1992. *Urban Labor Markets and Individual Opportunity*. Washington, D.C.: The Urban Institute Press.

Regional Alliance for Small Contractors. 1993. *Creating Growth Opportunities for Minorities and Women-Owned Businesses* (June).

Tweedie J., M. McDonald, and S. Sterett. 1992. "Minority and Women-Owned Firms in the New York State Agency Construction Markets," In *Opportunity Denied: A Study of Racial and Sexual Discrimination Related to Government Contracting in New York State*, Appendix E, Division of Minority and Women's Business Development, editors. Albany: New York State Department of Economic Development, 1992.

U.S. Department of Commerce, Bureau of the Census, *County Business Patterns* (1991, 1986, and 1981). Washington, D.C.

Waldinger, R. and T. Bailey. 1991. "The Continuing Significance of Race: Racial Conflict and Racial Discrimination in Construction," *Politics and Society* 19 (3) (September):291–323.

Wilson, W. 1987. *The Truly Disadvantaged*. Chicago: University of Chicago Press.

2

BLACK EMPLOYMENT, CRIMINAL ACTIVITY AND ENTREPRENEURSHIP: A CASE STUDY OF NEW JERSEY

Samuel L. Myers, Jr. and William E. Spriggs

INTRODUCTION

Current debates about crime and violence center on the effectiveness of sentencing reforms and incarceration in reducing crime. These punishment approaches to crime often ignore the evidence that employment also is an effective deterrent to crime and that in many respects crime can be viewed as a consequence of blocked legitimate earnings opportunities (Myers, 1983). There are important linkages between barriers to employment and the rise of criminal enterprise in African American communities. Many of these linkages can be viewed through the lens of northern states like New Jersey that experienced great transformation as a result of significant migration and demographic shifts during the first half of the twentieth century.

This chapter sketches a historical linkage between poor jobs, blocked employment opportunities, and the rise of criminal entrepreneurship. We suggest that this linkage may help to explain the low levels of self employment and business ownership in the current era. Although the story we tell is far from a definitive assessment of the failure to develop a strong African American business class in the post-World War II era, it does offer a glimpse of the apparent links crime, business ownership and employment.

We begin our story with some historical background on racial bias in employment in New Jersey. We then discuss the changing industrial structure in the post World War II period showing the roots of blocked employment paths for even professional blacks.

Blocked opportunities in particular industries contributed in part to the underrepresentation of African American businesses in those industries. To understand the underrepresentation of black businesses, however, requires an understanding of how a class of capitalists and entrepreneurs failed to emerge from the black middle class. We summarize the origins of the black middle-class in New Jersey. We sketch an hypothesis about why the black entrepreneurial class did not emerge from the black middle class. This permits us to examine empirically the ultimate impacts of the black professional/middle class on black business formation. We confirm, as our hypothesis would suggest, that at least in New Jersey with its legacy of a black middle class removed from business ownership, black business participation grew less rapidly there than it did elsewhere in the nation and that the size of the professional class among blacks has only a minor impact on black business participation rates. This has meant, ultimately, that other segments of society, including the black criminal class, remained as the principal heirs to entrepreneurship.

HISTORICAL BIAS AGAINST BLACK WORKERS IN NEW JERSEY

Ample evidence exists of long-standing patterns of discrimination against black workers in New Jersey. The New Jersey Historical Society relates:

> Of all New Jersey ethnic groups, Afro-Americans suffered most during the Depression of the 1930's. In 1932 black unemployment in the state was nearly twice that of whites. And once blacks lost their jobs they tended to remain unemployed longer than whites, so that they were more likely to become impoverished. In 1935 26 percent of the families on relief in the state were black, although black families constituted only five percent of the state's total family population. In 1937 the relief rolls in the state's eight largest cities revealed a disproportionate number of blacks; they were three to six times more likely to be relief recipients than whites in these cities. In Elizabeth, for example, where blacks constituted 4.2 percent of the family population, they accounted for 28.5 percent of the family relief cases.

> Black worker displacement was another feature of the Depression. White workers drove blacks out of certain positions they had held for decades. Waiters, hotel workers, elevator operators and others were replaced by young white women, while janitors and others were supplanted by white men (Wright, 1988:63).

In her historical analysis of the skilled working class in Newark, New Jersey, Susan Hirsch uncovers a persistent pattern of racial discrimination that has had enduring impacts on the structure of employment opportunities for blacks. The backdrop for this was the decline of the status of artisans as a result of industrialization:

> In pre-industrial Newark, an artisan class that included all craftsmen—apprentices, journeymen, and masters—was an important component of the class structure. Craftsmen had much status and power in local society; they were allied with a commercial class of merchants and professionals, and were above the class of laborers. Industrialization caused a split within the old artisan class between employers and employees and brought a new class structure and a new status structure to local society. The former artisan class was destroyed by industrialization since various former craftsmen were affected in different ways by the process. Those craftsmen who were employers joined merchants and professionals to form a capitalist class, while journey men and apprentices aligned themselves with workers. Few journeymen managed to rise to self-employment within their industry (Hirsch, 1978:xvii-xviii).

Hirsch's analysis focuses on a city, Newark, that by 1860 had become one of the leading industrial cities in the nation with 74 percent of the labor force employed in manufacturing (Hirsch, 1978:xix). Although initially an agricultural township, Newark became industrialized as an outgrowth of shoe making enterprises serving primarily the South. Road and bridge building efforts, along with expansion of shipping and credit linkages with New York City, combined with the production efforts of farmers in the off-season creating a massive shoemaking enterprise.

Before the 1830s, Newark was a largely homogeneous city, mostly Protestant, with strong values related to work and family, and with only one significant minority group: free blacks, representing about five percent of the population. Industrialization changed this. Economic development helped to spur the mechanization of production which "rendered craftsmen's skills obsolete (Hirsch, 1978:37)" and thus created a need for a pool of low wage labor. Hirsch argues that blacks were not deemed suitable to fill this role because:

> Community prejudice and the small number of blacks in Newark prevented manufacturers from using blacks as cheap labor. Few blacks were attracted to the town because of the negative effects of white racism on their job opportunities, social life, and civil rights. The black people of Newark comprised less than six percent of the total population between 1830 and 1860, and they formed a continually segregated group within the city. Prejudice against them was so strong that they were forced to have their own institutions: schools, churches, lodges, and the like. When a black person attended a pubic facility like the theater or library, there was an immediate pubic outcry by insulted whites. White fears of black equality caused Newark's first riot in July 1834 when enraged whites sought to disrupt an abolitionist lecture....blacks were often insulted or attacked by gangs of young white toughs who inhabited the street corners. The police did not interfere (Hirsch, 1978:38).

Hirsch argues that the major crafts were essentially all white and male. As for women, Hirsch contends:

> Manufactures did not open new jobs to women even though they worked for less, for women had many deficiencies as a work force. Above all, their employment violated the

values of Newarkers, who like Americans in general, viewed woman's domestic function as paramount (Hirsch, 1978:39).

Thus, low-wage labor in manufacturing industries was sought from immigrants, largely Irish and German males during the period 1830 to 1860, forestalling the economic advancement of African Americans who at that time were prohibited by state law from even voting.

Employment practices in the North, including those in New Jersey, differed sharply from those in the South where there was a pattern of segregated jobs — "good" jobs for whites (usually white men), and dirty, heavy work for blacks. In the North, however, the more common pattern was exclusion of blacks. In northern manufacturing it was common for there to be some work designated as "women's work," designed to meet the requirements of the state protective laws and paying less than male jobs. The dirty, heavy work performed by low paid blacks in southern factories was exclusive to white men earning higher wages in the north. Northern blacks were not hired at all.

Another important development that thwarted blacks' mobility within important occupations was the formation of industrial unions of immigrant workers. David Goldberg (1989) reviews the evolution of the Amalgamated Textile Workers of America in Paterson and Passaic, New Jersey in the aftermath of the massive textile worker strikes in 1919. He argues that these unions deviated from the craft structure of the earlier unions, which were composed largely of native-born workers. The interests of the immigrant workers often clashed (or appeared to clash) with those of native-born blacks, who were often used by northern firms as strike-breakers.

The best available statistics reveal that blacks held the lowest paying jobs requiring the fewest skills and were concentrated in the least desirable occupations in New Jersey in every decade from 1870 to 1940. However, much of this is a direct result of racist and sexist practices by the Census itself. When blacks or women moved into high-skilled occupations in non-trivial numbers, census enumerators merely reclassified the jobs as low-skilled ones. The following long quotation documents this:

> Census occupational statistics would therefore tend to be inaccurate in terms of those patterns which violated the rules for the whole. If there were, for example, blacks and women in skilled trades or high status occupations, the census data would tend to obscure them. Since most blacks and women worked at semiskilled and unskilled jobs, the census coder would classify an ambiguous return for a Black or female skilled worker in a lower status category. The gross patterns would probably be accurate though. Two examples will illustrate the issue.

> The dressmaking trade provides a sharp example of the problem of using census occupation statistics and the socio-economic status hierarchy to analyze women's work. In the occupation statistics for the ninth to the twelfth Censuses (1870–1900), dressmakers were listed as a "manufacturing" trade — 99 percent were women. In 1910 Edwards found it troublesome to list women workers among the skilled trade. Thus in his interpretive writings on the occupation statistics he moved dressmakers, who he conceded were "technically" skilled, to the ranks of the semiskilled, "because the enumerators returned

so many children, young persons, and women as pursuing the occupation." Since women worked at the job, the job could not be skilled. In 1940, when Edwards organized all occupations on the basis of socioeconomic status, he classified the dressmakers among the semiskilled operatives. An entire trade was downgraded, not because of structural changes in the job, but because of the group in the population who worked at it. Tailoring, by the way, remained a male, and a skilled, occupation.

The 1920 Census reports on shipbuilding workers are highly suspect, I think. It was an industry which as late as 1930 had over 50 percent of its work force in skilled trades, yet the 1920 Census listed shipbuilding workers under unskilled and semiskilled occupations. Thus the reports list 19,000 semiskilled and unskilled workers among the individual trades or misclassified skilled workers into the semiskilled and unskilled categories. Checking the appropriate skilled trades, one would expect to find some 19,000 extra workers in those jobs who in reality worked at the ship yards. There are no such inflated figures among the machinists, welders, heaters, carpenters, or other trades related to shipbuilding. Thus I would suggest that the census misclassified many skilled shipbuilding workers into unskilled and semiskilled positions because they were Black or immigrant.

Some verification of this hypothesis is possible by comparing the labor figures of the U.S. Shipping Board, Emergency Fleet Corporation against the census data. In September 1919 the Shipping Board reported the number of Black workers, skilled and unskilled, in the principal shipyard districts around the country. They reported 3,078 skilled and 2,426 unskilled Black workers in the yards in the Southern district. This encompassed the coast from Wilmington, North Carolina to the Mississippi River. The census taken four months later reported 7,833 unskilled Black workers and 1,581 Black semiskilled workers for the same region. In all, 17,500 workers were reported for the district. In other words, the census radically skewed the skill levels of the industry by making its occupational classifications on the basis of demographic data. Even if all the unskilled Black workers were in fact unskilled, and most of them are unemployed, and the semiskilled workers were in fact skilled, the census would still have underreported skilled black shipbuilding workers by 1,500 according to the Shipping Board figures (Conk, 1980).

The nature and scope of discrimination against better educated persons are more complex. There is the difficulty of determining whether the source of discrimination is race or gender on the one hand, or such permissible factors as performance, personality, attitude or motivation on the other. Since evaluators' perceptions of performance are often influenced by the race and gender of the worker, matters are clouded further. For example, the *Star Ledger* reported the following:

An Irvington woman who worked for AT&T for 23 years and filed a lawsuit claiming she was fired because of racial discrimination was awarded $465,000 in damages yesterday by a Superior Court jury in Newark.

... the jury rejected a claim that AT&T had discriminated against the plaintiff.... Her attorney had argued that Cary was replaced by a white women who was less qualified.

But the jury found that Cary had been defamed. Cary's attorney argued a superior had improperly altered positive evaluations of her work in order to justify firing her.

... AT&T said she was dismissed as part of widespread layoffs. (Dec. 19, 1991, p.38)

A more telling example where false evaluations cannot mask discriminatory behavior comes from the following case reported in the *Star Ledger*:

> A state appeals court ruled yesterday that Felicia Jamison, a black science teacher in Rockaway Township, had been a victim of racial discrimination when she was passed over for the position of assistant principal at Birchwood elementary School and the job was given to a less qualified white person.

> ... Jamison was rejected for the post after George Xenitelis, then the Birchwood principal, said some members of his staff could not work with her and added that he would not be responsible for parents' reaction if she were appointed assistant principal ... (April 25, 1990)

Without filing a lawsuit and uncovering discriminatory behavior, the two plaintiffs would have been viewed as disgruntled employees whose firings were justified. Because of the subjective nature of much decision-making in higher-level employment actions, racial discrimination in firing or other adverse employment actions appear difficult to prove.

Still, the vast majority of New Jersey employment discrimination cases to reach the federal court of appeals were filed by women and those in either professional or white-collar jobs. This despite the fact that there is widespread evidence of blatant and overt forms of prejudice and bigotry in blue-color employment. Employment discrimination, while operating in different ways for different groups, nonetheless affects blacks of all stripes.

INDUSTRY AND BLACK EMPLOYMENT

Blacks historically have been concentrated in industries that provided little opportunity for advancement into successful entrepreneurship. They were concentrated in industries that also limited opportunities for developing businesses that could contract with the state. They historically have been found in private household services and related services; they have been absent from construction, engineering, and legal professional services industries.

One can demonstrate this by computing a measure of "relative representation." To do this, first derive the ratio of employed minorities to employed whites for the entire state; then, compute the ratio of employed minorities to employed whites for the specific industry in the state. Taking these two and obtaining the ratio of the second to the first provides a measure of the relative representation of minorities in a particular industry. If minorities are distributed equally across industries, then this relative representation measure will be equal to one. That is, if minorities are found in a given industry in the same proportions as they are found in the labor force, then they are neither underrepresented nor concentrated in that industry. If the ratio is greater than one, then minorities are concentrated in an industry; if the ratio is less than one, then minorities are underrepresented in an industry.

This computation can be performed for any specific minority group. For example, in 1980, the ratio of American Indians employed to whites was .001551. That is, for every 10,000 whites, there were 15 Indians employed in New Jersey. In mining, however, the ratio of Indians to whites was .003136. In other words American Indians were twice as likely to be represented in mining, relative to whites, as in the labor force generally.

Using this criterion for measuring representation, we find that in 1980, blacks were heavily concentrated in service industries, private household service, hospitals, social service, religious, and membership organizations, health care and public administration. The only manufacturing industries among the top ten areas of overrepresentation were food and kindred products, transportation equipment and primary metals. They were also concentrated in public transportation. They were vastly underrepresented in wholesale trade, retail trade, construction and legal, engineering and other professional services.

How did this result come about? The concentration of blacks in service industries in the 1980s and their underrepresentation in important industries with which the State of New Jersey contracts, evolves from the slow development since World War II of the isolation of blacks in a handful of low-paying industries.

Black females historically have been concentrated in the "private household services" industry. That is, they were servants in the homes of whites. Of the 32,040 black females employed in the state in 1940, 23,621 were employed as domestics. They were 13 times more likely to be maids than were white women who worked. Black women were greatly concentrated in most of the non-professional services. Although they were often excluded from hospital work, they nonetheless were concentrated in health services, which at that time meant work as mid-wives and attendants to the elderly and infirm.

Their involvement in the retail industries was limited to eating places; there they worked primarily as cooks and dishwashers. They generally were excluded from conventional retail establishments, such as department stores and food stores, where they often could not even shop.

In 1940, black females were also excluded to a large extent from manufacturing industries, public utilities and wholesale trade. They were grossly underrepresented in the legal services professions and the finance, insurance and real estate industries, industries that could have served as the springboard for a future generation's movement into entrepreneurship.

The low numbers of black women in manufacturing are particularly revealing. In 1940 there were only 1,700 black women employed in all of the manufacturing plants in the state. By 1950, when there were 51,580 black women employed statewide, 11,961 worked in various manufacturing plants. As David Noble points out, this shift came about because of the production demands of World War II, when both black and white women were recruited for the major war manufacturing efforts (Noble, 1984).

At the same time, there were 22,657 black women employed in the private household services, about 1,000 less than a decade earlier. Black women shifted from domestic work to manufacturing after World War II. They were still over-represented in the private household services and vastly underrepresented in profes-sional business services. They remained largely absent from legal and engineering services, real estate, insurance and finance.

By 1960, when there were 79,177 black females employed in the state, 18,562 were in manufacturing, while 20,742 remained in domestic services. Although they were still underrepresented in various services, black women saw their representa-tion in professional services and public administration soar by the 1960s. They re-mained underrepresented in construction, wholesale trade, and in critical growth industries such as chemicals.

The movement into manufacturing was complete by 1970. Of the 124,567 black women employed in New Jersey, 34,582 were located in the various manufacturing industries. There was also continued growth of the middle class; a dramatic shift of black women from household service occurred as clerical and administrative jobs were opened to them. The numbers of black women in professional services rose substantially. There were almost as many black women in professional services (33,957) as there were in manufacturing that year; only 11,995 remained maids, half the number of earlier decades.

Despite the impressive move into professional employment, black women were virtually absent from many of the industries that would prove vital for state con-tracting and procurement in later years. They were severely underrepresented in printing and construction and were largely absent from engineering, legal services, banking and credit. Thus, precisely at the time that a sizable professional class among black women solidified its position in the labor market, barriers to entry in critical industries seemed to mount.

The 1970s saw some men's jobs (i.e. bank tellers) become women's jobs. Higher professional bank positions were filled by new MBA's instead of promotion of tell-ers from within, as had been true when white men were tellers. Just when doors of opportunity to black women opened, educational requirements for advancement multiplied.

By the 1980s, then, the die had been cast. Black professional women found themselves in public utilities, public administration, and in a handful of manufac-turing industries located near the decaying central cities: transportation equipment and railroads. They remained underrepresented in most "high-tech" industries and were also found in relatively few numbers in retail trade, wholesale trade, publish-ing, printing and the legal and engineering professions. Of the 175,087 black fe-male workers in 1980 residing in New Jersey, 63,683 were in professional services; 13,783 were in public administration.

The upshot of this 40–year transformation was that a managerial class had evolved, redefining the role of black women in the labor market. But these profes-sional women were concentrated in the public sector, not in the private sector, where they remained underrepresented. Many black women, formerly maids, simply withdrew from the labor market altogether. Those who remained in manufacturing faced bleak prospects because the industries in which they were concentrated—located as they were in the crumbling cores of metropolitan areas—were stagnant.

The story for black males is similar. They were concentrated in low-wage service industries and underrepresented in the high-wage growth industries that made New Jersey a leading producer of petroleum and chemical products. The difference is that blacks were disproportionately found in entertainment and recreation industries and several heavy industries, such as primary metals, that had already begun to face stiff international competition by the late 1970s. Steel workers have relatively high salaries—but only when they work. The concentration of black males in declining manufacturing industries was matched only by their underrepresentation in key professional service industries and in finance, credit, and business services.

THE BLACK MIDDLE CLASS OF NEW JERSEY

The underrepresentation of black firms in New Jersey is linked to the origins of the black middle class there. The history of black professional involvement in the medical and teaching professions devoted to uplifting the larger black masses is illustrative. This class stems largely from the growth of a free black population in the Delaware Valley. As is told in a New Jersey Historical Society tract:

> Facilitating the cultural metamorphosis of northern blacks was the "First Emancipation," the creation of a free black population. New Jersey's southern region in particular figured prominently in this development. It was a part of the Delaware Valley, where, due to a strong Quaker presence and influence, black slaves were first manumitted in very significant numbers (Wright, 1988:29).

Examples of the early success of these middle-class blacks are abundant:

> Dr. James Still (1812–1885), born in Shamong, Burlington County, was one of the earliest black medical doctors in New Jersey. Mainly self-educated, he specialized in the preparation and use of traditional medicines such as powders, tinctures, salves, liniments, teas and vegetable oils. His success enabled him to acquire considerable property and to build a large house and office in Medford (Wright, 1988:43).

> One [of the delegates to a black state-wide convention] was Dr. John S. Rock from Salem, a physician and dentist, who later became the first black attorney to practice before the United States Supreme Court. Another, Ishmael Locke of Camden County, was a teacher who had served as the principal of the Institute for Colored Youth in Philadelphia. (His grandson, Alain Locke, became the first black Rhodes Scholar, a philosopher and "guiding spirit" of the Harlem Renaissance in the 1920s.) The pastor of the church where the convention was held was the Reverend W.T. Catto. His son, Octavius V. Catto, a Philadelphia educator and a leader of the successful battle in the 1860s to end the city's streetcar segregation, was killed in 1871 in rioting after blacks voted under the newly acquired protection of the Fifteenth Amendment (Wright, 1988:34).

These successful blacks played prominent roles in the development of many institutions designed to serve the cultural and intellectual needs of the black community. Their energies were not devoted to business development or acquisition of capital; such would be a luxury affordable only when the masses of blacks were truly free. In this climate of considerable hostility directed towards blacks in New Jersey, even successful black professionals had much to fear.[1] Thus, they plunged into the difficult task of building institutions that had never before existed for the descendants of slaves in the Americas:

> The emergence of a free black population aided considerably the growth of black organizations and institutions of non-African nature and character. These new institutions sought basically to promote the race's general welfare and to ameliorate the harsh conditions of black life. They include fraternal lodges, benevolent societies, literacy societies and temperance organizations. The first four black fraternal lodges were organized between 1845 and 1847 in Trenton, Burlington, Camden and Salem. By the late 1860s Camden had a baseball team—the Blue Sky Club—which competed against other early black teams from Brooklyn, Philadelphia, Chicago, Washington, D.C. and Harrisburg.

The reason the middle class focused on black development was that the general black population faced such a precarious economic fate. Unlike other immigrant groups that either brought their own institutions with them or were assimilated into existing institutions that could provide the support for their economic well-being, blacks were in a unique state. Either they were free, but unwelcome by those whose institutions they hoped to join, or they were former slaves—forcibly broken off from their institutions and unaccustomed to the ways of the ones in their adopted home.

The unfavorable economic circumstances of the masses of blacks are worth remembering:

> One constant for New Jersey blacks down to 1870 was their dim economic prospect. Throughout the state most blacks were concentrated at the bottom of the occupational hierarchy, in low-income, menial work. In southern New Jersey many farmed for themselves or worked as farm laborers, often on Quaker-owned farms and large estates. In the towns and cities with sizable black populations, such as Newark, Trenton, Camden, Jersey City, Elizabeth and Princeton, they worked as unskilled laborers (for example, ditch diggers, hod carriers and porters) or were engaged in the domestic and service trades. By 1870 the labor supply offered by white immigrants had reduced the position of blacks in the skilled crafts and precluded their employment in the industrial concerns that were springing up in the state's urban centers (Wright, 1988:44).

---

[1] Wright documents the nature of these hostilities:
Examples of antipathy toward the darker race in New Jersey are easy to find. With the possible exception of New York, New Jersey had the most severe slave code of the northern colonies. In 1704, for example, a New Jersey law prescribed forty lashes and the branding of a T on the left cheek of any slave convicted of the theft of five to forty shillings. It dictated castration for any who attempted or had sexual relations with a white woman. A century later, New Jersey was the last northern state to enact legislation abolishing slavery; a law passed in 1804 established a system of gradual emancipation. This system actually allowed slavery to continue down to 1860's later by the domestic slave trade that relocated bondsmen in southern lands opened for cotton cultivation beginning in the early 1800s. Some were even delivered to southern markets, especially New Orleans, as late as the 1820s. From 1852 to 1859, the legislature appropriated $1,000 annually to transport free black New Jerseyans to Africa. op. cit., p. 14.

Things did not change much into the 20th century:

The masses of the race continued to occupy the lower rungs of the occupational ladder. In 1910 black urban males still tended to be laborers, delivery men, janitors, porters, teamsters, chauffeurs, waiters and servants. Women were heavily employed as laundresses, dressmakers and domestic servants (Wright, 1988:50).

By this period, however, the role of overt discrimination became apparent:

The prejudice of white employers and employees combined to exclude blacks from factory work and the skilled crafts. Comments from labor and management in the 1903 report of the Bureau of Statistics of Labor and Industries typify the mood of their period. "Their color and low instincts make them undesirable associates for white men," said an official of the carpenters' union in New Jersey. A representative of the glass bottle blowers declared, "[I] do not believe the average Negro is capable of acquiring the skill necessary to become a successful glass blower. They are naturally lazy and are not clean in their habits." A New Jersey brick manufacturer states, "[We] have no Negroes employed at our works and have made no attempt to use Negro labor. We prefer white foreign help such as Hungarians, Polanders, etc." And a manufacturer of hats reserved, "We do not employ Negroes in the hat manufacturing business; [we] do not believe they could be trained to do the work (Wright, 1988:51)."

The result of the depressed conditions of the general black population and the small numbers of black professionals was that there developed two distinct lines of businesses. On one hand, basic service shops evolved. The entrepreneurs who seized these service providing opportunities often had little education and even less initial capital. But they were able to thrive on the demand for their services from a black population with little cash. Much of the demand existed because white businesses would not serve blacks.

On the other hand, professional services were delivered by the doctors and dentists. These professionals suffered from exclusion from opportunities in the mainstream economy, but ironically benefited from the artificial monopoly created by the lack of professional services in the black community.

As the ghettos grew, more Afro-Americans were able to heed the age-old exhortations of black leaders and newspapers to go into business for themselves. Indeed, most of the state's black urban communities came to feature an array of black-owned establishments that catered mainly to blacks: building and loan associations, hotels, beauty parlors, dry cleaning shops, printing shops, funeral parlors, photography shops, pool halls, saloons, laundries, realty companies, employment agencies, shoe repair shops, confectioneries, butcher shops, ice houses, and dressmaking shops. The most successful tended to be barber shops, beauty parlors, restaurants, pool halls, and undertakers, which met needs normally ignored by white business in the ghetto. In contrast, small retail businesses owned by blacks were often unable to offer a wide variety of products and extend credit to customers, whereas their white competitors had the capital to offer these options to buyers (Wright, 1988:60).

The solidly entrenched middle class, however, did not enter entrepreneurship; they remained in professions needed as a result of continued racial segregation:

> The expanded ghetto economy also facilitated an increase of black professionals: teachers, physicians, nurses, dentists, lawyers, pharmacists and social workers. While the Great Migration's participants were largely poor and low in status, professionals also participated in the exodus North. Many of them helped organize such bodies as the New Jersey Association for Teachers of Colored Children, the Commonwealth Dental Association, and the North Jersey Medical Society (Wright, 1988:60).

In sum, the pre-World War II New Jersey black middle class largely devoted itself to establishment and enhancement of black institutions and provision of professional services and not to the development of major business enterprises. The result is that by the post-war period, the large and growing middle class did not usher in a booming entrepreneurial class.

WHY A BLACK ENTREPRENEURIAL CLASS FAILED TO EMERGE IN NEW JERSEY

Criminal Entrepreneurship

Ivan Light in his classic study, *Ethnic Enterprise in America*, identifies two characteristic experiences that have shaped the development of businesses of immigrant groups in America. One is the importance of credit and the role of traditional revolving credit associations found in many parts of the developing world. Another is the role of criminal activities both as a form of organization of enterprise and as a source of capital for the creation of immigrant businesses.[2]

More recent writings elaborate and extend this model for understanding the difference between African American and immigrant group experiences with entrepreneurship. For example, evidence from the 1980s shows that many immigrant groups have succeeded economically through entrepreneurship and self-employment. Balkin (1989) surveys this evidence showing that certain groups, like Eastern European Jews, Lebanese, Greeks, Koreans, Japanese and Chinese have self-employment rates significantly higher than the national average. Lower than average self-employment rates are found among Puerto Ricans, Dominicans, Haitians, Jamaicans, and persons of Subsahran African decent—meaning both Africans and African American. While the rate of self employment among Jamaicans is 60 percent higher than that among those of Subsaharan African descent, the rates of all

---

[2] Ivan Light, *Ethnic Enterprise in America,* 1972. Note, however, traditional revolving credit associations generally do not function as banks—making loans based on fractional reserves. As such, they do not create funds, they do not increase aggregate savings, nor do they necessarily increase individual saving rates. Thus, to the extent that these arrangements explain the success of immigrant groups, at least part of the explanation might lie in the higher initial wealth holdings of these immigrants.

blacks are found to be considerably lower than they are for most Asians and nearly all white groups (Balkin, 1989).

The explanation for the lower self-employment rates among native-born blacks as compared to immigrant groups, according to Light, is that they lack ethnic and class resources (Light, 1984). Access to capital—either obtained from conventional lenders or through revolving credit associations—is limited because of discrimination or absence of cultural or ethnic institutions supporting lending for black business development. The social networks and lending patterns observed among Koreans, Indians and Jews simply do not exist among native-born blacks, according to Balkin (op cit., p. 55). The problem is not one of lack of diligence, thriftiness, profit-seeking, or individualism—all classic determinants of entrepreneurial behavior. Rather, the problem is one of blocked legitimate opportunities and constrained resources. As a result, many of the entrepreneurial activities of native born blacks have been directed towards illegal pursuits (Myers, 1978; Light and Rosenstein, 1995).

Cultural explanations for differences in self-employment and entrepreneurship across different immigrant groups and across ethnicities and races, according to Light and Rosenstein (1995) are far from satisfactory. An alternative economic explanation for racial and ethnic differences in entrepreneurship is relative employment opportunities. Groups disadvantaged in the labor market—because of language or culture—may turn to entrepreneurship and self-employment as a substitute for conventional employment. Disadvantage in the labor market may be relevant but it has yielded to a broader class of explanations related to class and ethnic resources.[3] The theoretical synthesis of cultural explanations and labor market disadvantage views, called resource theory, posits that a range of ethnic factors including ethnic solidarity, social networks, ethnic institutions and social capital converge with class resources—such as investment capital and ownership of productive resources—to explain differences in entrepreneurship and self-employment across groups (Light and Rosenstein, 1995:25). Standing out in the midst of this convergence of ethnic and class resources, as Light originally hypothesized, are the characteristic roles of traditional credit associations and criminal enterprises.

The Case of New Jersey

These two characteristics—the presence traditional credit associations and the role of criminal activities—have important implications for understanding the under-representation of African American firms in New Jersey. First, for most of New Jersey's history, the vast majority of free blacks traced their roots to the American South and not to Africa or in later years the Caribbean where revolving credit asso-

---

[3] Light and Rosenstein (1995) only find limited support for this model because those who are most disadvantaged in the labor market are also those who have the least access to capital in order to pursue self-employment. When account is taken of *illegal* employment, however, particularly competitive street crimes like selling drugs, one finds greater support for the disadvantaged labor market model. See, Myers (1992).

ciations were common (Wright, op. cit.). Traditional credit associations failed to arise in black New Jersey largely because the memory of these associations long had vanished—or had been stolen—by the time African Americans arrived there.

However, this is also true of the nation as a whole. New Jersey's black population was much less heterogeneous than that of New York or Chicago, two locations known for their apparent success in attracting and nurturing black entrepreneurial talent from abroad. For many cities throughout the nation populated by descendants for slaves whose heritage and histories were long destroyed, there really was no sense of an indigenous saving institution.

Second, the residential segregation of much of New Jersey, the presence of all-black towns, the history of racialistic views in the state, all converged to create an artificial monopoly for black firms in the provision of goods and services to the black community. The effect of these monopolies, however, was not to create substantial, concentrated wealth. The monopolies were often based on licensing restrictions that were created by white businesses often devised to keep blacks from competing with whites.

Monopolistic enterprises included funeral parlors, medical and dental and law offices. These were professional services often unavailable to blacks in white communities. The paradox is that overt segregation brought with it the opportunity for a select few to capture monopoly rents from black consumers.

Whereas these providers of professional services often comprised the core of the black leadership class—in conjunction with teachers and preachers—they did not represent the majority of black business owners. Most such owners were mom and pop stores, barber shops, beauty parlors, and other enterprises that arose in response to the color prejudice and residential segregation patterns in the state (Wright, 1988:50).

These businesses had low revenues, little capital, and slim chances for growth, expansion and development. Even when black businesses had white customers from the nearby neighborhoods, those white customers did not frequent those businesses sufficiently to sustain them.

But even more relevant, is that these firms provided little opportunity for the development of an entrepreneurial class—a class that in the 1980s might have been willing, able and interested in pursuing the increased business opportunities available with the state.

There is another way in which residential segregation and color prejudice have contributed to the underdevelopment of an entrepreneurial class in New Jersey. These factors, while contributing to monopolies in professional services, also contribute to criminal monopolies. Both in the provision of illegal goods and services—gambling, prostitution, drugs and alcohol—and in the provision of capital for otherwise legitimate enterprises, criminal monopolies in black communities arose as a result of the willingness of the majority to permit the minorities to operate their own criminal activities. Although more akin to franchises than independently-owned businesses, these enterprises flourished over much of black America before the 1960s (Myers, 1978).

While these matters are difficult, if not impossible, to quantify, crime has been a major influence in the early development of African American businesses in New

Jersey. This is not because blacks themselves were exceptionally criminal, but because of the pervasiveness of crime in New Jersey.

There were several dimensions to this crime-entrepreneurship link. One was the role of corruption in local city government and its influence on the way business was done. Partisan supporters, and African Americans, were convinced for example that election fraud and corruption dominated Hudson County which includes Jersey City and East Newark. Jersey City Democrats in the late 1880s generally were elected illegally; there are several accounts of election frauds, including ballot stuffing (*New York Times*, November 16, 1887, page 8). Police efforts to raid illegal businesses (i.e., pool rooms) were often thwarted by "gangs" (*Ibid.*, July 28, 19889, page 2). Political leaders like the notorious Sheriff Robert Davis often had illegitimate business ties. The local clergy often spoke out against the political corruption even though they were frequently beneficiaries of gambling operations (*Ibid.*, December 17, 1889, page 6). For example, Hudson County was known for its gambling (pool selling, lottery tickets, etc.) in the late 19th century. These pool sellers "gave freely to charities and the churches and got the good will of the people. The Protestant and the Catholic churches receive[d] their favors" (*Ibid.*, December 17, 1889, page 6).

When Frank Hague entered office circa the late 1930s, a new "bossism" arose, having significant impacts on the ability of black businesses to effectively compete. In 1938, the *New York Amsterdam News* ran a series of articles on Jersey City Mayor Frank Hague. Blacks in Jersey City agreed that there was "no color line" in public places, however blacks had few jobs in the city. The only black City Hall employee was a porter (*New York Amsterdam News*, July 29, 1938, page 10). A small numbers banker (black) claimed that police smashed his business because he openly spoke out against Hague. Another businessman was severely beaten by white police officers. His case was thrown out of court, but the man did not react because he wanted to stay in business.

While these anecdotes reveal a pervasive set of corrupt practices that arguably affected both black and white enterprises, the absence of blacks in city hall and on the police forces (which conspired in many instances with city hall) created an environment disproportionately hostile to law abiding black businesses.

Robert Curvin, in his dissertation, *The Persistent Minority*, highlights the impacts of the criminal world on black entrepreneurship:

> The underworld system gave jobs to Black men as numbers runners and helped many of the Black social clubs, outlets for prohibition, to survive. Some of the men who worked in this system, one of the few open to them, emerged as the political leaders of the ward. Although the system provided a livelihood for some members of the Black community, the direct and indirect control by underworld forces over the emergence of Black political leadership had several destructive consequences. First, the underworld needed Black leaders who were corrupt or corruptible; it obviously would not tolerate leaders who might criticize or expose the damage and exploitation bestowed on the Black community through illicit activities. In addition, the underworld encouraged the kind of social behavior that was profitable to their businesses but damaging to Black community life (Curvin, 1975).

Another dimension of the crime-entrepreneurial link is the wide array of entertainment opportunities in the state with illicit underpinnings. For example, the black newspapers reported the operation of many black owned night-clubs (*New York Amsterdam News*, November 2, 1927) and "tea-rooms."[4] But they also reported the widespread incidence of criminal activities within these black-owned businesses. One notorious case involved the selling of drugs. It culminated in Federal agents arresting a black woman for selling marijuana in a "tea room" (*New York Amsterdam News*, October 16, 1937).

The center of much of this entertainment-related entrepreneurial activity was to some extent Atlantic City. The *New York Times* even noted the opening of a black-owned hotel there in 1923 (*New York Times*. August 20, 1923, page 12). This came about after many years of black employment in white-owned hotels. The New Jersey Historical Society writes:

> Atlantic City's rapid emergence as a major seaside resort explains the dramatic upsurge in its black population. The labor needed for the city's hotels and recreational facilities was largely black labor. The many service positions offered by the hotel-recreation industry—such as cook, waiter, bellman, porter, chambermaid—were within the occupational realm to which the black race had been customarily restricted. At the turn of the century the city's hotel-recreation labor force was about 95 percent black (Giles, op. cit., page 46).

There is ample evidence that elsewhere in the state other service related enterprises evolved, particularly in the period between the World Wars:

> The Apex Beauty Products Company in Atlantic City, a hair cosmetics firm, was by far the largest and most significant of New Jersey's black-owned businesses during this period. Established in 1919 by Sara Spencer Washington, it became one of the nations' leading black manufacturing companies. By the late 1930s its Atlantic City office and factory had eighty-seven employees, including chemists, clerks, bookkeepers, chauffeurs and beauty operators. The company also had eleven beauty schools in various cities. An estimated thirty-five thousands individuals throughout the world were dependent on the sales of its products and its methods of "Scientific Beauty Culture." (*Ibid.*, page 60).

The implication is that the few firms that succeeded in the inter-war years were those devoted to the provision of goods and services demanded by the black community, a community with low incomes and little capital. This business experience has not served well as the basis for the development of an entrepreneurial class able to avail itself of the increasingly attractive opportunities to do business with the state during the growth periods of the 1960s and 1970s. The sons and daughters of the black elite entered professions only to find that the fall of overtly discriminatory barriers had the paradoxical impact of eliminating the artificial monopolies their parents enjoyed because of racial discrimination. These persons entered managerial

---

[4] As early as 1923 there were black owned hotels, restaurants, and night clubs in Newark, Hudson County and Atlantic City. Blacks also managed many of these hotels. A black man was appointed manager of Liberty Apartment Hotel in 1927, according to *New York Amsterdam News* reports of the day. By the 1940s, hotels in New Jersey were owned by such notable blacks as Father Divine.

and professional positions in large organizations instead of seeking self-employment, but often were relegated to such jobs as personnel specialist or, worse, affirmative action officer—positions that in hindsight offered little opportunity for mobility into the top ranks of the corporate world, nor did they offer the opportunity to acquire business and management skills needed to conduct viable business, nor the managerial reputation that banks find creditable. Moreover, those managers and professionals who found employment in the public sector saw their careers limited to services to the poor and the black communities via jobs in welfare offices and social service agencies (Darity and Myers, 1986/87).

What this means is that while there was a small black entrepreneurial class in New Jersey prior to World War II, it was comprised of two groups, neither of which has reproduced a stronger more vibrant community from which entrepreneurial talent can be drawn. One group consisted of poor uneducated merchants who were either on the margin of economic existence or were heavily involved in illegal activities; the other consisted of an educated elite whose major advantage stemmed from the economic monopoly accompanying racial segregation and the color line during the earlier era.

The children of this generation certainly have highly valued professional and managerial skills, but not in the newly emergent technical and scientific fields requiring advanced degrees. Instead their skills are largely in areas related to public administration and personnel relations—stagnant areas of the economy. Because of "professional ghettos" in both the public and private sectors, they are grossly underrepresented among the computer scientists, the electrical engineers, the biotechnologists and geneticists, the applied mathematicians and physicists who are all making New Jersey an exciting national leader in the research and development of new technologies.

Indeed, it is in these industries that workers from other nations, including India and China, have been able to excel not only because of the underrepresentation of native-born minorities but also because of the short supply of native-born whites with these technical skills in science and technology.

The offspring of the black elite, then, are not necessarily concentrated in areas where the economy is growing. The offspring of the previous generations' merchants and small business owners may fare poorly if they do not have the technical and advanced degrees needed for the expanding economy. And the off-spring of criminal entrepreneurs are even worse off. Precisely at the time when there was a upswing in legitimate business opportunities with the state, there was a major increase in law enforcement efforts that resulted in increasing numbers of the black poor being incarcerated. Many of these blacks are the heirs to the criminal enterprises and the small business operations that, while marginal and inefficient, provided the training grounds for the entry into competitive business arrangements with the state.

Today, with crime rampant in black urban neighborhoods, guilt by association or guilt by proximity may make the modest but legitimate entrepreneur more suspect by law enforcement agencies and subject to closer scrutiny. Practices that are viewed as benign in other settings may be viewed with a more jaundiced eye when it comes to black entrepreneurs and individuals.

It may be that as economic conditions worsen, struggling businesspeople, like struggling individuals, resort to unorthodox and legally unsound means of surviving. Desperate times and zealous law enforcement may thus combine to eliminate all but the hardiest and most scrupulous entrepreneurs. In addition, the significance of increased incarceration and the marginalization of a core of potential entrepreneurs is far-reaching. These are the high-school dropouts, the graduates of vocational education curricula, the persons handy in classes in mechanical drawing, carpentry, and related building skills. And it is in building and construction skills that we observe the greatest potential for moving from a worker to a contractor. Yet these doors were closed to blacks in previous generations because of the refusal of the white unions to accept them. Although the overt barriers are gone, the sons and daughters of those thwarted in previous eras have little history and few contemporary models that would lead to entering the trades. The shortage is met largely by immigrant workers, often Hispanics, who bring a family tradition of involvement in the construction trades.

The consequence, then, is that in one area where it may have been possible for blacks to aspire to entrepreneurial careers by providing goods and services to the state not requiring extensive education or training—just talent and experience—the talent was destroyed through criminal justice policies and the experience was denied because of state acquiescence to the discriminatory practices of labor unions.

IMPACTS OF PROFESSIONAL/MANAGERIAL CLASS ON BUSINESS PARTICIPATION RATES

What factors contribute to the climate of black business ownership across many SMSAs in the United States? In particular, are there differences in black business participation between New Jersey SMSAs and SMSAs elsewhere? The main finding is that black business participation grew less rapidly in New Jersey than it did elsewhere in the nation and that the result was a widening of the already sizable ownership gap between New Jersey SMSAs and the rest of the nation between 1977 and 1982.

The details of these results are presented below. First, however, it is useful to concentrate on two key aspects the analysis. First, the size of the professional/managerial class among blacks has only a minor impact on black business participation rates. Second, blacks in New Jersey were less able to convert personal assets, educational attainment, or average levels of income into business ownership as compared to blacks in other SMSAs. Thus, a large portion of the underrepresentation of blacks among business owners in New Jersey could not be explained by blacks' under endowments of assets or education or lack of professional and managerial experience. This analysis answers the question: "Even if blacks had higher proportions of professional or managerial workers, would that translate into more black businesses?" The answer, based on aggregate data, is "No."

It is important to draw out the implications of the analysis for understanding the role of employment disparities in contributing to the low rates of business participation among blacks in New Jersey. If we had found that blacks were discriminated against in managerial and professional occupations and that this discrimination had contributed to the underrepresentation of blacks among managers and professional workers, then this source of bias would justify race-based strategies for remedying black business underutilization, when there was a direct impact of black managerial/professional employment on black business participation. In the aggregate, at least, no such impact is found.[5]

The question, then, that must be answered for black professionals in New Jersey, is: "Why is it that the sizable black middle-class, including many professional and managerial workers, has been unable (or unwilling) to translate its resources into business participation?" The answer, we conclude from our discussion above, stems partly from the pervasiveness of state and local corruption from the earliest days of blacks' attempts to enter business in the state. Black professionals, who often faced severe restrictions on their employment until recent times, simply chose to work for themselves or their communities—as doctors, clergy, teachers or social workers—rather than to fight the ugly battles needed in order to break into the often violent and complex world of machine politics and local business contracting.

We are interested in the conditions within an area that help promote the success of African-American owned business. To measure this success, our measure is the probability of observing an African-American as a business owner. We want to see how that probability varies as the characteristics of the area change. The area unit of analysis that we have chosen is the SMSA. For most small businesses, this is their relevant market area. The characteristics that we are most interested in are the ones identified in other portions of this project, they include: income, asset ownership, education and occupation.[6] These variables have been identified as key to the individual success of African-American business owners.

An ecological view is concerned not with the individual characteristics that lead to individual success, but the *community* characteristics that lead to individual success. As opposed to the individual characteristic—or micro data—analysis that shows the relationship of an individual's income, wealth or education to business success, we are concerned with how does the community's income, wealth or education level contribute to business success. This is an important view because policies that systematically deny educational opportunities to a group will easily show in community based statistics. However, a study of individuals may not show this pattern. As an example, if New Jersey systematically discriminated in its provision of education opportunities to African-Americans, it is could still be possible to observe

---

[5] To be sure there is ample evidence that on the *individual* level being a professional/managerial worker enhances your chances of business or entrepreneurial success, if only because skill gained in such occupations are vital to business success. Thus, we do not contradict the findings of Bates.

[6] The measure used in this paper is distinct from the probability that a business is owned by an African-American. In this paper, the denominator of the probability fraction is the adult African-American population. In the latter, the denominator would be all businesses. The approach taken by this paper is meant to be the ecological analog of Timothy Bates (1991). That is, Bates was concerned with the self-employment rate of African-Americans and used micro-level data to predict the probabilities of self-employment. This paper is concerned with that same variable, but looking at community level variables. This paper uses measures similar to Bates', but at the community level.

individual African-Americans with substantial educational credentials. Their existence would not counter the existence of systematic discrimination, but could mask its potential effects. One might still observe African-Americans as successful business owners if individual initiative alone was important. Yet, if the success of a business also relies on the health of the whole community, the systematic discrimination would show up in lower education or income levels for the average community member. The poorer position of the African-American community may be the key impediment to successful business ownership—and not the efforts of the individual alone.

To model the probability of African-American business ownership, we have chosen the logistic curve, expressed as the following function:

$$Y_i = \frac{1}{1+\exp(\alpha + \beta'X_i + \varepsilon_i)}, \text{ where}$$

Y_i = the probability of business ownership for the ith SMSA,
α = a constant term
β = a vector of coefficients showing how the community characteristics effect the probability,
X = a vector of community variables,
ε = a stochastic error term, and
exp = the base of the natural logarithm = 2.71828....

Unfortunately, that function is difficult to estimate with data aggregated over individuals. So, we are estimating the equation in a linear form. This is achieved by taking the natural logarithm of both sides of the equation. Doing this gives the following function:

$$\log[Y_i / (1 - Y_i)] = a + b'X_i + e_i .$$

The left hand side of the equation is now the logarithm of the odds-ratio. So, the coefficients of our equation will tell us how our right hand side variables effect changes in the logarithm of the odds-ratio.

The probability of owning a business is the number of businesses divided by the adult population.[7] If multiplied by 1,000, this yields a measure called the "Business Participation Rate."[8] For this study, the probability of owning a business for Afri-

---

[7] The numerator here is the number of firms. This does not necessarily equal the number of business owners since an individual could own more than one firm. It is also possible, as in the case of a Subchapter S corporation that more than one person can own a business. However, this is likely to be only random noise in the measure, and given the fraction size, extremely unlikely to change the measure much. In 1982, 95.0% of firms in the sample were individual proprietorships. Only 1.7% of firms were subchapter S corporations. In any case, it is not likely to be a problem more severe for New Jersey than for non-New Jersey.
[8] A measure proposed by Fratoe and Meeks (1986). In his report, Bates multiplied the probability by 100, to convert it to a percentage. Y_i could be converted to the Business Participation Rate, by changing the

can-Americans was calculated using two different periods in the numerator—1977 and 1982. The number of minority-owned businesses was surveyed by the Census Bureau for 1977 and 1982. The surveys made use of tax information merged with economic census data. The tax and social security files of individuals were used to identify race and sex characteristics of business owners. The individual owners themselves were not contacted for the information,[9] except through the economic census.

The Reagan midterm recession began in July 1981 and continued to November 1982. A time period caught by the 1982 data. The survey includes "any legal entity engaged in economic activity during any part" of 1982 that filed an IRS form 1040, Schedule C; 1065; or 1120S (U.S. Department of Commerce). So that firms that failed in 1982 would have been included. However, firms that failed to formalize because of the recession would—of course—not be included. The issue of interest in this paper is the extent to which community level economic data contribute to business formation. So, for the recession to affect this analysis, it would have to be the case that the recession impacted different communities differently—a definite possibility as to the industries hurt. But more specific to the point of this research, is whether New Jersey was more adversely impacted than other states. A stronger case can be made that New Jersey was not more adversely affected by the recession than can be a case made that New Jersey was unique in the recession.

Data collected by the Federal Reserve Board from its Survey of Consumer Finances shows that in 1983, 16.1 percent of white non-Hispanic households versus 5.4 percent of non-white and Hispanic households had equity interest in a business—including limited partnerships, other partnerships, corporations, sole proprietorships, and other private businesses (Kennick and Shack-Marquez, 1992).

SMSA level data on community characteristics are not available except from the decennial census. So, the denominator for calculating the probability of African American business ownership (the number of African-Americans over age 25,) and the right hand side variables are drawn from the 1980 census. Some of the data—such as per capita income, refer to 1979. Because these are community based statistics, changes in community averages from 1977 to 1980, or 1980 to 1982 should not be too great. Of course 1980 cannot "predict" in the causal sense events in 1977. However, the best measure of the 1977 levels for the community variables is more likely to be in the 1980 data than in the 1970 data for the SMSAs. So, when 1977

---

numerator of the logistic function from 1, the maximum for the probability, to 1,000, the maximum for the participation rate; or to Bates' self-employment rate by changing the numerator to 100. However, because of the linear transformation, the logarithm of the odds-ratio is more straightforward to interpret than the transformation of the business participation or self-employment rates.

[9] The information on race and sex came from the Social Security Administration. Race is coded as White, Black, Other. Individuals with typical Hispanic or Asian last names, or who checked race as other, are mailed a questionnaire to determine their race. A sample of all business owners is also chosen to determine if Hispanic or Asian business owners were missed using the surname and race classification data. A black business owner who is also Hispanic, will be included as both black and Hispanic. So, estimates of African-American and female business ownership is less likely to include the sampling error inherent in the identification process for Asians and Hispanics. Persons applying for a social security card after 1981 are coded as (a) Asian, Asian-American or Pacific Islander, (b) Hispanic, © black, (d) Northern American Indian or Alaskan Native, and (e) White.

data is used in the numerator, the denominator and the other variables are meant to proxy the 1977 level of these variables.

The right hand side variables serve as our explanatory variables. The coefficients tell us how changes in these variables effect changes in the logarithm of the odds-ratio of African-American business ownership. These included:

The proportion of African-American workers who listed either professional or managerial occupations.

1. The median home value of African-American owner-occupied housing, weighted by the proportion of all African-American households that are owner-occupied. Thus, this gives the average home value across the community.[10]

2. The median value of mortgages of African-American households, weighted by the proportion of all African-American households that carry a mortgage. Thus, this gives the average home debt across the community.

3. The proportion of African-Americans over 25 years of age who have completed college.

4. The per capita income of the white community.

5. The per capita income of the African-American community.

6. The size of the African-American population.

Table 2.1 gives the mean of these variables for the entire sample and for the SMSAs in New Jersey included in the sample. The mean of the logarithm of the odds-ratio is smaller in the New Jersey SMSAs than for the entire sample. In 1977, the logarithm of the odds-ratio of African-American business ownership is -4.2029 in New Jersey. This translates to an odds-ratio of 0.015[11] and also a probability of 0.015.[12] The corresponding business participation rate is 15.17.[13] For the entire sample, the figure is -3.9627, or an odds-ratio of 0.019, and a business participation rate of 18.65. Similarly in 1982, the logarithm of the odds-ratio for New Jersey is -3.8899, or 0.020 and for the entire sample the figures are -3.5658 or 0.028 (with

---

[10] In 1983, the Federal Reserve estimates that 42.2 percent of non-white and Hispanic households had their principle residence as a nonfinancial asset. The only more common nonfinancial asset was motor vehicles (64.4 percent.) Checking accounts (46.4%), savings accounts (44.9%) and retirement accounts (10.2%) were the most common financial assets that non-white and Hispanic households held. In terms of median value, however, ownership of principle residence was clearly the most important wealth asset of non-whites and Hispanics. For this reason, it was chosen as a measure of non-business wealth among African-American households. Using this measure, and not a measure of total wealth avoids the simultaneity bias of including business equity.

[11] The odds-ratio, w, is exp (log (w)). In this case: exp (-4.2029).

[12] The odds ratio, w, is P/ (1 – P). The probability, P, is w/ (1 + w). In this case, 0.01495/1.01495. For small values of P (i.e., P < 0.10), the difference between w and P is also small.

[13] The business participation rate is 1,000 * P.

business participation rates of 20.04 and 27.50—a difference of fifteen businesses for every 2,000 in population.)

Table 2.1. Means of Variables Used in this Analysis.

Variables	All	New Jersey*
Proportion of African-American Workers who are Professionals and Managers	0.145 (0.032)	0.149 (0.027)
Average African-American Household Home Value	$13,228.000 (5,820.500)	$9,741.300 (5,607.800)
Average African-American Household Mortgage Debt	92.052 (31.680)	79.773 (39.742)
Proportion of African-American Adults who Completed College	0.091 (0.035)	0.080 (0.022)
White Per Capita Income	$8,039.000 (1,114.500)	$8,347.100 (701.220)
African-American Per Capita Income	$4,633.400 (776.320)	$4,875.600 (507.060)
Size of African-American Population (In millions)	0.132 (0.238)	0.355 0.656
Logarithm of Odds-Ratio of Business Ownership 1977	−3.963 (0.303)	−4.203 (0.219)
Logarithm of Odds-Ratio of Business Ownership 1982	−3.566 (0.352)	−3.890 (0.213)

*Standard errors of means are in parentheses. *The nine New Jersey SMSAs analyzed are: Atlantic City; Jersey City; Long Branch-Asbury Park; New Brunswick-Perth Amboy-Sayrevill; New York, NY-N.J.; Paterson-Clifton-Passaic; Philadelphia, PA-N.J.; Trenton; Wilmington, DE-MD-N.J.*

The lower odds of African-American business ownership in New Jersey could be a function of communities in New Jersey having fewer of the characteristics necessary for African-American business ownership. It could also be that with the same characteristics New Jersey communities are doing something we have not measured that discourages the formation of African-American business ownership. In either case, the discrepancy could be the result of discriminatory behavior. For instance, Table 2.1 shows that the average household's personal asset of home value in the entire sample is $13,228. But, in the New Jersey SMSAs, this value is $9,741. If the community's wealth is important to business formation, then discrimination against African-Americans in the housing market in New Jersey could lead to lower business formation. But, in all other aspects relating to business formation there may be no discrimination. So, it could appear that there is no discrimination in New Jersey given the approach of this research.

A similar problem is that all jurisdictions may discriminate against African-American business formation in one form or another. Thus, even if this analysis does not find any difference between New Jersey and other communities, it at best means that New Jersey does not discriminate any more than do other communities.

Two approaches to estimating the regression were taken. The first was to estimate separate equations for New Jersey and the remainder of the sample and then to test whether this yielded significantly different answers to running the regression with the data pooled together. This was done for 1977 and 1982 data. The results are in Table 2.2. The second approach was to run the data pooled together, but to include a dummy variable for New Jersey. A dummy variable (coded New Jersey = 1) would show the effects of variables not included in the equation, but that were unique to New Jersey. The results of this estimation are in Table 2.3.

Table 2.2 shows that there is no statistically significant difference between the New Jersey equation and the equation for the remainder of the sample for the 1977 regression. This is shown in the results of the Chow Test. The significance level for a test that the New Jersey and Non-New Jersey samples yield different results than the pooled regression is 0.37.[14] Thus, the null hypothesis that samples yield similar results cannot be rejected. This means that the effects of the individual variables are similar for New Jersey and the rest of the U.S. For the 1977 regression, it would be appropriate to estimate the sample together with a dummy variable for New Jersey. Looking at the pooled regression, several of the variables are significant in predicting changes in the logarithm of the odds-ratio. If the average household home value increases by $10,000, then the logarithm of the odds-ratio will increase by 0.28. Evaluated at the mean probability of 0.019, this would mean an increase to a probability of 0.025—an increase of almost one-third over the mean probability. In a population of 190,000 adult African-Americans (the average for the New Jersey communities being studied,) that would mean a difference of 1,140 African-American owned businesses. An effect that is even more dramatic, an increase in the average household mortgage debt of $100, would decrease the logarithm of the odds-ratio by 0.36. Again evaluated at the mean probability of 0.019, this would mean a decrease to a probability of 0.013—a decrease of almost one-third over the mean probability. An increase of $1,000 in the per capita income of African-Americans would increase the logarithm of the odds-ratio by 0.12. An increase in the African-American population of one million would decrease the logarithm of the odds-ratio by 0.198.[15]

---

[14] The reader is cautioned that there are nine New Jersey communities in the study, and there are seven independent variables used. Thus, including the intercept, this leaves only one degree of freedom for the New Jersey equation. Thus the high R^2 value for the New Jersey regression should be interpreted with caution. Even controlling for the one degree of freedom, the adjusted R^2 value is misleadingly high at 0.9627 for the 1977 data. However, the Chow Test is based on the residual sum of squares for the New Jersey and Non-Non Jersey sample compared to the residual sum of squares of the combined sample. It is the Chow Test that is of importance here.

[15] While the size of the African-American population had a negative influence on the level of the probability of business ownership, it significantly increased the probability of business formation from 1977 to 1982.

Table 2.2.

Dependent Variable:	Log Odds-Ratio of Business Ownership 1977			Log Odds-Ratio of Business Ownership 1982		
Independent Variables	New Jersey	Non-New Jersey	Pooled Both Samples	New Jersey	Non-New Jersey	Pooled Both Samples
Intercept	-6.2822* (0.278)	-4.7669*** (0.242)	-4.7321*** (0.223)	-5.0848* (0.387)	-4.6114*** (0.209)	-4.5652*** (0.182)
Proportion of Workers who are Professionals and Managers	13.7155* (0.999)	0.7377 (1.706)	0.6234 (1.588)	1.8012 (1.393)	-0.1848 (1.4000)	-0.4183 (1.283)
Average Household Home Value (In ten thousands)	0.4850* (0.038)	0.2549*** (0.065)	0.2797*** (0.058)	0.3592† (0.053)	0.4490*** (0.063)	0.4645*** (0.058)
Average Household Mortgage Debt (In hundreds)	-0.7827* (0.033)	-0.3713** (0.122)	-0.3572** (0.115)	-0.2049 (0.045)	-0.4416*** (0.119)	-0.4096*** (0.123)
Proportion of Adults who Completed College	-19.4221* (1.491)	0.4317 (1.002)	0.5454 (0.904)	1.3416 (2.077)	1.9315* (0.960)	2.2045* (0.895)
White Per Capita Income (In thousands)	0.0605 (0.010)	0.0046 (0.032)	0.0049 (0.028)	0.0972† (0.014)	-0.0442 (0.033)	-0.0451 (0.029)
African-American Per Capita Income (In thousands)	0.2725 (0.067)	0.1432* (0.068)	0.1230† (0.067)	-0.0330 (0.094)	0.2362*** (0.046)	0.2141*** (0.047)
Size of African-American Population (In millions)	-0.2360* (0.024)	-0.2160 (0.136)	-0.1984* (0.067)	-0.0493 (0.033)	-0.1598 (0.146)	-0.1124† (0.068)
R^2	0.995	0.323	0.327	0.990	0.690	0.680
Mean Square Error	0.042	0.002	0.002	0.059	0.002	0.002
Number of Observations	9	114	123	9	114	123
Chow Test F-statistic $_{(8,107)}$			1.105			1.755
Significance Level			0.366			0.094

Standard errors in parentheses.
Significance levels indicated by: † = 0.10, * = 0.05, ** = 0.01, *** = 0.001
All regressions estimated using least squares, but consistent estimates of the covariance matrix allowing for heteroskedasticity was done following Halbert White, "A Heteroskedasticity-Consistent Covariance Matrix Estimator and Direct Test for Heteroskedasticity," Econometrica, *Vol. 48 (1980): pgs. 817–838.*

The regression for 1982 showed a much better fit than did the data for 1977. In the pooled sample regression the amount of variance in the logarithm of the odds-ratio explained by the community variables increased from almost one-third (0.327) to roughly two-thirds (0.680.) It was also the case that the separate equations for New Jersey and the rest of the sample were statistically different from the pooled sample regression—the Chow Test had a significance level of 0.09, so at the 0.10 level of significance one could reject the null hypothesis that the two samples had equal results to the pooled sample. In the New Jersey regression, two variables were significant in predicting the logarithm of the odds-ratio. First, as was true in the

previous model, is the average household's home value. This variable was also significant in the non-New Jersey sample. In New Jersey, increasing the average
household's home value by $10,000 would increase the logarithm of the odds-ratio
by .359, while in the non-New Jersey sample, the ratio would increase by .449—a
bigger impact. Evaluated at the pooled sample mean probability of 0.028, in New
Jersey this would be an increase to a probability of 0.039, and in the non-New Jersey sample an increase to 0.042 (a difference of almost ten percent.) Again taking a
community of 190,000 adult African-Americans, this means that given the same
amount of community wealth, the New Jersey community would have 570 fewer
African-American businesses than a community not in New Jersey for each $10,000
increase in home value. In the New Jersey sample, the per capita income of the
white community was significant, though it was not in any of the other models.
Oddly, the coefficient on African-American per capita income is negative—though
not statistically, significantly different from zero. A negative coefficient means that
increases in African-American income lowered the odds of business ownership.

In the non-New Jersey model, in addition to the average household's home value,
the average household's mortgage debt, the proportion of African-Americans over
age 25 with college degrees and African-American per capita income were all significant predictors of the logarithm of the odds-ratio of business ownership. This is
similar to the result of the pooled regression for 1977. A big difference, however, is
in the magnitude of the effects of these variables. For instance, in 1982 a $100 in-
crease in average household mortgage debt decreased the logarithm of the odds-
ratio by 0.442. An increase in African-American per capita income of $1,000 in-
creased the logarithm of the odds-ratio by 0.236. A ten percentage point increase in
the proportion of adult African-Americans with college degrees increased the logarithm of the odds-ratio by 0.193. For 1982, using the whole sample, the standard
error of the mean of the logarithm of the odds-ratio was 0.352. So, many of these
changes are quite large when compared to the standard error.

In 1982, then, the difference between the logarithm of the odds-ratio of business
ownership for New Jersey and the entire sample shows that the community based
variables had significantly different effects on the odds-ratio. In the New Jersey
sample communities were not as likely to convert personal assets into business assets; and, neither increases in educational attainment nor income could significantly
increase the odds of business ownership. In the non-New Jersey sample, increases in
the community's pool of highly educated adults and in income did significantly increase the odds of business ownership; and, increases in personal assets had a
greater influence on the creation of businesses.

Table 2.3 shows the results of the last method of estimating the logarithm of the
odds-ratio. In this case, the samples have been pooled, and a dummy variable has
been used to capture the effects of the New Jersey SMSAs. For 1977, the previous
test concluded that the pooled sample would be appropriate because the effects of
the community variables were the same in both the New Jersey and non-New Jersey
samples. The results are very similar to the pooled regression for 1977 shown in
Table 2.2. Again, the average household's home value and mortgage debt are significant, as is African-American per capita income, and the size of the African-
American population. The coefficient on the New Jersey dummy variable means

that, controlling for all other community characteristics, the odds-ratio would be reduced by 18.34 percent because the community is among the New Jersey SMSAs.[16] This result is significantly different from zero at the 0.003 level of significance. Again using the sample mean probability of 0.019 and a community of 190,000 adult African-Americans, this means that if a New Jersey and non-New Jersey community were alike in income, home values, home debt, education and occupation, the New Jersey community would have 708 fewer African-American owned businesses.

A similar model was estimated using 1982 business data. However, for 1982 it is important to remember that the previous test showed that community variables had different effects in New Jersey than in non-New Jersey SMSAs. So, the dummy variable does not capture all of the differences between the two samples. It is, nonetheless, interesting to see that the coefficient on the dummy variable for New Jersey is negative and statistically, significantly different from zero. In this model, controlling for all other community characteristics, the odds-ratio would be reduced by 21.07 percent because the community is among the New Jersey SMSAs.[17] Again using the sample mean probability of 0.027 and a community of 190,000 adult African-Americans, this means that if a New Jersey and non-New Jersey community were alike in income, home values, home debt, education and occupation, the New Jersey community would have 1,224 fewer African-American owned businesses.

Table 2.4 shows the difference in the means of the variables for the New Jersey communities, compared to the pooled sample. Those differences are then used with the coefficients from the pooled regression to show how the difference in the means of the variables can result in lower African-American business ownership. The difference in the means is multiplied by the pooled coefficient to yield the difference in the logarithm of the odds-ratio. This is evaluated at the mean of the logarithm of the odds-ratio reported in Table 2.1, to calculate the difference in probabilities. The probabilities are then multiplied by 1,000 to convert them to business participation rates. The business participation rate, evaluated at the mean, for 1977 was 18.657, and 27.497 for 1982.

For 1977, New Jersey communities would have performed above average because of their higher proportion of professionals and managers, the lower average debt carried on their homes, the higher per capita white and African-American per capita income. They would have performed worse than average because of lower home values and the proportion of adults with college degrees. Because of the importance of home value, the net effect is that New Jersey communities would have a business participation rate 0.37 lower than other communities because of their lower home values and educational attainment. In a community of 190,000 adults that means 70

---

[16] This calculation is made as: [exp (b) – 1] * 100, where b is the regression coefficient. In this case b = -0.2026705.

[17] Using the average number of businesses for 1977 and 1982 as the numerator of the probability fraction, the Chow Test for the equality of the New Jersey and non-New Jersey sample is accepted. So, in a pooled sample, with a dummy variable for New Jersey, the results are very much the same. In that regression, the odds-ratio would be reduced by 19.78 percent because the community is among the New Jersey SMSAs. The regression coefficient, b = -0.2203675 (the standard error is 0.052135) and has a probability value of 0.000024.

fewer African-American businesses.[18] However, in 1977, the business participation rate was 3.925 lower for New Jersey communities. That means that beyond the lower home values and lower proportion of adults with college degrees are other factors that account for the lower rate in New Jersey.

Table 2.3.

Dependent Variable: Log Odds-Ratio of Business Ownership	1977 Pooled Both Samples	1982 Pooled Both Samples
Independent Variables		
Intercept	-4.7643^{***} (0.227)	-4.6029^{***} (0.185)
Proportion of Workers who are Professionals and Managers	0.8360 (1.673)	-0.1702 (1.364)
Average Household Home Value (In ten thousands)	0.2572^{***} (0.059)	0.4382^{***} (0.058)
Average Household Mortgage Debt (In hundreds)	-0.3580^{**} (0.109)	-0.4105^{***} (0.110)
Proportion of Adults who Completed College	0.3239 (0.946)	1.9460^{*} (0.904)
White Per Capita Income (In thousands)	0.0077 (0.029)	-0.0419 (0.029)
African-American Per Capita Income (In thousands)	0.1315^{*} (0.066)	0.2241^{**} (0.045)
Size of African-American Population (In millions)	-0.1599^{*} (0.067)	-0.0675 (0.074)
New Jersey (Dummy Variable, New Jersey = 1, Otherwise =0)	-0.2027^{**} (0.0691)	-0.2366^{***} (0.0519)
R^2	0.354	0.707
Mean Square Error	0.002	0.002
Number of Observations	123	123

Standard errors in parentheses.
Significance levels indicated by: † = 0.10, * = 0.05, ** = 0.01, *** = 0.001
All regressions estimated using least squares, but consistent estimates of the covariance matrix allowing for heteroskedasticity was done following Halbert White, "A Heteroskedasticity-Consistent Covariance Matrix Estimator and Direct Test for Heteroskedasticity," Econometrica, *Vol. 48 (1980): pgs. 817–838.*

---

[18] Business participation rate is 1,000 * P. So to project for a community of 190,000, this would be the business participation rate times 190.

Table 2.4.

	Differences between NJ and Pooled Means	Pooled Co-efficient	Difference in Log Odds-Ratio	1977		
				Business Participation Rate		
				NJ	Pooled Mean	Difference
Proportion of Workers who are Professionals and Managers	0.003	0.6234	0.002	18.697	18.657	0.040
Average Household Home Value	–$3,486.700	0.2797	–0.098	16.953	18.657	–1.704
Average Household Mortgage Debt	–12.279	–0.3572	0.044	19.477	18.657	0.820
Proportion of Adults who Completed College	–0.011	0.5454	–0.006	18.551	18.657	–0.106
White Per Capita Income	$308.100	0.0049	0.002	18.685	18.657	0.028
African-American Per Capita Income	$242.200	0.1230	0.030	19.210	18.657	0.553
Size of African-American Population (In millions)	0.223	–0.1984	0.000	18.657	18.657	0.000
Logarithm of Odds-Ratio of Business Ownership 1977	–0.240		Sum of Effects of Means			–0.369
			Total Effect	14.732	18.657	–3.925
1982						
Proportion of Workers who are Professionals and Managers	0.003	–0.4183	–0.001	27.458	27.497	–0.039
Average Household Home Value	–$3,486.700	0.4645	–0.162	23.482	27.497	–4.015
Average Household Mortgage Debt	–12.279	–0.4096	0.050	28.874	27.497	1.377
Proportion of Adults who Completed College	–0.011	2.2045	–0.023	26.878	27.497	–0.619
White Per Capita Income	$308.100	–0.0451	–0.014	27.128	27.497	–0.369
African-American Per Capita Income	$242.200	0.2141	0.052	28.918	27.497	1.421
Size of African-American Population (In millions)	0.223	–0.1124	0.000	27.497	27.497	0.000
Logarithm of Odds-Ratio of Business Ownership 1982	–0.324		Sum of Effects of Means			–2.244
			Total Effect	20.038	27.497	–7.459

In 1982 the mean business participation rate was 27.497. Based on that rate, communities in New Jersey would have performed above the mean because of lower debt on African-American homes, and because of higher African-American per capita income. However, lower home values and a reversal in the effect of occupation again meant that on net the effect of the difference in the mean value of the independent variables would have predicted a lower business participation rate in New Jersey communities. The net effect was 2.244 lower business participation rate for New Jersey communities. Again, in a community of 190,000 adults, that meant 426 fewer African-American owned businesses. The difference in the business participation rate for New Jersey and the pooled sample was 7.459. So, again, the difference in the means does not tell the whole story. The results using the 1982 data in Table 2.2 showed that increases in home value produced less effects in New Jersey than in the non-New Jersey sample. And, some variables that were helpful outside of New Jersey, were not helpful in New Jersey.

Thus, we can conclude that among the 128 SMSAs with the largest number of African-American owned businesses, there are unique factors in New Jersey that lower the probability of African-American business ownership. These factors significantly lower the probability of African-American business ownership, on the order of one-fifth. This is in relation to other communities and without having attempted to control for patterns of discrimination that may be common to all communities. Therefore, this should be considered a lower limit as a measure of the discriminatory impact of the uniqueness of New Jersey. It remains probable that in comparison to a world without discrimination, the probability of African-American business ownership is harmed by more than one-fifth.

CONCLUSION

Blocked employment paths can lead to entry into illegitimate business pursuits. The effect is the draining of talent that could be directed towards productive activities in the legitimate economy. We have argued that the pervasiveness of crime in New Jersey thwarted the movement of professional blacks into entrepreneurial activities beyond private medical and law practices well into the post-World War II period. Those blacks—often from the working class—who did enter businesses during the era were caught in the web of crime and corruption that was characteristic of the era. This suggests a complex interaction between crime, entrepreneurship and blocked employment opportunities.

The historical record surveyed in this chapter documents important linkages between barriers to employment and the rise of criminal enterprise in African American communities. We suggest that these linkages may help to explain the low levels of self employment and business ownership in the current era. While the evidence comes from one state, it reveals the limited role played by the black middle class in creating potential capitalists and developing entrepreneurs in the minority community. While the origins of the black middle-class in New Jersey may be unique, the case certainly invites comparisons to other cities, like Atlanta or Durham, where the black middle-class has played a prominent role in the evolution of the entrepreneurial class. (Butler, 1989).

The employment barrier is more direct. Ample evidence exists of long-standing patterns of discrimination against black workers in New Jersey. Blacks historically have been overrepresented in those industries were there are few contracting opportunities with the state; they have been underepresented in those industries for which there are many contracting opportunities.

Black professionals, involved in the medical and teaching professions, did not form the core for a substantial entrepreneurial class. What ever entrepreneurial class existed was largely concentrated among small shops and illegitimate businesses.

We argue that crime has been a major influence in the early development of African American businesses in New Jersey, but not because blacks themselves were exceptionally criminal, but because of the pervasiveness of crime in New Jersey. The result is that black business participation grew less rapidly in New Jersey than it did elsewhere in the nation and this contributed to a widening of the already sizable ownership gap between New Jersey SMSAs and the rest of the nation between 1977 and 1982. We demonstrate that had the professional/managerial class among blacks been larger, there still would not have been much of a change in the growth of black businesses in New Jersey. A large portion of the underrepresentation of blacks among business owners in New Jersey could not be explained by blacks' under endowments of assets or education or lack of professional and managerial experience. We conclude that the very nature of the criminal enterprises in the state and the corruption in local politics combined to deter African American professionals from entering businesses and thus to reduce the pool of firms prepared to compete for state and local government contracts when new opportunities emerged in the 1980s.

REFERENCES

Abadinsky, Howard. 1981. *The Mafia in America: An Oral History*. New York: Praeger Publishers.

Albert, Kenneth J. 1977. *How to Pick the Right Small Business Opportunity*. United States: McGraw-Hill Book Company.

Alexander, Herbert E. and Gerald E. Caiden, eds. 1985. *The Politics and Economics of Organized Crime*. Lexington, MA: Lexington Books.

Balkin, Steven. 1989. *Self-Employment for Low-Income People* New York: Praeger.

Bates, Timothy. 1991. "Discrimination and the Capacity of New Jersey Area Minority and Women-Owned Businesses" (August).

Becker, Gary S. 1971. *The Economics of Discrimination*. Chicago and London: University of Chicago Press.

Bloch, Farrell E. et. al. 1977. *Equal Rights and Industrial Relations Research Association*. Wisconsin: Industrial Relations Research Association.

Block, Alan A. 1991. *Perspectives on Organizing Crime*. Boston: Kluwer Academic Publishers.

Blumrosen, Alfred W. 1969–1972. *Enforcing Equality in Housing and Employment through State Civil Rights Laws*. Newark, NJ: The Administrative Process Project, Rutgers Law School.

_____. 1971. *The Duty to Plan for Fair Employment: Plant Location in White Surburbia*. Rutgers Law Review.

Burggraf, Fred and Orland, Herbert P. eds. 1962. *A Key to Change Urban Transportation Research*. Washington, D.C.: National Academy of Sciences, National Research Council.

Cantor, Milton, ed. 1989. *A Social History of Economic Decline*. New Brunswick: Rutgers University Press.

Chambliss, William J. 1988. *From Petty Crooks on the Take to Presidents*. Bloomington & Indianapolis: Indiana University Press.

Commission on Sex Discrimination in the Statutes. 1983. *An Analysis of Wage Discrimination in New Jersey State Service*. New Jersey.

Conk, Margo Anderson. 1980. *The United States Census and Labor Force Change*. Ann Arbor, MI: UMI Research Press.

Crammer, H. Jerome. 1964. *New Jersey in the Automobile Age: A History of Transportation*. New York, NY: D. Van Nostrand Company, Inc.

Cunningham, Barbara , ed. 1977. *The New Jersey Ethnic Experience*. Union City, NJ: Wm. H. Wise & Co.

Curvin, Robert. 1975. *The Black Political Experience in Newark*. Diss. Princeton, NJ: Princeton University.

Darity, William and Myers, Samuel. 1986/87. "Public Policy and the Fate of the Black Family," *Humboldt Journal of Social Relations* 14 (1&2) (Fall/Winter & Spring/Summer).

Davidson, Marilyn J. and Jill Earnshaw, eds. *Vulnerable Workers: Psychosocial and Legal Issues*. New York: John Wiley & Sons.

Department of Conservation and Development. 1950. *Development Plan for New Jersey*.

Dickson, Paul. 1985. *On Our Own: A Declaration of Independence for the Self-Employed*. New York: Facts on File, Inc.

Dubinsky, Irwin. 1973. *Reform in Trade Union Discrimination in the Construction Industry: Operation Dig and Its Legacy*. New York: Praeger Publishers.

Emerson, M. Jarvin and F. Charles Lamphear, eds. 1975. *Urban and Regional Economics: Structure and Change*. Boston: Allyn and Bacon, Inc.

Falcocchio, John C. and Cantilli, Edmond J. 1974. *Transportation and the Disadvantaged: The Poor, the Young, the Elderly, the Handicapped*. Lexington, MA: Lexington Books.

Fratoe, Frank and Ronald Meeks. 1986. "Income of Self-Employed Persons Among the 50 Largest U.S. Ancestry Groups," Research Division, Office of Advocacy, Research and Information, Minority Business Development Agency, U.S. Department of Commerce (March).

Fin, Gary M., ed. 1977. *Labor Unions*. Connecticut: Greenwood Press.

Fox, Stephen R. 1989. *Blood and Power; Organized Crime in Twentieth Century America*. New York: William Morrow and Company, Inc.

Franklin, James. 1981. *Modeling State Growth: New Jersey*. New Brunswick, NJ: Center for Urban Public Policy.

Friedland, Seymour. 1963. *The Financing and Manufacturing in the State of New Jersey*. Report No. 8.

Gage, Nicholas. 1971. *Mafia is not an Equal Opportunity Employer*. New York: McGraw-Hill Book Company.

Goldberg, David J. 1989. *A Tale of Three Cities*. Edited by Milton and Bruce Laurie Cantor. New Brunswick: Rutgers University Press.

Gould, William B. 1977. *Black Workers in White Unions*. London: Cornell University Press.

Grodin, Joseph R. 1961. *Union Government and the Law: British and American Experiences*. Los Angeles: University of California Institute of Industrial Relations.

Halle, David. 1984. *America's Working Man:Work, Home, and Politics among Blue-Collar Property Owners*. Chicago and London: The University of Chicago Press.

Hausman, Leonard J., et. al. eds. 1977. *Equal Rights and Industrial Relations*. Madison, WI: Industrial Relations Research Association.

Hill, Herbert. 1977. *Black Labor and the American Legal System: Race, Work, and the Law*. Washington, D.C.: The Bureau of National Affairs, Inc.

Hirsch, Susan E. 1978. *Roots of the American Working Class: The Industrialization of Crafts in Newark*. University of Pennsylvania Press.

Humphrey, Melvin. 1973. *Employment Profiles of Minorities and Women in the SMSA's of 17 Large Cities, 1971*. Washington, D.C.: Equal Employment Opportunity Commission.

James, Franklin J. and Hughes, James W. 1980. *Modeling State Growth: New Jersey*. Center for Urban Policy Research, Rutgers University, The State University of New Jersey.

Jones, David W., Jr. 1985. *Urban Transit Policy: An Economic and Political History*. Englewood Cliffs, NJ: Prentice-Hall.

Kassell, Paula. 1974. "Few Jobs for Women New Direction Continues Research." *New Direction for Women in New Jersey* 3 (1) (Winter).

Kennickell, Arthur and Janice Shack-Marquez. 1992. "Changes in Family Finances from 1983 to 1989: Evidence from the Survey of Consumer Finances," *Federal Reserve Bulletin*, January, p. 8.

Lake, Issac Beverly. 1947. *Discrimination By Railroads and Other Public Utilities*. North Carolina: Edwards and Broughton Company.

Leavitt, Judith A. 1982. *Women in Management: An Annotated Bibliography and Sourcelist*. Phoenix and Canada: Oryx Press.

Lester, Richard A. 1980. *The Economics of Trade Unions*. Princeton: Princeton University Press.

Liepmann, Kate K. *The Journey to Work*. Edited by Dr. Karl Mannheim. Oxford University Press, 1944.

Light, Ivan. 1972. *Ethnic Enterprise in America*. Berkeley: University of California Press.

_____. 1984. "Immigrant and Ethnic Enterprise in America," *Ethnic and Racial Studies* April: 195–16.

Light, Ivan and Carolyn Rosenstein. 1995. *Race, Ethnicity, and Entreprenuership*, New York: Aldine de Gruyther.

Lindley, Robert M., ed. 1980. *Economic Change and Employment Policy*. New York: Holmes and Meir Publishers, Inc.

Marshall, Ray. 1965. *The Negro and Organized Labor*. New York: John Wiley & Sons, Inc.

Mincer, Jacob. *Schooling, Experience, and Earnings*. New York: National Bureau of Economic Research.

Myers, Jr., Samuel L. 1978. "The Economics of Crime in the Urban Ghetto," *Review of Black Political Economy* (9): 43–59

_____. 1983. "Estimating the Economic Model of Crime: Employment vs. Punishment Effects," *Quarterly Journal of Economics* 98 (1) (February):157–166.

_____. 1992. "Crime, Entrepreneurship, and Labor Force Withdrawal," *Contemporary Policy Issues* 10 (April): 84–97.

National Advisory Commission on Civil Disorders. 1969. *The Kerner Report:The 1968 Report of the National Advisory Commission on Civil Disorders*. New York: Pantheon Books.

New Jersey Commission on Civil Liberties. 1948. *Civil Liberties in New Jersey, A Report Submitted to Governor Driskell*.

New Jersey Department of Education. 1949. *Report on a Survey of 85 General Hospitals in New Jersey*.

New York Amsterdam News. July 29, 1938. p. 10.

New York Amsterdam News. November 2, 1927.

New York Amsterdam News. October 16, 1937.

New York Times. August 20, 1923. p. 12.

New York Times. November 16, 1887. p. 8.

York - New Jersey Transportation Agency. 1964. *Journey to Work: Manhattan Central Business District*. New York: New York - New Jersey Transportation Agency.

Noble, David. 1984. *Forces of Production: A Social History of Industrial Automation*. University Press.

Permanent Subcommittee on Investigations. 1984. *Waterfront Corruption*. Washington, D.C.: U.S. Government Printing Office.

Peterson, Florence. 1945. *American Labor Unions: What They are and How They Work*. New York: Harper & Brothers Publishers.

Rees, Albert. 1962. *The Economics of Trade Unions*. Chicago: University of Chicago Press.

_____. 1989. *The Economics of Trade Unions*. Chicago and London: University of Chicago.

Ruchames, Louis. 1953. *Race, Jobs, and Politics: The Story of FEPC*. New York: Columbia University Press.

Ruffin, David C. 1986. "Parren Mitchell's Sixteen years: A Legislative legacy." *Black Enterprise* 16 (June): 59.

Sapiro, Virginia. 1990. *Women in American Society*. California: Mayfield Publishing Company.

Schwartz, Rosalind M., ed. 1978. *Equal Employment Opportunity Enforcement: One Law - One Agency or Multiple Jurisdiction?* University of California Institute of Industrial Relations.

Seidman, Joel. 1943. *Union Rights and Union Duties*. New York: Harcourt, Brace and Company.

Servadio, Gaia. 1976. *Mafioso: A History of the Mafia from its Origins to the Present Day*. New York: Stein and Day.

Smith, Dwight C., Jr. 1975. *The Mafia Mystique*. New York: Basic Books, Inc. Publishers.

Stanfied, George. 1983. *New Jersey: A Geography*.

Stansfield, Charles A. "The Metropolitan State." In *New Jersey: A Geography*, 161–179. Colorado: Westview Press.

State of New Jersey Commission of Investigation. *Organized Crime in Boxing*. New Jersey.

Sterling, Claire. 1990. *Octopus:The Long Reach of the International Sicilian Mafia*. New York: W.W. Norton & Company.

Sternlieb, George and Alex Schwartz. *New Jersey Growth Corridors Site Selection and Locational Satis-
    faction of New Firms in Selected Employment Growth Areas: A Survey of Industrial Location*, 1–
    109. Center For Urban Policy Research.
Subcommittee on Urban and Minority Owned-Business Development. 1990. *Hearing*. The U.S Government
    Printing Office.
Subcommittees of the Committee on Appropriations House of Representatives. 1970. *Hearings*. Ninety-First
    Congress 2nd Session. Washington, DC: U.S Government Printing Office.
Taylor, Andrew J. 1989. *Trade Unions and Politics*. New York: St. Martin's Press.
The New York State Organized Crime Task Force. *Corruption and Racketeering in the New York City
    Construction Industry*. New York: New York State School of Industrial and Labor Relations Cornell
    University.
The Port of New York Authority. 1963. *Metropolitan Transportation-1980*. New York: The Port of New
    York Authority.
The United States Equal Employment Opportunity Commission. 1980. "On Job Segregation and Wage Dis-
    crimination." In *Hearings*. Washington, D.C.
Troy, Leo. *Labor Organization in New Jersey*. 1965. New Brunswick, NJ: Institute of Management and
    Labor Relations Rutgers — The State University.
U.S. Civil Rights Commission. 1962. *Hearings Before the Commission*. Newark, NJ, September 11–12.
U.S. Department of Commerce. Bureau of the Census. 1990. *1987 Economic Censuses: Survey of Minority-
    Owned Business Enterprises—Black*, MB87–1 (July) A-1.
United States Senate Committee on Governmental Affairs. 1984. "Profile of organized Crime Mid-Atlantic
    Region." In *Report*. Washington, D.C.: U.S. Government Printing Office.
Wagenheim, Kal and Wagenheim, Olga Jimenez, eds. *A Documentary History: The Puerto Ricans*. New
    York: Praeger Publishers, 1973.
Waldinger, Roger. "Structural Opportunity or Ethnic Advantage? Immigrant Business Development in New
    York." *International Migration Review* 1: 48–73.
Wallace, Phyllis A., ed. 1976. *Equal Employment Opportunity and the AT&T Case*. Cambridge and Lon-
    don: MIT Press.
Willihan, James. 1985. *Union Government and Organization in the United States*. Washington, D.C.: The
    Bureau of National Affairs, Inc.
Wright, Giles R. 1986. *Arrival and Settlement in a New Place*. Edited by Howard L. Green. Trenton, NJ:
    New Jersey Historical Commission.
_____. *Work*. 1987. Edited by Howard L. Green. Trenton: New Jersey Historical Commission.
_____. *The Journey from Home*. 1986. Edited by Howard L. Green. Trenton, NJ: New Jersey Historical
    Historical Commission.
_____. 1986. *The Reasons for Migrating*. Edited by Howard L. Green. Trenton, NJ: New Jersey Historical
    Commission.
_____. 1986. *Looking Back: Eleven Life Histories*. Edited by Howard L. Green. Trenton, NJ: New Jersey
    Historical Commission, Department of State.
_____. 1988. *Afro-Americans in New Jersey: A Short History*. Trenton, NJ: New Jersey Historical Com-
    mission.
Wright, William C., ed. 1974. *Economic and Social History of Colonial New Jersey*. Trenton, NJ: New
    Jersey Historical Commission.

Part II

Racial Wage Inequality and Discrimination

3

MEASURING WAGE DICRIMINATION DURING PERIODS OF GROWING OVERALL WAGE INEQUALITY

William M. Rodgers III

INTRODUCTION

The decline in the relative earnings of African Americans during the 1980s is now well documented.[1] However, much debate as to the causes still remains. Becker's (1971) theory of discrimination, based on human capital theory, stresses the importance of racial differences in "productive" characteristics, such as years of schooling. In the theory's purest form, where free entry and exit of firms exist, blacks and whites have the same average productivity, and white's tastes for discrimination are given, Becker's model predicts that racial differences in wages should not persist over time. Yet, in their reviews of the empirical literature, Mason (1992), Darity (1982), and Darity and Williams (1985) conclude that large and persistent gaps exist.

To reconcile these differences, human capital theorists either relax the assumption that markets are perfectly competitive or the discriminatory tastes of whites are given. By doing this, they depart from their strict neoclassical view of the world and

---

[1] See, for example, Smith and Welch (1989), Bound and Freeman (1992), Juhn, Murphy and Pierce (1992), Rodgers (1994), and Card and Krueger (1992).

base their explanations on market power and imperfect information.[2] For many human capital economists, these modified models are just as problematic as models that interpret the persistent wage gaps as the amount of discrimination present in the labor market.

In response to this deficiency, researchers now drop the assumption that blacks and whites enter the labor market with the same average productivity. They argue that the inferior school and family environments of African Americans lead to lower average productivity, and if these "cultural" differences are not adequately controlled for in empirical studies, then the econometrician might conclude that labor market discrimination plays a key role in explaining the relative earnings of African Americans. The overall benefit of this approach is that it allows for the existence of persistent wage gaps, but within a "skills" framework.

O'Neill (1990), Neal and Johnson (1995), Maxwell (1994), and Ferguson (1994) attempt to capture the impact that the inferior family and school environments of African Americans have on their wages. These researchers use the Armed Forces Qualification Test (AFQT), a test of cognitive ability to proxy for an individual's family and school environments. Their empirical results indicate that the lower scores of African Americans explain the remainder of the black-white wage gap. As a result, they conclude that the "social and cultural skills hypothesis" is the missing link for explaining why it appears that racial wage gaps persist over time. The key implication of their results is that discrimination within the labor market plays a minor role in generating the relative wage outcomes of African Americans.

However, Currie and Thomas (1995) and Korenman and Winship (1995) provide compelling evidence that questions the overall quality of the AFQT as a measure of cognitive ability. Further, Rodgers and Spriggs (1995) provides evidence that suggest that the AFQT score is not a racially unbiased predictor of wages. As a result, they conclude that the existence of persistent wage gaps can be attributed to labor market discrimination.[3]

Another human capital explanation argues that the expansion in persistent wage gaps can be attributed to the widening of the overall U.S. wage distribution. Juhn, Murphy, and Pierce (1991) and Reardon (1995) argue that shifts in labor demand toward better educated and better skilled workers hurt less-educated and less-skilled workers regardless of race. As a result, empirical research on racial inequality that does not take into account the increased dispersion in the wage distribution overstates the role that labor market discrimination plays in generating labor market outcomes of African Americans.

More specifically, Juhn, Murphy, and Pierce (1991) argue the following. In 1979, the median black male was at the 31st percentile of the white earnings distri-

---

[2] Market power includes bargaining, dominance, and coercion explanations. For an excellent discussion of these models, see for example, Darity (1982).

[3] Their conclusion is consistent with the decline in federal resources devoted to enforcement of Affirmative Action and anti-discrimination laws, and evidence from matched-pair studies. See, for example, Anderson (1994) who documents the decline in resources allocated to EEOC during the 1980's. Also see Darity and Myers (1995) and Leonard (1990). Matched-pair studies such as Galster et al (1994) and Turner, Fix and Struyk (1991) have been quite successful in providing solid evidence that African Americans and other minorities are discriminated against in the hiring process.

bution. Because of a shift in labor demand toward better skilled workers during the 1980's, the lower third of the white distribution lost ground relative to the average white male. This shift also caused the average black to lose relative to the average white. Thus, they conclude that a large fraction of the erosion in the relative earnings of African Americans should not be attributed to labor market discrimination. It is just due to the fact that low-skilled workers regardless of race lost ground because they were employed in industries that either experienced labor saving technological change, or increased international competition.[4]

Thus, as Juhn, Murphy and Pierce (1991) point out, using the residual wage difference between African Americans and whites with identical observable characteristics to conclude that pay discrimination exists within the labor market is inappropriate, especially during the 1980s, when the residual wage distribution of white men expanded at a faster rate than in earlier periods. The key insight of their work is that researchers who use the residual due to race from a typical human capital wage equation may severely overstate the magnitude of wage discrimination that many African Americans face in the labor market. Furthermore, if Juhn, Murphy, and Pierce are correct, their work provides empirical support for a shift of the government's finite resources out of efforts to create equal opportunity in the labor market and to non-race based skill augmenting programs.

Juhn, Murphy, and Pierce (1991) develop a quite ingenious set of mean regression and mean decomposition techniques to indirectly account for the growing white residual wage inequality; however, their findings and subsequent interpretation overstate the ability of expanding residual inequality to explain the recent African American experience in the U.S. labor market. Assuming that this explanation applies to the average black is problematic, especially when only segments of the white residual wage distribution illustrate dramatic changes. It is quite reasonable to argue that the inequality explanation is limited to particular skill levels as measured by different segments of the residual wage distribution.

This paper first provides an overview of Bound and Freeman and Juhn, Murphy, and Pierce, two influential empirical studies on the erosion in the relative earnings of African American men during the 1980s.[5] Both utilize data from the Current Population Surveys to document and explain the erosion in the relative wages of African American men. I then replicate and update Juhn, Murphy, and Pierce's analysis for the following years: 1963, 1970, 1979, 1987, and 1992. The first four years represent the breakpoints that they used in their analysis. The evidence presented in this chapter challenges Juhn, Murphy, and Pierce's result that white residual wage inequality growth explains a sizable portion of the change in the gap. The chapter concludes with an application of the distributional methodology developed in Rodgers (1994) to selected years of the March Current Population Survey Annual Demographic Files. The evidence from the distributional analysis strongly indicates that the inequality growth hypothesis does not explain the typical labor market experience of African American men during the 1980s.

[4.] See, for example, Krueger (1991), Katz and Murphy (1992), Murphy and Welch (1991).
[5.] See Cain (1986) for a review of earlier empirical tests for the presence of wage discrimination.

MEASURING DISCRIMINATION DURING THE 1980S

Bound and Freeman (1992) and Juhn, Murphy, and Pierce (1991) have had the largest impact on recent literature that examines racial inequality. Bound and Freeman (1992) use the May and Merged Outgoing Rotation Group files from 1973 to 1989 to construct a series of cross-section estimates of the black-white wage gap. They focus on describing and explaining the experience of new entrant males (0 to 10 years of potential experience). From their decompositions, Bound and Freeman conclude that the decline in relative earnings of African American men has no uni-causal explanation.[6] One factor cannot completely describe the African American experience during the 1980s. For example, the decline in the real value of the minimum wage and the decline in the importance of unions are key contributors to the gap's expansion among less-skilled workers, while the rapid increase in the supply of black college graduates is a key contributor to the dramatic erosion in their earnings.

Juhn, Murphy, and Pierce (1991) provide an alternative explanation for the erosion in the relative earnings of African Americans. Following the work of Smith and Welch (1989), they pursue the hypothesis that race has little to do with the erosion. A large portion of the erosion is due to the fact that the overall white wage distribution expanded. Many researchers attribute this expansion to a shift in labor demand away from less-skilled workers, as measured by individuals at the lower tail of the residual wage distribution. This shift has hurt both less-skilled blacks and whites, and thus the overall decline in the mean black-white wage gap has little to do with race. However, their study has two major problems. First, their work fails to explicitly identify this newly important skill.[7] Second, they apply mean regression and decomposition techniques to a problem that is purely distributional in nature, and then use the mean result to describe the typical African American experience.

More specifically, increasing inequality has not been distributed evenly throughout the white residual wage distribution. For example, Figure 4–5 in JMP suggests that the expansion during the 1980s was concentrated at the lower segment of the wage distribution. In an effort to disentangle these distributional effects, Rodgers (1994) developed three procedures that allows one to decompose changes in the black-white wage gap at various segments of the residual wage distribution into the component due to expanding inequality, and the portion that is typically associated with wage discrimination. Rodgers' results which are generated from the CPS Merged Outgoing Rotation Group file and thus focus explicitly on the 1980s clearly indicate that Juhn, Murphy, and Pierce's findings overstate the importance of their non-race based explanation.

[6.] Also see, for example, Rodgers (1994).

[7.] In an effort to formally or explicitly document this skill, O'Neill (1990), Ferguson (1994), Ferguson (1995), and Neal and Johnson (1995) use the National Longitudinal Survey of Youth. Although a small sample relative to micro data from the CPS and decennial censuses, the perceived benefit of the NLSY is its wealth of family background, school quality, and the AFQT score, an index of the skills acquired in the family and school. O'Neill (1990), Maxwell (1994), Ferguson (1995), Ferguson (1994), and Neal and Johnson (1995) began to add the AFQT score in earnings equations. A recent paper by Rodgers and Spriggs (1995) cast serious doubt on the importance of the AFQT score.

DATA AND METHODOLOGY

The data comes from the 1964, 1970, 1980, 1988, and 1993 March Current Population Survey Annual Demographic Files. The samples consist of white and black males who worked at least 39 weeks in the previous calendar year, were employed in the public or private sector, and were at least 18 years of age. The basic human capital wage equation that is estimated throughout this paper is the following:

$$\ln W_i = X_i'\beta + e_i, \tag{1}$$

where $\ln W_i$ denotes individual i's logarithm of weekly wages, X_i denotes a set of human capital and sociodemographic characteristics such as education, potential experience, metropolitan and census division of residence.[8] Weekly wages are constructed from the ratio of income and salary and weeks worked during the previous calendar year.[9]

I use Bound and Freeman's specification for education. The specification for education is linear until 7 completed years, and then is unconstrained from 8 to 18. Specifically, X_i contains the following education dummy variables: 8, 9, 10, 11, 13, 14, 15, 16, 17 and 18. High school graduates are the excluded group. An additional education variable is included which takes the actual value of education if it is less than 8, and 0 if education exceeds 7. Dummy variables for individual years of potential experience are included in X_i along with dummy variables for race, central city residence and suburban residence. Eight census divisional dummy variables are also included.[10,11]

The last portion of this section describes the procedure that I use to determine whether Juhn, Murphy, and Pierce's results fail to explain the labor market experiences of the typical African American. For each period, with special focus on 1979 to 1987, the task is to pinpoint in the wage distribution where rising wage inequality's contribution to the expanding mean black-white wage gap is the greatest. The first step is to construct a prediction of the wage in year t' which the median black

---

[8.] Potential experience equals Min(Age - 18, Age - Education - 6).

[9.] I do not adjust the data for the presence of topcoding. Median regression estimates which are robust to topcoding yield similar results to the mean regression results. These estimates are presented in Appendix Table 3.A.1.

[10.] The divisions are New England, Mid-Atlantic, East North Central, West North Central, South Atlantic, East South Central, West South Central, Pacific. The Mountain divisional dummy variable was excluded.

[11.] In 1992, the Bureau of the Census changed the format of the education variable. The new question provides detailed information about an individual's post high school educational attainment. Along with affecting the education specification for the 1992 cross-section, this change also affects the construction of potential experience. In an attempt to maintain comparability with years prior to 1992, this paper recodes 1992 educational attainment as the following: some college = 15, vocational and academic AA = 14, BA = 16, MA and Professional school degrees = 17, and PhD = 18. These categories are adhoc; however, the mapping seems to perform quite well. The 1992 educational attainment question also brackets education for values below 9 years of schooling. I recode individual's with 1 to 4 years of schooling as a 4, individuals with 5 to 6 years as 6, and individuals with 7 to 8 years of schooling as 8. My empirical results are not influenced by this scheme. Less than 5 percent of the young male sample has values of educational attainment between 1 and 9 years.

in year t would receive given that his position in the year t white wage distribution does not change. Second, I construct the predicted change in the black-white gap between years t and t' which equals the difference between the predicted year t' median gap and the actual year t median gap. I then compare the predicted change in the gap to the actual change in the black-white median gap. For ease of interpretation, a ratio of the predicted and actual changes is constructed. A value of 0 indicates that Juhn, Murphy, and Pierce's hypothesis explains none of the change in the black-white wage gap, and a value of 1 indicates that their hypothesis explains all of the gap's change. Ratios are also constructed for the 10th, 25th, 75th and 90th percentiles.

The procedure used in this paper compares the black and white residual wage distributions, where the regression line for whites is used to generate residual wages. The key assumption is that in a nondiscriminatory world, white prices would prevail; however, this assumption is still quite controversial.

More formally, the procedure starts with estimating a weekly wage equation in year t using only the white male subsample. Controls for individual years of schooling, potential experience, region and metropolitan residence are added. The estimated coefficients are used to construct white and black residual distributions. The location of the year t median black residual is found in the year t white residual distribution. Denote this location as the qth quantile. Now using the year t' white residual distribution, find the white residual which corresponds to the qth quantile. This residual is interpreted as the predicted year t' black wage residual assuming that the median black's initial year t position is preserved.

Analytically, we can think of the procedure as follows. In year t, we have a log weekly wage equation for whites:

$$\ln W_{iw} = X'_{iw}\beta_w + e_{iw}, \qquad (2)$$

where X_{iw} is a $k \times 1$ vector containing the observable characteristics of the ith white male, and β_w gives the coefficients on these characteristics.[12] The ith white residual is the following:

$$\varepsilon^t_{iw} = \ln W_{iw} - X'_{iw}\beta_w, \qquad (3)$$

and the ith black residual, if he is paid like a white, is:

$$\varepsilon^t_{ib} = \ln W_{ib} - X'_{ib}\beta_w, \qquad (4)$$

The median black residual wage, Med (ε_b), is found in the black residual wage distribution. Let $\varepsilon_{b,.5}^t$ denote the value of the year t median black residual wage. Now find the quantile, q^*, where $\varepsilon_{b,.5}^t$ is located in the white residual distribution. This is where $\varepsilon_{w,q^*}^t = \varepsilon_{b,.5}^t$.

[12.] A constant is also included.

Using the year t' data, estimate equation (2) for whites. Construct the white and black residuals in equations (3) and (4). Now find $\varepsilon_{w,q*}^{t'}$. This is the year t' white residual wage at the quantile q^*, or the predicted year t' black residual wage. Also calculate $\varepsilon_{w,.5}^{t'}$ and $\varepsilon_{b,.5}^{t'}$, the year t' white and black median residual wages, respectively. The residuals $\varepsilon_{w,.5}^{t}$, $\varepsilon_{b,.5}^{t}$, $\varepsilon_{w,q*}^{t'}$, $\varepsilon_{w,.5}^{t'}$ and $\varepsilon_{b,.5}^{t'}$ are used to construct the year t and t' actual gaps, and the year t' predicted median gap. They are the following:

$$Agap_t = \varepsilon_{b,.5}^{t} - \varepsilon_{w,.5}^{t} \tag{5}$$

$$Agap_{t'} = \varepsilon_{b,.5}^{t'} - \varepsilon_{w,.5}^{t'} \tag{6}$$

$$Pgap_{t'} = \varepsilon_{w,q*}^{t'} - \varepsilon_{w,.5}^{t'} \tag{7}$$

To determine wage dispersion's contribution to the expansion of the median black-white wage gap, the ratio of the predicted and actual changes is constructed as follows:

$$\frac{Pgap_{t'} - Agap_t}{Agap_{t'} - Agap_t} \tag{8}$$

I also evaluate equation (8) at the 10th, 25th, 75th, and 90th percentiles.[13,14] Before generalizing this approach to segments of the wage distribution, I provide a numerical example of how to measure rising inequality's contribution to the growth in the median black-white wage gap. After estimating equation (2) using data for whites in year t, I construct $\varepsilon_{w,.5}^{t}$, the median white residual wage and $\varepsilon_{b,.5}^{t}$, the median black residual wage. Suppose that the median white residual equals 0.0 and the median black residual equals -.22 log points. From this, $Agap_t$, the actual median gap in year can be constructed. In this example, the actual median black-white gap equals -.22 log points. Before shifting to the year t' data, I locate q^*, the location of the median black residual in the white year t residual wage distribution. In this example q^* equals 31, the thirty-first percentile of the white residual wage distribution.

Equation (2) is now estimated using data for whites in year t'. I first construct the $\varepsilon_{w,.5}^{t'}$ and $\varepsilon_{b,.5}^{t'}$, the actual median white and black residuals. In this example,

---

[13.] The ratio in Equation (8) decomposes the actual gap's change (denominator) which is known to be nonzero into its portion due to rising wage inequality.

[14.] To provide an indication of the statistical qualities of the estimates, I conducted a bootstrap procedure and used the percentile method to construct 95 percent confidence intervals. The bootstrap procedure basically replicated the experiment 500 times using random samples of the population. The results indicated that conducting the procedure at specific points may provide misleading results. In many cases, the predicted change in the black-white gap due to a rise in white residual inequality actually declined. Thus, indicating that at particular quantiles (e.g., .10, .25, or median) rising inequality actually helped lead to a narrowing in the gap. Another indication of the poor reliability of utilizing a particular point was that the confidence intervals constructed from the bootstrap procedure were quite large.

they equal 0.0 and -.26 log points. This leads to an actual year t' gap, $Agap_{t'}$ of -.26 log points. Thus, from year t to t', the median black-white wage gap expanded by .05 log points. I now locate the residual in the white year t' wage distribution, $\varepsilon_{w,q*}^{t'}$ that corresponds to q^*, the 31st percentile. The value corresponds to the residual that the median black would have in year t' if he or she had maintained their position in the year t white residual wage distribution. Let $\varepsilon_{w,q*}^{t'}$ equal -.24 log points. As a result, $pgap_{t'}$, the year t' predicted gap equals -.24 log points.

To construct the ratio in equation (8), the contribution of general wage inequality to the expansion in the black-white wage gap, I compute two changes: the difference between actual gaps in year t and t', and the difference between the predicted gap in year t' and the actual gap in year t. The first change equals -.05 log points, and indicates that the median black-white wage gap increased by 5 log points. The second change equals -0.03 log points, and indicates the median black-white wage gap would have only expanded by 3 log points if the median black's position had been preserved in the white residual wage distribution. Thus, the value of the ratio equals .60 (-0.03/-0.05), and thus indicates that growth in general residual wage inequality explains 60 percent of the actual increase in the median black-white wage gap.

To provide a broader description of rising inequality's contribution at various segments or skill levels of the distribution, I conduct the procedure for each quartile of the wage distribution. The procedure for the lowest quartile (5th to 25th percentiles) is as follows. I locate the positions of the 5th to 25th percentile blacks in the year t white residual wage distribution, and then find the year t' white residuals which correspond to these percentiles. The mean of these residuals is the year t' average predicted wage for blacks at the lowest quintile, assuming that their year t positions in the white distribution are preserved. I then compute the year t and year t' averages of the white 5th to 25th percentile residual wages. The ratio in equation (8) is the difference between the predicted year t' mean gap and the actual year t mean gap divided by the change in the actual year t' and year t mean black-white wage gaps.

THE RESULTS

Table 3.1 contains estimated black-white weekly wage gaps from four specifications. Panel A presents the results for males of all experience levels and Panel B presents the results for males who have 0 to 10 years of potential experience. The estimates labeled "unadjusted" come from regressions of the logarithm of weekly wages on a constant and a dummy variable that equals 1 if the individual is black, and 0 if the individual is white.[15] These estimates are identical to the gaps presented in Juhn, Murphy, and Pierce, and thus exhibit the slowdown in black-white conver-

---

[15.]These are just the gaps that one obtains from calculating the difference between the average logarithm of the weekly wages of African Americans and whites.

gence.[16] For all males, the unadjusted gap starts at 59 percent in 1963, falls to 44 percent in 1970, and falls to 30 percent in 1979. From 1979 to 1987, the unadjusted gap expands to 32 percent and after 1987 falls 7 percentage points to 25 percent. The unadjusted gaps for young males exhibit a similar pattern; however, the levels of the gaps are smaller.[17] The next three rows of each panel contain estimated gaps from specifications that first include educational attainment, then add potential experience, and finally add census division and metropolitan residence. Even after controlling for racial differences in these observable characteristics, the slowdown in black-white convergence is still quite apparent.

Table 3.2 provides the motivation for focusing on the residual wage distribution instead of the overall wage distribution. The table contains the ratio of the difference between the 90th and 10th percentile residual log weekly wage distribution and the difference between the 90th and 10th percentile unadjusted log wage distribution. A value of 1 indicates that residual inequality in a given year explains all of overall wage inequality and a value of 0 indicates that residual inequality explains none of overall wage inequality. To construct the residual wage distributions, I use the coefficients that come from regressions of the logarithm of weekly wages on educational attainment, potential experience, race, census division of residence, and metropolitan residence.

The ratios reveal that as a fraction of total wage inequality, residual inequality grows in importance during the 1980s for men of all experience levels and for new entrants. The 90–10 ratios for men of all experience levels start at .88 in 1963, rise to .93 in 1970, and jump further to .97 in 1980 and 1987. The majority of this rise in relative importance has occurred at the among less-skilled workers as measured by the larger increase in the 50–10 versus the 90–10 spread. For new entrant men, the 90–10 ratios start at .93 in 1963, and rise to .98 in 1970, and rise slightly to .99 in 1979. The ratio remains at this level throughout the 1980s and early 1990s. Again, as measured by the 90–50 and 50–10 spreads, the increases in relative importance also tend to be among less-skilled workers.

Table 3.3 describes the location of African Americans in the white residual wage distribution. These calculations are another way to demonstrate the dramatic slowdown in black-white convergence. I construct the residual wage distributions for blacks and whites from coefficients that come from regressions of the logarithm of white weekly wages on their educational attainment, potential experience, census division of residence, and metropolitan residence.[18] I then compute the 10th, 25th, median, 75th and 90th percentile black residuals and find the percentile in the

---

[16.]Juhn, Murphy, and Pierce (1991) further restrict their sample to males who worked at least one week, usually worked full-time, and met several other criteria, which they do not list in their text. They go on to say that their conclusions are not sensitive to these sample criteria.

[17.]This is the typical result found in this literature. For a more detailed discussion see, for example, Card and Krueger (1992).

[18.]Juhn, Murphy, and Pierce make the controversial assumption that in the absence of discrimination, the prices that whites receive in the labor market would prevail. The suggested specifications in Oaxaca and Ransom (1994) could also be utilized to determine whether Juhn, Murphy, and Pierce's findings are sensitive to different choices of prices.

white residual wage distribution that they correspond to.[19] From 1963 to 1979, the average male jumps from the 19th to the 35th percentile of the white residual wage distribution, with the bulk of these gains occurring from 1963 to 1970. The gains occur at all segments of the distribution.

Table 3.1. Estimated Black-White Weekly Wage Gaps, Selected Years (Standard Errors in Parentheses).

Panel A: All Experience Levels					
Specification	1963	1970	1979	1987	1992
Unadjusted	−0.5909 (0.0198)	−0.4446 (0.0142)	−0.3031 (0.0153)	−0.3173 (0.0182)	−0.2464 (0.0178)
Education	−0.4548 (0.0194)	−0.3044 (0.0139)	−0.2164 (0.0148)	−0.2350 (0.0172)	−0.1620 (0.0165)
Education/ Experience	−0.4184 (0.0179)	−0.2954 (0.0127)	−0.2321 (0.0135)	−0.2460 (0.0157)	−0.1805 (0.0148)
Education/ Experience/ Geographic	−0.3960 (0.0178)	−0.2848 (0.0129)	−0.2060 (0.0140)	−0.2316 (0.0162)	−0.1625 (0.0151)
Panel B: New Entrants, 0 to 10 Years of Potential Experience					
Specification	1963	1970	1979	1987	1992
Unadjusted	−0.5550 (0.0500)	−0.3030 (0.0333)	−0.2086 (0.0255)	−0.2230 (0.0338)	−0.1045 (0.0357)
Education	−0.3718 (0.0480)	−0.1911 (0.0319)	−0.1457 (0.0241)	−0.1565 (0.0308)	−0.0877 (0.0336)
Education/ Experience	−0.3636 (0.0410)	−0.1961 (0.0262)	−0.2104 (0.0211)	−0.1941 (0.0275)	−0.1374 (0.0298)
Education/ Experience/ Geographic	−0.3320 (0.0413)	−0.1940 (0.0267)	−0.1807 (0.0219)	−0.1794 (0.0283)	−0.1301 (0.0307)
Sample Sizes	1963	1970	1979	1987	1992
All Males	12492	26383	29317	25345	24705
New Entrants	2654	6717	10577	8106	5856

Notes: Calculated using the CPS March Annual Demographic files for the following calendar years: 1964, 1970, 1980, 1988, and 1993. The samples consist of black and white males who fit the following criteria: (1) at least 18 years of age, (2) worked at least 39 weeks in the previous calendar year, and (3) employed in the public or private sector.

[19.] The values presented in this paper are higher than those found in Juhn, Murphy, and Pierce. They construct their residual wage distributions from regressions that only include education and potential experience. Adding controls for census division and metropolitan residence removes the relative wage disadvantage that African Americans experience due to living in lower wage central cities and census divisions.

Table 3.2. Ratio of Residual Wage and Total Wage Inequality.

Panel A: All Experience Levels					
Spread	1963	1970	1979	1987	1992
90–10	0.88	0.93	0.97	0.97	0.98
90–50	1.00	0.97	0.97	0.97	0.96
50–10	0.80	0.91	0.96	0.98	1.00
Panel B: New Entrants, 0 to 10 Years of Potential Experience					
Spread	1963	1970	1979	1987	1992
90–10	0.93	0.98	0.99	0.99	0.97
90–50	0.96	0.98	0.93	0.98	0.93
50–10	0.91	0.98	1.04	1.00	1.01

Notes: See text for description of procedure. Components of ratio are available upon request from the author.

New entrant African American males experience a sharp improvement in their positions. The bulk of their gains which are distributed throughout the distribution also occur during the 1963 to 1970 period. However, after 1970, their gains at the median and below cease. From 1979 to 1987, the average African American male maintains his position in the white residual wage distribution. The calculations at various points in the distribution indicate that the maintenance of position occurs throughout the distribution. Finally, since 1987, the typical African American male makes modest improvements in his position.

Table 3.3 shifts to describing changes in within group wage inequality for the four sub-periods. Three measures of inequality are presented: 90–10, 90–50, and 50–10 spreads. The entry labeled "90–10" refers to the change in the difference between the logarithm of the 90th and 10th percentile weekly wages. The entry labeled "90–50" refers to the change in the difference between the logarithm of the 90th percentile and median weekly wages, and the entry labeled "50–10" refers to the change in the difference between the logarithm of the median and 10th percentile logarithm of weekly wages. The half spreads allow one to pinpoint the location in the wage distribution where changes may have occurred. Further, if the percentiles represent skill levels, where the 90th percentile corresponds to the highest skill, then the changes can be interpreted as changes in the relative price of skill.

For white men of all experience levels, wage inequality expands in every period, with the largest increases during the 1970 to 1979 and 1979 to 1987 periods.[20] Note

---

[20.] An initial reaction to the results in Table 3.3 is that the increase during the 1963–70 sub-period is inconsistent with previous research. However, Table 3.2: Part 2 of Levy and Murnane (1992) shows that Juhn, Murphy, and Pierce obtain similar results as shown in Table 3.3. The variance of log weekly wages for their sample of white, male, year-round, full-time workers jumps from .469 in 1963 to .494 in 1970. The variance of log weekly wages for white males in my sample increases from .339 to .402. The vari-

that their is no acceleration in white residual inequality growth. The spreads indicate that growth actually slows. This finding is detrimental to the Juhn, Murphy,
and Pierce explanation. In order for their explanation to make sense, white residual
inequality must have accelerated in the 1980s.[21] For the 1970 to 1979 period, the
half spreads indicate that the growth in inequality is distributed at the lower part of
the residual wage distribution, while the 1979 to 1987 changes are distributed
evenly throughout the wage distribution. African American inequality also expands
during the 1970 to 1979 and 1979 to 1987 periods. The most interesting changes
occur during the 1963 to 1970 and 1987 to 1992 periods. Inequality at the lower
segment of the distributions narrow dramatically.

In terms of new entrant white men, residual wage inequality accelerates from
1979 to 1987. This growth is concentrated at the upper tail of the wage distribution.
For other periods, changes in inequality are not evenly distributed throughout the
white residual wage distribution. From 1963 to 1970 and 1987 to 1992, inequality
growth occurs at the lower tail, while from 1970 to 1979, growth occurs at the upper tail. For new entrant African Americans, inequality growth also accelerates
during the 1980s. After making tremendous gains in previous periods, African
Americans located at the lower tail of their residual wage distribution lost relative to
the median African American.

The evidence presented in Table 3.4 illustrates the dramatic improvement in the
relative positions of African Americans from 1963 to 1979; however, the pace of
these change slows. For the 1980s, this slowdown is significant because the upward
movement of African Americans in the white residual wage distribution had previously offset the general trend in white male inequality growth for men of all experience levels, and was not present to offset the acceleration of wage inequality growth
among new entrant white men. To formally demonstrate this relationship and assess
the relative magnitudes, I use Equation 4–3 of Juhn, Murphy, and Pierce (1991) to
decompose convergence in the black-white wage gap into the components due to a
narrowing in observable skills, a narrowing in the prices of observable skills, rising
overall inequality, and convergence due to blacks changing their location in the
white wage distribution.

Juhn, Murphy, and Pierce (1991) write the convergence in the average black-
white wage gap, $D_{t'} - D_t$ between years t' and t as:

$$D_{t'} - D_t = (\Delta X_{t'} - \Delta X_t)\beta_t + \Delta X_{t'} (\beta_{t'} - \beta_t) + (\Delta\theta_{t'} - \Delta\theta_t)\sigma_t + \Delta\theta_{t'} (\sigma_{t'} - \sigma_t) \quad (9)$$

---

ance of log weekly wages for African American males remains unchanged at .451. Of the remaining male
studies on wage inequality that Levy and Murnane highlight, Bluestone (1989) is the only one in which
inequality expands during the 1963 to 1970 period. He finds that the variance of log wages (annual wages
and salary income) falls from 1.471 to 1.428. His results differ because he includes part-time and part-
year workers in his samples.
[21] This finding is completely consistent with Bernstein and Mishel (1995). They find that no acceleration
in technology change, which is viewed as one of the key contributors to increasing residual wage inequality occurs during the 1980s.

Table 3.3. Location of African Americans in the White Residual Wage Distribution.

Panel A: All Experience Levels					
Year	1963	1970	1979	1987	1992
Mean	18.96	27.06	35.14	34.53	38.53
10	0.73	4.24	7.48	6.01	7.93
25	9.01	15.49	20.63	19.48	20.98
Median	24.51	32.26	40.68	38.08	41.28
75	45.68	52.17	60.28	59.13	63.01
90	64.35	69.21	74.21	74.41	77.90
Panel B: New Entrants, 0 to 10 Years of Potential Experience					
Year	1963	1970	1979	1987	1992
Mean	27.45	36.39	37.12	38.95	41.04
10	1.87	6.18	5.66	5.72	7.55
25	14.95	21.10	19.34	21.09	24.18
Median	34.08	42.41	41.32	44.83	44.87
75	54.62	60.07	62.23	64.57	67.36
90	70.73	77.18	81.07	78.93	81.80

Notes: Calculated using the CPS March Annual Demographic files for 1964, 1970, 1980, 1988, and 1993. The samples consist of black and white males who fit the following criteria: (1) at least 18 years of age, (2) worked at least 39 weeks in the previous calendar year, and (3) employed in the public or private sector. I construct residual wage distributions for whites and blacks from coefficients that come from regressions of the logarithm of white weekly wages on their educational attainment, potential experience, census division of residence, and metropolitan residence. I then compute the .10, .25, median, .75 and .90 black residuals and find the percentile in the white residual wage distribution that they correspond to.

where the first term on the right side of the equation measures convergence based on observable quantity changes at fixed prices, $(\Delta X_{t'} - \Delta X_t)\beta_t$. The second term measures convergence due to price effects, The third term measures convergence due to changes in the position of African Americans in the white distribution, $(\Delta \theta_{t'} - \Delta \theta_t)\sigma_t$, and the fourth term measures convergence due to changes in white residual wage inequality, $\Delta \theta_{t'} (\sigma_{t'} - \sigma_t)$. The third term captures changing discrimination in the labor market, and the fourth term which is Juhn, Murphy, and Pierce chief concern, captures the role that general changes in white residual wage inequality affect the gap's convergence.

Table 3.4. Changes in Within Race Residual Wage Inequality

Panel A: All Experience Levels				
White	1963–1970	1970–1979	1979–1987	1987–1992
90–10	0.1054	0.2117	0.1912	0.1068
90–50	0.0497	0.0116	0.1037	0.0565
50–10	0.0557	0.2001	0.0875	0.0503
Black	1963–1970	1970–1979	1979–1987	1987–1992
90–10	−0.2646	0.1474	0.1526	−0.0888
90–50	−0.0070	0.0915	0.0584	0.0194
50–10	−0.2576	0.0560	0.0942	−0.1081
Panel B: New Entrants, 0 to 10 Years of Potential Experience				
White	1963–1970	1970–1979	1979–1987	1987–1992
90–10	0.0764	0.0030	0.2005	0.0237
90–50	0.0263	0.1034	0.1421	−0.0096
50–10	0.0501	−0.1004	0.0584	0.0332
Black	1963–1970	1970–1979	1979–1987	1987–1992
90–10	−0.1910	−0.0256	0.2232	0.0308
90–50	−0.0010	0.1098	0.0490	−0.0023
50–10	−0.1901	−0.1353	0.1742	0.0332

Notes: Calculated using the CPS March Annual Demographic files for the following calendar years: 1964, 1970, 1980, 1988, and 1993. The samples consist of black and white males who fit the following criteria: (1) at least 18 years of age, (2) worked at least 39 weeks in the previous calendar year, and (3) employed in the public or private sector. The entry labeled "90–10" measures changes in the difference between the logarithm of the 90th and 10th percentile weekly wages. The term labeled "90–50" measures changes in the difference between the logarithm of the 90th percentile and median weekly wages, and the term labeled "50–10" measures changes in the difference between the logarithm of the median and 10th percentile logarithm of weekly wages. Tables A1 and A2 contain the spreads for each year.

To deal with the index number problem, Juhn, Murphy, and Pierce use the average over all years as their benchmark instead of year t characteristics and estimated coefficients. My interest is in explaining the relative importance of the residual wage inequality hypothesis within each sub-period. Thus, t' and t correspond to end and beginning period values of the characteristics and coefficients. Using a different benchmark from Juhn, Murphy, and Pierce also serves as a form of sensitivity analysis.

The rates of convergence for men of all experience levels are presented in the first row of Panel A of Table 3.5.[22] They indicate that the actual black-white weekly wage gap for men of all experience levels narrows by 15 percent from 1963 to 1970 and 14 percent from 1970 to 1979. Between 1979 and 1987, the gap actually expands by approximately 1 percent. However, since 1987, the actual gap narrows by 7 percent. The contribution of unobservable prices is not important in explaining changes in the gap and its slowdown in convergence. In each of the three subperiods from 1963 to 1987, the inequality term contributes only 2 to 3 percentage points to the gap's expansion. A narrowing in the observable racial differences in quantities and the upward movement of African Americans increases the importance of the Juhn, Murphy, and Pierce residual inequality term. From 1963 to 1970 and 1970 to 1979, the Gap term, or movement of blacks in the white distribution contributes 14 and 10 percentage points to the gap's narrowing, while from 1979 to 1987, the Gap term basically contributes nothing. Although not as large as in earlier periods, the Gap term since 1987, returns to play a key role in elevating the position of African American men of all experience levels, and even though it is quite small, expanding white residual wage inequality raises the relative wages of African Americans.

Panel B contains the decomposition results for new entrants. The actual black-white weekly wage gap narrows by 25 percent from 1963 to 1970 and 9 percent from 1970 to 1979. Between 1979 and 1987, the gap expands by approximately 1 percent. However, since 1987, the actual gap narrows by 12 percent. The Unobservable Price term is only important in explaining an increase in the gap and its slowdown in convergence during the 1979 to 1987 period. The term contributes 3 percentage points to the erosion. The Gap term is the key contributor. The term indicates that the slowdown in the improvement of African Americans' positions in the white residual wage distribution leads to the apparent growth in the relative importance of unobservable prices. From 1963 to 1970, the term suggests a 14 percent narrowing, while from 1970 to 1979 and 1979 to 1987, the term suggests a 1 and 3 percentage point narrowing in the black-white wage gap. Since 1987, the Gap term returns to play a role in elevating the position of African Americans; however, the major contributor to the recovery is a narrowing of racial differences in observable quantities and prices.

These results clearly illustrate the limited role that white residual inequality growth plays in explaining changes in the black-white wage gap and its slowdown in convergence. The key contributor to the slowdown was the slowdown in the upward movement of African Americans in the white residual wage distribution. This is the term that researchers attribute to changing discrimination. Hence, these results are consistent with the decline in the vigor of enforcement of antidiscrimination and affirmative action laws that took place in during the late 1970s and all of the 1980s.[23]

[22.] These correspond to taking differences in Table 3.1 of the columns labeled "unadjusted" gaps.

[23.] See, for example, Anderson (1994) and Leonard (1990).

Table 3.5. Decomposition of Black–White Convergence, 1963–70, 1970–79, 1979–87, and 1987–92

Panel A: All Experience Levels	(1) 1963–70	(2) 1970–79	(3) 1979–87	(4) 1987–92	Difference (1)–(2)	Difference (2)–(3)	Difference (3)–(4)
Total	0.146	0.142	−0.014	0.071	0.004	0.156	−0.085
Observables	0.031	0.064	0.010	0.003	−0.033	0.054	0.007
Quantities	0.031	0.076	0.018	0.005	−0.045	0.058	0.013
Prices	0.000	−0.012	−0.008	−0.002	0.012	−0.004	−0.006
Unobservables	−0.029	−0.024	−0.022	0.016	−0.005	−0.002	−0.038
Gap	0.144	0.102	−0.002	0.052	0.042	0.104	−0.054
Panel B: New Entrants	(1) 1963–70	(2) 1970–79	(3) 1979–87	(4) 1987–92	Difference (1)–(2)	Difference (2)–(3)	Difference (3)–(4)
Total	0.252	0.094	−0.014	0.118	0.158	0.108	−0.132
Observables	0.103	0.068	−0.009	0.081	0.035	0.077	−0.090
Quantities	0.071	0.095	0.008	0.046	−0.024	0.087	−0.038
Prices	0.032	−0.027	−0.017	0.035	0.059	−0.010	−0.052
Unobservables	0.008	0.006	−0.030	0.008	0.002	0.036	−0.038
Gap	0.141	0.020	0.025	0.029	0.121	−0.005	−0.004

Notes: See text for detailed explanation of the procedure.

The remainder of this section presents results from my distributional procedure and demonstrates that Juhn, Murphy, and Pierce's hypothesis, especially during the 1980s is only applicable to limited parts of the wage distribution. Table 3.6 contains the results for men of all experience levels, and Table 3.7 contains the results for new entrants. The procedure is done for the four sub-periods. For the first two periods, the actual change in the wage gap declines monotonically as we move up the distribution from the lower to higher quartiles. The gains from 1970 to 1979 are smaller at all segments of the distribution. The predicted changes are consistent with expanding residual white wage inequality. Two important results emerge. First, with the exception of the second quartile from 1970 to 1979, the absolute size of the predicted erosion is quite small. Second, the predicted increases are located at the lower or middle part of the residual wage distribution. Expanding white residual wage inequality had a modest impact on slowing the rate of convergence in black-white wage gaps for less-skilled African Americans.

Table 3.6. Distributional Decomposition for All Experience Levels

Panel A: 1963–1970				
Statistic	5–25	26–50	51–75	76–90
Agap$_{63}$	−0.5768	−0.3751	−0.3191	−0.2975
Agap$_{70}$	−0.3664	−0.2710	−0.2373	−0.2205
Pgap$_{70}$	−0.6022	−0.3865	−0.3175	−0.2938
Pdgap	−0.0254	−0.0114	0.0016	0.0037
Adgap	0.2104	0.1041	0.0818	0.0770
Ratio	−0.1208	−0.1095	0.0191	0.0476
Panel B: 1970–1979				
Statistic	5–25	26–50	51–75	76–90
Agap$_{70}$	−0.3664	−0.2710	−0.2373	−0.2205
Agap$_{79}$	−0.2429	−0.2171	−0.1848	−0.1691
Pgap$_{79}$	−0.3989	−0.3453	−0.2734	−0.2194
Pdgap	−0.0325	−0.0743	−0.0361	0.0010
Adgap	0.1235	0.0538	0.0525	0.0514
Ratio	−0.2636	−1.3798	−0.6869	0.0201
Panel C: 1979–1987				
Statistic	5–25	26–50	51–75	76–95
Agap$_{79}$	−0.2429	−0.2171	−0.1848	−0.1691
Agap$_{87}$	−0.2871	−0.2591	−0.2146	−0.1908
Pgap$_{87}$	−0.2511	−0.2381	−0.2037	−0.1872
Pdgap	−0.0082	−0.0209	−0.0189	−0.0181
Adgap	−0.0442	−0.0420	−0.0298	−0.0217
Ratio	0.1857	0.4983	0.6351	0.8354
Panel D: 1987–1992				
Statistic	5–25	26–50	51–75	76–95
Agap$_{87}$	−0.2871	−0.2591	−0.2146	−0.1908
Agap$_{92}$	−0.1611	−0.1989	−0.1643	−0.1563
Pgap$_{92}$	−0.2853	−0.2611	−0.2223	−0.1962
Pdgap	0.0018	−0.0020	−0.0077	−0.0054
Adgap	0.1261	0.0603	0.0502	0.0345
Ratio	0.0146	−0.0332	−0.1536	−0.1567

Notes: See text for a detailed description of the procedure.

Table 3.7. Distributional Decomposition for New Entrants

Panel A: 1963–1970				
Statistic	5–25	26–50	51–75	76–90
$Agap_{63}$	−0.5651	−0.3482	−0.2792	−0.2285
$Agap_{70}$	−0.3111	−0.1891	−0.1570	−0.1252
$Pgap_{70}$	−0.5209	−0.3598	−0.2763	−0.2363
Pdgap	0.0443	−0.0116	0.0029	−0.0078
Adgap	0.2540	0.1591	0.1223	0.1034
Ratio	0.1743	−0.0726	0.0240	−0.0751
Panel B: 1970–1979				
Statistic	5–25	26–50	51–75	76–90
$Agap_{70}$	−0.3111	−0.1891	−0.1570	−0.1252
$Agap_{79}$	−0.2146	−0.1799	−0.1864	−0.1392
$Pgap_{79}$	−0.2729	−0.2202	−0.1911	−0.1313
Pdgap	0.0382	−0.0311	−0.0341	−0.0061
Adgap	0.0965	0.0092	−0.0294	−0.0140
Ratio	0.3958	−3.3802	1.1608	0.4393
Panel C: 1979–1987				
Statistics	5–25	26–50	51–75	76–90
$Agap_{79}$	-0.2146	-0.1799	-0.1864	-0.1392
$Agap_{87}$	-0.2811	-0.1862	-0.1450	-0.1211
$Pgap_{87}$	-0.2276	-0.1944	-0.2011	-0.1507
Pdgap	-0.0130	-0.0145	-0.0147	-0.0115
Adgap	-0.0664	-0.0063	0.0414	0.0180
Ratio	0.1949	2.2909	-0.3555	-0.6401
Panel D: 1987–1992				
Statistic	5–25	26–50	51–75	76–90
$Agap_{87}$	-0.2811	-0.1862	-0.1450	-0.1211
$Agap_{92}$	-0.1516	-0.1291	-0.1217	-0.0984
$Pgap_{92}$	-0.2774	-0.1964	-0.1604	-0.1246
Pdgap	0.0037	-0.0102	-0.0154	-0.0035
Adgap	0.1295	0.0571	0.0232	0.0228
Ratio	0.0282	-0.1779	-0.6634	-0.1530

Notes: See text for detailed description of procedure

Between 1979 and 1987, wage inequality growth's ability to explain the expansion in the black-white gap grows due to the small decline in the relative wages of African Americans. Wage inequality growth explains 19 percent of the rise in the black-white wage gap at the first quartile (5th to 25 percentiles), 50 percent at the second quartile, 64 percent at the third quartile, and 84 percent of the change in the black-white wage gap at the upper most quartile. The shift in labor demand toward better-skilled men explains more of the gap's widening at the upper tail of the wage distribution. Employees viewed better skilled African Americans as being more deficient in the newly important skills than observationally equivalent whites.

The remainder of this section describes the results of the distributional analysis for new entrants. From 1963 to 1970 and 1970 to 1979, new entrant African Americans also experience improvements in their relative wages. These gains are greatest at the lower tail of the distribution and are smaller in the 1970 to 1979 period. The predicted change in the gap provides mixed results. Although small, expanding white residual wage inequality helps to raise the relative wages of African Americans at the lowest quartile. For all other quartiles, expanding inequality leads to a monotonically decreasing expansion of the gap. Again, in both absolute and relative terms the predicted increases are small.

For 1979 to 1987, a 1 to 2 percentage point expansion in the black-white wage gap could be attributed to expanding white residual wage inequality at all points of the distribution. Its importance is limited to the first two quartiles. Finally, the 1987 to 1992 results indicate that a tremendous narrowing occurs at the first and second quartiles. The actual gap narrows by 13 and 6 percentage points. This result is quite consistent with the increases in the federal minimum wage in 1989 and 1990. The predicted changes due to expanding inequality have small effects at the second and third quartiles; however, the actual narrowing is large enough to offset the negative effects of growing white residual wage inequality.

CONCLUSION AND DISCUSSION

Juhn, Murphy, and Pierce (1991) develop a quite ingenious set of mean regression and mean decomposition techniques to indirectly account for growing overall inequality; however, their findings and subsequent interpretation overstate the importance of these unobservable prices in explaining the relative decline of African American wages. I first show that our basis for concern with the role that residual differences play in explaining black-white wage gaps is due to the growing importance of residual wage inequality relative to overall wage inequality. The implication of this result is that future policies that continue to attempt to narrow racial differences in educational attainment will have limited success in lowering the black-white wage gap. Focusing solely on skill differences as measured by residual wages, I then present results from a distributional methodology developed in Rodgers (1994). The evidence challenges Juhn, Murphy, and Pierce's conclusion that white residual wage inequality growth explains a sizable portion of the change in the gap and that it explains the typical labor market experience of African American men during the 1980s. I find that the predicted increases in the black-white wage gap are quite small in both absolute and relative sizes, and that these losses are limited to a very small fraction of African American men. More specifically, better skilled African American men are the only group that is significantly affected by the growth in white residual wage inequality.

At a more general level, the results presented in this paper indicate that the standard mean regression and decomposition approaches of Juhn, Murphy, and Pierce (1991) clearly mask the underlying variation in wage inequality growth's contribution to changes in the black-white gap and its convergence. The lesson to be learned from this paper is that as applied researchers, we must resist the temptation to globally apply results generated from mean regression techniques to all individuals. Distributional analysis of the kind presented in this paper, may force us to report and digest more statistics, but having the additional information provides a more detailed and richer picture on which to base public policy decisions.

REFERENCES

Anderson, B. 1994. "Affirmative Action Policy Under Executive Order 11246: A Retrospective View." Unpublished Paper, U.S. Department of Labor (October).

Becker, G. 1971. *The Economics of Discrimination*. Chicago: The University of Chicago Press. (Original Edition, 1957).

Bernstein, J. and L. Mishel. 1994. "Is the Technology Black Box Empty?: An Empirical Examination of the Impact of Technology on Wage Inequality and the Employment Structure." Unpublished paper. Washington, D.C.: Economic Policy Institute (April).

Bluestone, B. 1989. "The Chaning Nature of Employment and Earnings in the U.S. Economy: 1963–1987." Paper prepared for the conference on "Job Creation in America." Chapel Hill, N.C.: University of North Carolina (April 10).

Bound, J. and R. Freeman. 1992. "What Went Wrong? The Erosion of Relative Earnings and Employment Among Young Black Men in the 1980's." *The Quarterly Journal of Economics* 107 (February): 201–232.

Cain, G. 1986. "The Economic Analysis of Labor Market Discrimination: A Survey." In *Handbook of Labor Economics, Volume I*, O. Ashenfelter and R. Layard, eds., *(PAGES)*. Elsevier Science Publishers BV.

Card, D. and A. Krueger. 1992. "School Quality and Black-White Relative Earnings: A Direct Assessment." *The Quarterly Journal of Economics* 57 (1) (February):151–200.

Currie, J. and D. Thomas. 1995. "Race, Children's Cognitive Achievement and the Bell Curve." *NBER Working Paper #5240*. Cambridge, MA (August).

Darity, W. 1982. "The Human Capital Approach to Black-White Earnings Inequality: Some Unsettled Questions." *The Journal of Human Resources* 17 (Winter): 73–93.

Darity, W. and R. Williams. 1985. "Peddlers Forever?: Culture, Competition, and Discrimination." *The American Economic Review* 75 (May): 256–261.

Darity, W. and S. Myers. 1995. "The Widening Gap: A Summary and Synthesis of the Debate on Increasing Inequality." Unpublished paper. Chapel Hill, NC: University of North Carolina and Minneapolis, MN: University of Minnesota.

Ferguson, R. 1994. "New Evidence on the Growing Value of Skill and Consequences for Racial Disparity and Returns to Schooling." Unpublished paper. Cambridge, MA: John F. Kennedy School of Government, Harvard University (September).

Ferguson, R. 1995. "Shifting Challenges: Fifty Years of Economic Change Toward Black-White Earnings Equality." *Daedalus* 124 (Winter): 37–76.

Freeman, R. and L. Katz. 1993. "Rising Wage Inequality: The U.S. vs. Other Advanced Countries." Washington, D.C.: Presented at the NBER Working Under Different Rules Conference (May 7).

Galster, G. et al. 1994. "Sandwich Hiring Audit Pilot Program Report to the Rockefeller Foundation." Unpublished Paper. Washington, D.C.: The Urban Institute (March).

Juhn, C., K. Murphy, and B. Pierce. 1991. "Accounting for the Slowdown in Black-White Convergence." In *Workers and Their Wages: Changing Patterns in the U.S.*, M. Kosters, ed., 107–143. Washington, D.C.: The AEI Press.

Juhn, C., K. Murphy, and B. Pierce. 1989. "Wage Inequality and the Rise in Returns to Skill." *(LOCATION):* Paper presented at the Universities Research Conference "Labor Markets in the 1990s" (November 13).

Korenman, S. and C. Winship. 1995. "A Reanalysis of the *Bell Curve*." NBER Working Paper #5230. Cambridge, MA: National Bureau of Ecomic Research (August).

Leonard J. 1990. "The Impact of Affirmative Action Regulation and Equal Employment Law on Black Employment." *The Journal of Economic Perspectives* 4 (Fall): 47–64.

Levy, F. and R. Murnane. 1992. "U.S. Earnings Levels and Earnings Inequality: A Review of Recent Trends and Proposed Explanations." *Journal of Economic Literature* 30 (September): 1333–1381.

Mason, P. 1992. "The Divide-and-Conquer and Employer/Employee Models of Discrimination: Neoclassical Competition as a Familial Defect." *The Review of Black Political Economy* (Spring): 73–89.

Maxwell, N. 1994. "The Effect on Black-White Wage Differences of Differences in the Quantity and Quality of Education." *Industrial and Labor Relations Review*, 47 (January): 249–264.

Neal, D. and W. Johnson. 1995. "The Role of Pre-Market Factors in Black-White Differences." NBER Working Paper #5124. Cambridge, MA: National Bureau of Economic Research (May).

Oaxaca, R. and M. Ransom. 1994. "On Discrimination and the Decomposition of Wage Differentials." *Journal of Econometrics* 61: 5–21.

O'Neill, J. 1990. "The Role of Human Capital in Earnings Differences Between Black and White Men." *The Journal of Economic Perspectives* 4 (Fall): 25–45.

Reardon, E. 1995. "Demand-Side Changes and Black Relative Economic Progress: 1940–1990." MIJCF Working Paper 95–2. Santa Monica, CA: *(ORGANIZATION)* (February).

Rodgers, W. M. III. 1993. "Male Black-White Wage Gaps, 1979–1991: A Distributional Analysis." Unpublished Paper. Williamsburg, VA: The College of William and Mary.

Rodgers, W. M. III. and W. Spriggs .1995. "What Does the AFQT Really Measure: Race, Wages and Schooling and the AFQT Score." Unpublished Paper. Williamsburg, VA: The College of William and Mary and Washington, D.C.: Joint Economic Committee, U.S. Congress.

Smith, J. and F. Welch. 1989. "Black Economic Progress After Myrdal." *The Journal of Economic Literature* 27 (June): 519–564.

Turner, M., M. Fix, and R. Struyk. 1991. Opportunities Denied, Opportunities Diminished: Racial Discrimination in Hiring, Urban Institute Report 91–9. Washington, D.C.: Urban Institute Press.

Table 3.A.1. Estimated Median Black-White Weekly Wage Gaps, Selected Years (Standard Errors in Parentheses).

Panel A: All Experience Levels					
Specification	1963	1970	1979	1987	1992
Unadjusted	−0.5390 (0.0006)	−0.4055 (0.0050)	−0.2877 (0.0083)	−0.3361 (0.0019)	−0.3032 (0.0335)
Education	−0.4055 (0.0037)	−0.2894 (0.0024)	−0.2231 (0.0001)	−0.2578 (0.0062)	−0.2215 (0.0035)
Education/ Experience	−0.3793 (0.0123)	−0.2678 (0.0055)	−0.2151 (0.0088)	−0.2542 (0.0077)	−0.2064 (0.0063)
Education/ Experience/ Geographic	−0.3600 (0.0138)	−0.2566 (0.0111)	−0.1844 (0.0131)	−0.2361 (0.0165)	−0.1823 (0.0129)
Panel B: New Entrants, 0 to 10 Years of Potential Experience					
Specification	1963	1970	1979	1987	1992
Unadjusted	−0.5108 (0.0096)	−0.3151 (0.0338)	−0.2151 (0.0319)	−0.2290 (0.0292)	−0.0612 (0.0350)
Education	−0.4391 (0.0306)	−0.1839 (0.0191)	−0.1613 (0.0193)	−0.1671 (0.0116)	−0.0392 (0.0275)
Education/ Experience	−0.3522 (0.0295)	−0.1807 (0.0202)	−0.2142 (0.0130)	−0.1988 (0.0221)	−0.1206 (0.0353)
Education/ Experience/ Geographic	−0.3075 (0.0325)	−0.1648 (0.0197)	−0.1818 (0.0184)	−0.1678 (0.0260)	−0.1152 (0.0359)

Table 3.A.2. Within Race Wage Inequality

Panel A: Unadjusted Weekly Wages					
White	1963	1970	1979	1987	1992
90–10	1.2040	1.3122	1.5084	1.6740	1.7716
90–50	0.5108	0.5529	0.6077	0.6931	0.7615
50–10	0.6931	0.7593	0.9008	0.9808	1.0100
Black	1963	1970	1979	1987	1992
90–10	1.7380	1.3962	1.4912	1.6662	1.5802
90–50	0.6190	0.5208	0.6061	0.7119	0.7234
50–10	1.1189	0.8755	0.8850	0.9543	0.8569
Panel B: Residual Weekly Wages					
White	1963	1970	1979	1987	1992
90–10	1.1456	1.2510	1.4628	1.6540	1.7607
90–50	0.5129	0.5627	0.5743	0.6781	0.7345
50–10	0.6327	0.6883	0.8884	0.9759	1.0262
Black	1963	1970	1979	1987	1992
90–10	1.5796	1.3150	1.4624	1.6150	1.5262
90–50	0.5140	0.5069	0.5984	0.6568	0.6762
50–10	1.0656	0.8081	0.8640	0.9582	0.8500

Table 3.A.3. New Entrant Within Race Wage Inequality

Panel A: Unadjusted Weekly Wages					
White	1963	1970	1979	1987	1992
90–10	1.5104	1.6014	1.5388	1.7918	1.8233
90–50	0.4916	0.5162	0.6178	0.7503	0.7861
50–10	1.0188	1.0852	0.9210	1.0415	1.0372
Black	1963	1970	1979	1987	1992
90–10	1.9769	1.5527	1.5581	1.7707	1.7750
90–50	0.5906	0.5404	0.6419	0.7344	0.6763
50–10	1.3863	1.0123	0.9163	1.0364	1.0986
Panel B: Residual Weekly Wages					
White	1963	1970	1979	1987	1992
90–10	1.4696	1.5460	1.5490	1.7495	1.7732
90–50	0.4755	0.5018	0.6052	0.7474	0.7378
50–10	0.9941	1.0441	0.9437	1.0021	1.0354
Black	1963	1970	1979	1987	1992
90–10	1.7643	1.5733	1.5477	1.7709	1.8017
90–50	0.5145	0.5135	0.6233	0.6723	0.6699
50–10	1.2498	1.0598	0.9244	1.0986	1.1318

Part III

Health

4

WILL GREATER COMPETITION IMPROVE THE MARKETS FOR HEALTH CARE SERVICES AND THE HEALTH OUTCOMES FOR BLACK AMERICANS?

Wilhelmina A. Leigh, Ph.D.*

INTRODUCTION

As a prominent feature in the organization of U.S. society, race has interacted with the two central ideological forces of the 20th century — the commitment to individual freedom and, at least in the abstract, the commitment to equality — to yield systems and market mechanisms that generate a variety of health outcomes (Fuchs, 1993). Tension has always existed between these two ideological forces, with the emphasis on individual opportunity and achievement prevailing most of the time, but with the egalitarian emphasis much in evidence in the 1930s and 1960s, when such programs as federally assisted housing, Social Security, and Medicaid and Medicare (federal programs for health insurance) were implemented. The egalitarian ideology, however, has focused more on equality of social status, equality under the law, and equality of opportunity than on equality of outcomes. This chapter focuses on the equality (or inequality) in access to health care and in health outcomes between black and white Americans.

The chapter begins with definitions of health and health-care services and with measures of health outcomes by race. It then examines the markets for health-care services and discusses proposals to alter these marketplaces, as the way to achieve broader societal goals. A discussion of likely implications of reform proposals for the health care and outcomes of African Americans concludes the chapter.

HEALTH OUTCOMES AND RACE

No single concept of health is ideal for all purposes (Fuchs, 1993). Health is multidimensional and has been studied as a function of medical care, income, education, age, sex, race, marital status, environmental pollution, and personal behavior (such as cigarette smoking, diet, and exercise). Health is difficult to trade interpersonally, and, relatedly, initial endowments are extremely important (Fuchs & Zeckhauser, 1987). Economists treat health as an object of choice, subject to constraints, such that in the getting and spending of income, individuals make choices that affect their health (Fuchs, 1993). Inequality in health outcomes is partly the result of initial endowments and partly the result of individual behavior and choices and of random shocks.

Health has been modeled as both a consumption good that directly affects utility and as an investment good that contributes to the production of other commodities and services. Because health is probabilistically produced from initial endowments through lifestyle choices of individuals, its production function is peculiar (Fuchs, 1993; Fuchs & Zeckhauser, 1897). Whereas most commodities are produced by specialists and then sold to the general public, an individual's health status is largely self-produced, being strongly affected by his or her consumption of other commodities. Achieving and maintaining health also requires patients and health professionals to work cooperatively rather than as adversarial buyers and sellers. Thus the model of atomistic competition is not appropriate for health. Together, these conditions imply that individuals will not value health equally at the margin. Even if there were no income inequalities, individuals would have dramatically different values for the same health output.

Significant externalities of the conventional sort afflict health, and significant interdependent utilities affect its valuation (Fuchs & Zeckhauser, 1987). For example, industrial production often results in negative externalities both for the health of employees involved in the production process and for the health of those living near sites where toxic by-products are dumped or buried (Dula, Kurtz & Samper, 1993). Black lung disease, asbestosis, lead poisoning, and certain types of cancers are examples of diseases that may result from these externalities. External benefits to others, on the other hand, may arise because their health depends, in part, on your health (as in the case of communicable diseases), or your ill health may simply be a source of disutility to them. Conversely, because of the significant externalities from good health — an improvement in your health benefits others, and there is no feasible way of arranging compensation for that benefit — a free-market approach may result in suboptimal levels of health, and collective intervention (through subsidies or other means) may be justified to achieve a more efficient allocation of resources in the health sector (Fuchs, 1993).

HEALTH-CARE OR MEDICAL-CARE SERVICES

Arrow (1963) defines health-care (or medical-care) services as the complex of services that center around physicians (in both private and group practice) and hospitals, and that relate to public health. Health care sometimes is characterized as an intermediate good in the production of health because it can involve the preservation of life, or, at least, have major effects on the quality of life.

Despite some differences between health care and other goods and services, similarities stem from the fact that it is produced with resources that are scarce relative to human wants. Thus, every society must have control mechanisms to determine how much health care to produce, how to produce it, and how to distribute it among the population. Fuchs (1993) finds that, in principle, only three types of mechanisms are available: the market, central direction, and traditional norms.

Medical services also are of three main types. First, are those services that the consumer gets frequently enough to be able to judge quality and know price (e.g., pediatric office visits for preschoolers). Second, are those services that the consumer buys infrequently but the provider furnishes commonly, for which a reputation in principle can develop — i.e., perfect reputation goods. Third, are those services that are rare for everyone and for which, even in the best of circumstances, reputation or track record will be hard to determine — i.e., imperfect reputation goods. Because of the nature of the differences in these three types of services, the market for medical care is almost as much a market for information as it is a market for specific services (Pauly, 1988). The definitional differences in the types of medical services illustrate the informational asymmetries that abound in the relationships among providers and consumers in the market for medical care services.

Moreover, even with accurate diagnostic information, there is considerable randomness in the relation between health care and health outcomes. It is difficult to measure the true marginal productivity of a medical care intervention, which may in turn differ for patients with specific characteristics (age, race, gender). Phelps (1992) notes that there can be patient-specific effects (almost unmeasurable), doctor-specific effects, and even time (experience) effects. Thus, the quality of treatment received in a particular instance cannot be easily inferred from the outcome, and precise "performance guarantees" cannot be given (Blomqvist, 1991: 411). As Arrow (1963) has observed, recovery from disease is as unpredictable as its incidence.

Medical care is in many respects, the quintessential service industry (Fuchs, 1993). It is extremely difficult to measure output. The stochastic nature of the demand for hospital care results in excess capacity, and the problem is exacerbated by systematic variation in demand according to day of week and month of year. The market for medical services is unlike most markets with excess capacity, however, in which prices tend to fall sharply and some firms are forced out of business. By contrast, in many health-care markets there are excess supplies of hospital beds, high-tech equipment, and certain surgical and medical specialists, but charges and fees remain high and the excess capacity persists for decades (Fuchs, 1993).

HEALTH OUTCOMES BY RACE

Attempts to measure and analyze differences in health across individuals and populations have typically focused on self evaluations of health status, morbidity (as evidenced by symptoms or diagnosed illnesses), and mortality (especially age-specific and age-adjusted death rates). By all of these measures, the health of African Americans is worse than that of whites. African Americans have more undetected diseases, higher disease and illness rates, and more chronic conditions (such as hypertension and diabetes) than whites (Leffall, 1990).

African Americans are more likely than whites to rate their health as fair or poor (see National Center for Health Statistics [NCHS], 1995). In each year between 1987 and 1993, between 8 and 9 percent of White Americans rated their health as fair or poor, while between 15 and 17 percent of African Americans did likewise. In the three age groups, "under 15 years," "15–44 years," and "45–64 years," in virtually all years, the percentage of African Americans rating their health fair or poor was more than double the percentage of whites doing so. For the age groups "65–74" and "75 years and over," in all years, although less than double the white rate, the share of African Americans reporting fair or poor health remained more than the share of whites.

Lifestyle and behavior influence the incidence of certain illnesses and even death. A prime example is cigarette smoking, which is a contributing factor in cardiovascular diseases and cancer, the two major killers of all Americans. Although the percent of all persons 25 years of age and older who reported that they were current smokers declined for most gender and race groups between 1974 and 1993, in 1993, higher percentages of both Black and White males — than of African American and white females — reported smoking (NCHS, 1995). In 1993, 36 percent of African American males were smokers, as opposed to 26 percent of White males. Since 1990, the percentages for female smokers have been very close, with 23 percent of white females and 22 percent of Black females indicating that they were current smokers in 1993.

Obesity — defined as excess body weight relative to height — has implications for many health problems. Although the incidence of obesity generally is greater among women than men, Black women have an exceptionally high incidence (NCHS, 1995). Over the 1988–1991 period, among persons ages 20–74, half of Black females (49.6 percent) were obese, whereas about a third (33.5 percent) of white females were. Thirty-two percent of both African American males and white males also reported obesity.

Hypertension, or elevated blood pressure, a major contributing factor in heart disease, is more prevalent among African Americans than among white Americans (NCHS, 1995). In the period 1988–1991, one-fourth of white males (25.1 percent) and nearly one-fifth of white females (19.0 percent) reported hypertension. Over the same period, nearly a third (31.3 percent) of black females and close to two-fifths (37.4 percent) of black males reported the condition.

Cancer incidence at all sites was highest among African American males and lowest among African American females between 1973 and 1991 (NCHS, 1995). In 1991, at all sites, the number of new cases per 100,000 population ranged from 598 for black males to 334 for black females. Also in 1991, among white males, the number of new cases was 495, whereas for white females, it was 348.

Death, or mortality, is the clearest indicator of health status, and life expectancy re-flects this same measure in a slightly different way. Despite improvements in health care for African Americans since the 1960s, according to the Council on Ethical and Judicial Affairs of the American Medical Association (1990), African Americans have twice the infant mortality rate of whites and a life expectancy 7 years shorter than that of whites (see also NCHS 1995). Excess deaths — the difference between the number of deaths observed in a subpopulation and the number of deaths that would have occurred if that group had experienced the same death rates as the white population — by black males and females due to all causes accounted for over half of all such deaths in 1991 (see NCHS n.d.). African Americans continue to have a one-and-a-half times higher overall age-adjusted death rate than do whites (Blendon et al. 1989; Windom, 1989).

When we look at specific causes, we find greater death rates for Blacks than for whites for many of them. For example, in 1992, diseases of the heart were responsible for 264 deaths per every 100,000 black males, but for only 190 deaths for every 100,000 white males (NCHS, 1995). In the same year, diseases of the heart were the reported cause of death for 98 out of every 100,000 white females and 162 per 100,000 black females. For all types of cancers combined, higher age-adjusted death rates per 100,000 population are reported among black males (238) than among white males (157), and among black fe-males (137) than among white females (110) (see NCHS 1995). This is so in spite of the lower cancer incidence among black females. Greater 5–year survival rates for whites than for African Americans with all cancers (except cancers of the pancreas and stom-ach) in the 1983–90 period may explain this differential (see NCHS 1995). African American males under the age of 70 reported 5,238 excess deaths and African American females in the same age group reported 2,589 excess deaths from all types of cancers in 1991 (NCHS n.d.).

Both the incidence of HIV infection and deaths from AIDS are disproportionately high among African Americans. For example, although white women are 75 percent of all women ages 15–44, in 1994, only 3.8 cases of AIDS were reported per 100,000 white women. African American women, who are only 13 percent of all women ages 15–44, reported 62.7 AIDS cases per 100,000 population (see Leigh 1994a; Centers for Disease Control and Prevention 1994). From the early 1980s through the end of 1994, deaths from AIDS among black females totaled 17,911, compared to 7,846 such deaths among white females.

Because of the extent of racial differentials in health outcomes, researchers have tried to disentangle the many causative factors. Blendon et al. (1989) suggest that the fact that African Americans, on average, are in poorer health than whites may be a consequence of a life-course deficit in access to medical care, as well as their generally lower standard of living (reflected in differences in average incomes and other indicators of socioeco-nomic status). For example, in a 1986 survey, one in 11 African Americans reported not receiving health care for economic reasons, while only 1 in 20 Whites reported the same. The life-course deficit in access to medical care and the generally lower standard of liv-ing are attributable in part to racial discrimination in the markets for health-care services and for education and labor, respectively. The health-care services utilization patterns of African Americans may be influenced both by cultural phenomena and/or by a realistic assessment of the assistance available to them, which may be restricted by institutional-ized and systematic forms of discrimination (White-Means & Thornton, 1989).

Although adverse health indicators reflecting lifestyle/behavior choices, such as cigarette smoking, correlate inversely with socioeconomic status, it is not always possible to isolate the effects of occupation, income, and education (Nickens, 1991). In addition to its relationship to socioeconomic status and its influence on lifestyle/behavior choices, the generally lower educational attainment of African Americans than whites, for example, may restrict the ability of some African Americans to gain access to and to negotiate effectively for the best medical treatment available (Council on Ethical and Judicial Affairs, 1990). Lower educational attainment decreases the ability to comprehend written information and instructions from physicians, from health-care facilities, from third-party payers, and on medications.

Socioeconomic factors also strongly influence hospital use and are associated with a large share of the geographic variation in hospital medical and surgical admissions. One study found that two-thirds of this variation was associated with socioeconomic factors (U.S. Department of Health and Human Services [USDHHS], 1993b). Specifically, communities whose residents were more educated were found to have lower rates of hospitalization.

MARKETS

The presence of competition in a market, and the existence of a competitive equilibrium where all commodities are priced relative to their costs or utilities, has several generally agreed upon preconditions (Fuchs, 1993). There must be a large number of buyers and sellers in the market, no one of whom is so big as to have a significant influence on market price. Collusion to fix prices or quantities must not exist among the buyers or sellers. There must be relatively free and easy entry into the market by new buyers and sellers, and there must not be governmentally imposed restraints on prices or quantities. Both buyers and sellers in a perfectly competitive market also must have reasonably good information about prices and quality. Without competition, sellers with monopoly power or buyers with monopsony power could take advantage of their customers or their suppliers with results that are neither efficient nor equitable.

Most health-care markets depart substantially from competitive conditions, sometimes inevitably and sometimes as a result of deliberate public or private policy (Fuchs, 1993). The pricing practices of the medical industry depart sharply from the competitive norm, primarily because the price paid by insured consumers when health-care services are demanded can be set separately from the price paid to providers for the services supplied (Ellis & McGuire, 1993; Arrow 1963). Thus, price discrimination exists in the market for medical care services. Price discrimination by income, which exists when the price of zero is charged for sufficiently indigent patients, is also a source of nonoptimality in the market for health-care services.

Much of the competition in the U.S. health-care system has centered around expensive and sophisticated medical technologies. Hospitals have wooed physician specialists and patients with the newest medical equipment and procedures, with a resulting proliferation of such equipment and facilities that often are used far below capacity (Sisk and Glied, 1994). As Arrow (1963) observes, the special structural characteristics of the medical-care market are largely attempts to overcome its lack of optimality due to the nonmarketability of the bearing of suitable risks and the imperfect marketability of information. Compensatory institutional changes, with some reinforcement from the usual profit motive, largely explain the observed noncompetitive behavior of the medical-care market.

The rest of this section looks at markets for three specific health-care services — insurance, physician services, and hospital services. How African Americans operate in each of these markets is discussed as well.

MARKET FOR HEALTH INSURANCE

Two kinds of risk are involved in medical care: the risk of becoming ill, and the risk of incomplete or delayed recovery (Arrow, 1963). From the point of view of the welfare economics of uncertainty, both are risks against which individuals would like to insure. Individuals normally are assumed to be risk-averters; in fact, health insurance is sometimes explained as the attempt of risk averse individuals to maximize their expected utility (Pauly, 1986). It is, however, impossible to draw up insurance policies that sufficiently distinguish among risks; thus, incentives to avoid losses are diluted. The nonexistence of suitable insurance policies for either type of risk implies a loss of welfare.

Because of the inability to insure for the risks noted above, insurance markets in medical care are themselves different from conventional insurance markets (Pauly, 1986). The cost of medical care constitutes only part of the loss due to illness. It also consists of discomfort and the loss of productive time during illness, and, in more serious cases, prolonged deprivation of normal function, or death. Not only is the level of the loss-probability for a particular individual sometimes unknown to the insurer, the actual loss in real income or well-being also is unknown. Ignorance about probabilities means that the insurer may have difficulties in determining which purchasers of insurance are at which levels of risk. Adverse selection by insurers, of those deemed least likely to need services, may result. Ignorance about the actual loss in well-being suffered and/or the actual illness of the individual may force insurers to base benefits on the level of expenditures, which is a proxy for the effects of illness, but which also is partly under the control of the insured.

Moral hazard arises whenever an individual's behavior that affects the expected loss is altered by the quantity of insurance he/she obtains (Pauly, 1986). Moral hazard can occur because insurance affects either the probability of an event associated with a loss, or the size of the loss conditional on the occurrence of the event. The first sort of moral hazard arises when the purchase of health insurance encourages individuals to spend less on preventive medical care. The second sort occurs when the purchase of insurance induces an individual who has experienced an illness to spend more resources on its treatment. Various forms of cost-sharing have been implemented to reduce this inefficient use of financial incentives by consumers and doctors, but all forms of cost-sharing include some greater exposure to risk before the share has been paid. For example, an insured patient typically faces an annual deductible ($475 for a family on average in 1991), followed by a coinsurance rate (usually 20 percent) up to an out-of-pocket maximum (usually less than

$2000). Only after the out-of-pocket maximum has been reached does the marginal cost to the individual of each additional service fall to zero and has risk exposure for the consumer disappeared (Cutler, 1994a). An alternative approach to limit moral hazard would be to maintain full coverage but to control use by rationing via nonprice mechanisms. That is, the control over use would generally take the form of refusal to pay benefits in certain circumstances.

The framework for virtually all of the empirical work on insurance effects on demand for medical care has been the very simple model of insurance coverage of a homogeneous medical service, where insurance cuts the user price and thereby increases the physical quantity of services used (Pauly, 1986). This model ignores the fact that, other things being equal, types of medical care associated with low-probability, high-loss events, such as hospitalization, are more likely to be insured for than are types of medical care associated with high-probability, low-loss events, such as routine physician services. Traditional health insurance is more complete for large losses, which in turn account for the bulk of spending on health-care services.

Under ideal insurance, medical care will always be undertaken in any case in which the expected utility, taking account of the probabilities, exceeds the expected medical cost. This would lead to an economic optimum (Arrow, 1963). Under conventional programs of insurance and reimbursement, "buyers" of health care — patients — bear only a fraction of the cost; therefore, neither patients nor health-care entrepreneurs have the incentive to assess whether a given medical innovation "saves gasoline but increases the price of the car" (Fuchs, 1993, 195). Economic research suggests that up to one-third of many common medical procedures have less benefit than risk to the patient (Cutler, 1994b). In addition, the tax treatment of health insurance has warped the choice process for it, resulting in the purchase of insurance that, at the market level, is both excessive in quantity and distorted in form (Pauly, 1986). Increases in the level and form of insurance coverage have the effect of distorting the demand for medical care.

Three different methods of coverage of the costs of medical care have arisen: prepayment, indemnities according to a fixed schedule, and insurance against costs, whatever they may be (Arrow, 1963). In hypothetically perfect markets, these three forms of insurance would be equivalent. The indemnities stipulated would, in fact, equal the market price of the services, so that the value to the insured would be the same if he were to be paid the fixed sum, or the market price, or were given the services free.

The inefficiency of conventional third-party insurance and fee-for-service remuneration of doctors is due not just to information asymmetry between physicians and patients but also to information asymmetry between doctors and the providers of health insurance (Blomqvist, 1991). Thus, even if doctors can be induced to act as perfect agents for their patients, first-best indemnity-type contracts (or complete contingent contracts) can not exist as long as the information asymmetry between doctors and insurers has not been altered. Conversely, although an insurance mechanism such as that inherent in the contract structure for a health maintenance organization, or HMO, may resolve the problem created by the information asymmetry between doctor and insurer, it does not yield an efficient solution unless the HMO can be induced to also (through their physicians) act as the patient's agent. This could in principle be accomplished through some type of performance guarantee or liability rule.

AFRICAN AMERICANS IN THE MARKET FOR HEALTH INSURANCE

Although health insurance provides access to health-care services and thereby influences health status, about half of African Americans under age 65 are uninsured or covered by Medicaid, the state-administered program of health insurance for low-income persons, in which the federal government matches state expenditures for covered services and administrative costs (Leigh, 1994b; Nickens, 1991). Nearly a quarter of African Americans under age 65 are uninsured compared to 16 percent of whites. African Americans with health insurance are less likely to be covered by a private carrier, with their generally more generous policies, than are Whites — 75 percent of whites versus 51 percent of Blacks in 1993 (NCHS, 1995). In addition, African Americans are significantly more likely to reside in states with the least generous Medicaid programs, those in the South and the Southwest (Blendon et al., 1989).

This background information on the type of health insurance coverage of African Americans allows one to ask — but, unfortunately, not find the answer to — the following questions about how they fare in the market for health insurance. First, why are African Americans less likely to have health insurance than whites? Employment in industries that do not typically offer health insurance accounts for part but not all of the disproportionate lack of health insurance coverage by African Americans (Leigh, 1994b). Are African Americans less likely to have health insurance than whites because blacks and whites differ in the way they assess the probability and loss associated with health events? Or, phrased another way, are Blacks less risk averse than Whites with respect to health events? Finally, do Blacks and Whites value what is forgone (in payments for health insurance premiums and time spent seeking care) to obtain an increment of health differently? Only partial answers to these questions are known.

Second, do African Americans, because of greater lack of insurance and greater Medicaid coverage, face a different set of informational asymmetries when seeking health care than do whites? In 1993, twenty-three percent of African Americans had Medicaid, and African Americans are estimated to be 40 percent of all Medicaid enrollees (Leigh, 1994a; NCHS, 1995). In addition to the asymmetries noted previously between physicians and insurers, and physicians and patients, are there yet other informational asymmetries between Medicaid patients and their insurers (the federal and state governments), or between physicians (who treat Medicaid patients) and the federal and state governments, which diminish the ability of sizable percentages of African Americans to get care? Little, if anything, is known about these possible asymmetries.

Finally, if insurance begets moral hazard and, thereby, generates more demand for health- care services than it is optimal to provide, does this suggest that initiatives to close the insurance gap for African Americans might be stymied by the Congressional mood of cost consciousness? In addition, if discounted future earnings are calculated to value and insure human life (as economist would prefer), given the lower earnings of African Americans than Whites, what does this suggest about the valuation of the life and health of African Americans and the likelihood that providing health insurance coverage to all Americans will gather widespread political support?

MARKET FOR PHYSICIAN SERVICES

Weisbrod (1991) finds that physicians and other health-care providers select the resources used to treat any particular patient within the technologically feasible set and subject to revenue constraints. The coordination of supply and demand and the rationing of resources are accomplished directly by physicians as they advise their patients on the use of services that they (the physicians) also produce and sell (Farley, 1986). McCarthy (1985) characterizes the typical self-employed, office-based physician as a utility maximizer of net income and leisure. The physician sells a product differentiated by its dollar price-time, price-amenity mix, and the physician's patients are sensitive to these price/attribute combinations.

Physicians are expected to behave differently than the typical businessman. For example, advice given by physicians as to further treatment by himself or others is supposed to be completely divorced from self-interest (Arrow, 1963). It is at least claimed that treatment is dictated by the objective needs of the case and not limited by financial considerations. While the ethical compulsion is surely not as absolute in fact as it is in theory, we can hardly suppose that it has no influence over resource allocation in this area. Charity treatment in one form or another exists because of this tradition of the human right to adequate medical care.

Despite expectations of non-self-interested behavior by physicians, economists have analyzed the demand creation hypothesis. This hypothesis, as framed by Pauly (1986), holds that physicians can and do alter the content of the advice they provide to patients in order to increase the quantity demanded (and their net incomes) at any price, and that physicians alter their advice to a greater extent when the number of physicians per capita is high. The primary evidence in favor of this hypothesis is the finding, in some empirical studies, that the use of medical care is related to the supply of physicians, when user price and other demand determinants are held constant. The literature suggests that demand inducement may occur in the market for surgical services, but that its extent is less than previously estimated. Little evidence for demand inducement is found in the primary-care physician services market (Feldman & Sloan, 1988; Pauly 1986; Newhouse 1992).

The primary-care physician services market in large metropolitan areas has been shown to be consistent with monopolistic competition (McCarthy, 1985). Empirical evidence to support this claim is provided by: consumer sensitivity to dollar and time prices; the direct competitive effect of new physician entry; and the finding that physicians are forced to offer shorter waiting times if higher dollar prices are to be introduced. A positive association between physician density and price charged for services also has been noted in large urban-suburban settings. Some researchers suggest that in physician dense areas, patients may be managed differently, with more emphasis on referrals, consultations, and additional diagnostic tests. Whether this style reflects a self-selection process by physicians who prefer to practice in areas where other medical resources are also concentrated, or whether it is imposed by patient preferences, can not be determined. Feldman and Sloan (1988) attempted to explain the positive association by arguing that consumers have difficulty getting information about a particular doctor in physician-rich areas. This lack of information enhances the monopoly power of physicians and leads to higher prices in these places.

Individual physicians in deciding what courses of action to recommend for each patient tend to follow the norms for care in the community. According to Pauly (1986), those norms in turn will be related to the predominant or average demand in the community, and hence will be related to the average or predominant level of insurance coverage. Phelps (1992) finds that regional patterns of medical practice may result when 'schools of thought' get established in specific localities and the costs of gathering relevant evidence to alter those beliefs are large, if not prohibitive. Since medical care is generally a local service industry (with a few exceptions involving regional or national referral patterns for highly specialized surgery), one does not find the usual market forces driving out inefficient modes of production (in this case incorrect treatment strategies) with the same vigor as one finds, say, in national markets for manufactured goods.

The services provided by a physician are appropriately judged from a patient's perspective in terms of the net benefit or utility of the treatment after the bill is paid. Therefore, according to Farley (1986), the idea that physicians are altruistically concerned about their patients is best formalized by assuming that the utility of each patient is an argument in a physician's utility function. If the utility function of all patients is assumed to be identical, then Pareto optimality will result from the allocation of resources in this market. If the more realistic assumption is made, however, that patients do not have identical utility functions, then an efficient allocation is optimal only if the physician is able to charge a different price to each different type of patient (i.e., in accordance with each patient's willingness to pay) for the marginal unit of service. Otherwise, a trade-off between efficiency and the welfare of patients takes place.

AFRICAN AMERICANS IN THE MARKET FOR PHYSICIAN SERVICES

There is some evidence that the health outcomes for African Americans noted in an earlier section result in part from — limited access to physicians, dissatisfaction in the patient/physician relationship, and differences in the treatments recommended by physicians for African Americans and Whites with comparable illnesses. Blendon et al. (1989) have found that, even after taking into account a person's income, health status, age, sex, and whether he/she had one or more chronic or serious illnesses, African Americans have a statistically significantly lower mean number of annual ambulatory visits and are less likely to have seen a physician in a year than are Whites. This lack of physician visits may be explained by the lack of physicians in predominantly African neighborhoods. McCord and Freeman (1990) noted that in Harlem during the 1980s, the number of primary-care physicians per 1,000 people was 74 percent lower than the average for New York City as a whole.

African Americans who see a physician are more likely than Whites to report that their physician failed to do the following: (1) inquire sufficiently about their pain; (2) tell them how long it would take for prescribed medicine to work; (3) explain the seriousness of their illness or injury; and (4) discuss test and examination findings (Blendon et al., 1989). Blacks consequently were less likely than Whites to be satisfied with their most recent ambulatory care visit.

The dissatisfaction noted by African patients may reflect the findings of several recent studies — that African Americans receive less aggressive treatments than Whites for a number of medical conditions. If diagnosed with heart disease, African Americans were less likely to undergo coronary artery bypass graft surgery than were Whites with a comparable diagnosis (see USDHHS 1993a). Among HIV/AIDS patients for whom the Public Health Service recommends drug therapy to prevent other opportunistic viral infections, while 68 percent of Whites received such therapy, only 48 percent of African Americans did (USDHHS, 1994a). If diagnosed with kidney disease, Blacks are less likely to receive long-term hemodialysis or a transplant than are Whites (Council on Ethical and Judicial Affairs, 1990).

How does one explain these patterns of care for African Americans within the market for physician services? The physician's utility function contains the utility of his/her patients as an argument, and the physician maximizes patient health subject to revenue constraints. How does the utility of the African patient enter into the utility function of his/her physician? Does this differ with the race of the physician? Some medical experts have suggested that physicians are more likely to treat aggressively those patients who are wealthier, more productively employed, and more assertive, because such patients are viewed as more likely to respond successfully to therapy and to be more valuable to society (Council on Ethical and Judicial Affairs, 1990). Because African Americans are less likely to be wealthy or productively employed (or, concomitantly, insured) than are Whites, they may receive less aggressive medical treatment disproportionately, for this reason.

One of the assumptions underlying the specification of the market for physician services in the preceding section could be questioned, and maintaining this assumption could result in some of the inappropriate treatment of African Americans in the market for physician services. The assumption is that the utility functions of all consumers of physician services are identical. The failure to reflect the heterogeneity among consumers of physician services has led to a single "Grade A" measure of quality as the norm, instead of safe and appropriate minimum standards for care, along with a range of standards between minimum and "Grade A." Because of the existence of only this "Grade A" standard of care, if physicians offer this to African American patients and the African American patients reject it — perhaps for reasons related to cultural preferences, or because of the lack of income or insurance — the physician often has nothing else to offer. Thus, the Black patient who might have preferred a "Grade B" standard of care may not get care at all for a given condition and then would be reflected in statistics such as those cited above about racial differences in treatment for selected conditions. Some of the racial disparities in treatment by physicians indeed may result from the revealed preferences of heterogeneous patient consumers. Unfortunately, we know little today about the degree of heterogeneity of preferences among consumers of physician services and other medical care (Pauly, 1988).

Finally, the issues of community norms for treatment and demand inducement need to be addressed. As noted in the discussion of the market for physician services, individual physicians may not tailor their advice entirely to the insurance coverage of each patient. They may instead follow the norms for care in the community. Although physicians in resource-rich areas have been observed to have somewhat different styles of practice, involving numerous referrals, consultations, and additional diagnostic tests, there is little evidence on the practice of physicians in resource-poor areas (such as Harlem) and the norms they follow. In addition, are physicians in resource-poor areas able to induce demand for their services, even in the case of surgery, which provides the strongest evidence of induced demand?

MARKETS FOR HOSPITAL SERVICES

One of the main factors that influences the market behavior of hospitals is the extensive insurance coverage of patient hospital bills, which renders consumers of hospital services relatively insensitive to price (Noether, 1988). In addition, physicians play a major role in determining both the supply of and demand for hospital services through their influence on hospital input and production decisions, as well as through their role as patients' agents. Since patients have poor information about competing hospitals and physician objectives may not coincide with the maximization of the objectives of hospitals, physicians may alter hospital behavior. Finally, the hospital industry is composed primarily of nonprofit firms, whose incentives are not clearly understood, but for whom profit maximization is not the only explicit objective.

The dominance of the hospital sector by nonprofit firms has several implications. Subsidies received from private philanthropy, in addition to the favorable tax status of nonprofit hospitals, raise barriers to the entry of for-profit hospitals into the market and engender inefficiency in hospital operations and in the market for hospital services (Newhouse, 1970). A nonprofit hospital might be run more inefficiently than and yet be able to charge a price equal to or below that charged by a hypothetical for-profit hospital, with the difference being made up by a subsidy. Consumers may prefer nonprofit hospitals because these facilities are thought to be less willing to constrain quality in order to increase profits (Pauly, 1988).

The objective function for a hospital has been variously specified in the economic literature. Davis (1972) postulates that a voluntary or nonprofit hospital aims to maximize the welfare of society by serving as many people as possible, subject to certain constraints, one of which is that the size of its deficit not exceed specified limits. A variant of this objective function, suggested by Newhouse (1970), would add as a constraint that the quality of care be the best possible with the available equipment and personnel. Davis (1972) also notes that this quantity-quality maximizing hospital is noted to provide a lesser quantity of care than the quantity- or profit-maximizing hospital.

The tradeoff between quantity and quality as maximands in the objective function of hospitals is strongly influenced by the unwillingness to produce lower quality care, even though this care is demanded by a certain segment of the population (Newhouse, 1970). This bias against producing lower qualities does not exist for a profit-maximizing firm. Thus, the hospital decision maker may pick a point on the quantity-quality tradeoff curve that is optimal for his facility but is not necessarily socially optimal. In other words, lower qualities of hospital services (i.e., wards v. semi-private rooms) may have negative marginal benefit to the decision maker and therefore not be produced.

Hay (1983) proposes an alternative view of economic behavior that treats the hospital as a physicians' producer cooperative whose objective is to maximize the net incomes of its physician staff. The first order conditions imply that the physician-controlled hospital will operate like a profit-maximizing hospital with respect to its pricing and output policies in both the public and private sectors, when the government uses a cost-based reimbursement policy. The hospital will produce private hospital services at the point where marginal revenue equals average cost and will restrict output. From yet another perspective, Frank and Salkever (1991) put forth the pure altruism model, which assumes that a nonprofit hospital maximizes an objective function whose two arguments are net revenue and the amount of unmet need for care among the indigent (i.e., a public "bad").

What type of market structure do hospitals operate within in the U.S.? Noether (1988) finds it difficult to test models of hospital competition for at least two reasons. First, the definition and measurement of quality or complexity in the market is elusive because of the many unpriced product attributes such as response time, precautions taken, excess capacity, and amenities. Second, most theories imply that hospital markets are differentiated oligopolies, a market structure that is notoriously difficult to model. At a minimum, though, the structural preconditions for a competitive market among hospitals seem to be violated. The hospital market has a limited number of providers, who are protected by regulatory barriers to entry, and who produce differentiated products that are purchased by relatively uninformed consumers (Feldman & Dowd, 1986).

All economic models proposed to explain hospital pricing and output policy assume that the hospital has some degree of local monopoly power — i.e., that the demand for hospital services is less than totally elastic. In the simplest models, hospitals are assumed to be monopolistic profit-maximizers (Hay, 1983). Other models assume that hospitals behave like Cournot oligopolists, and the market continuously becomes more competitive as the number of firms increases (Noether, 1988). Feldman and Dowd (1986) model hospitals as price discriminating monopolists that sell a common product to different market segments, each effectively insulated from one another and each with a different price elasticity of demand.

For several reasons, a model with price discriminating monopolists is chosen as a reasonable approximation to the market for hospital services. First, patient cost-sharing for hospital services differs dramatically among insurance plans, and cost-sharing is expected to influence the price elasticity of demand. Second, the appropriate purchaser of hospital care may be the health plan rather than the individual patient, and some health plans, especially health maintenance organizations, or HMOs, restrict the use of hospitals felt to be expensive. Finally, since hospital care is both non-durable and non-tradable, different market segments can be kept separate from one another.

AFRICAN AMERICANS IN THE MARKET FOR HOSPITAL SERVICES

Access to hospital services depends in part on access to a physician and on the proximity of a hospital for emergency care. Although numerous hospitals to serve African Americans have been established since the late 1800s, few continue to operate today (Rice & Winn, 1991). Currently, nongovernmental hospitals are sited primarily in areas less likely to generate unprofitable cases, rather than in places with unmet needs (Weisbrod, 1991). In other words, the inner cities of major metropolitan areas and other places with high percentages of people in poverty attract few new hospitals. Additionally, hospitals in counties with a decline in population, an increase in the unemployment rate, and/or low per capita income face greater odds of closure (Lillie-Blanton et al., 1992).

In addition, trends in the closure of hospitals in medically underserved areas may be related to the more rapid decline in days of hospital care (per 1,000 population) observed for the poor (relative to the nonpoor) and for African Americans (relative to Whites) between 1981 and 1986. Access surveys conducted by the Robert Wood Johnson Foundation in 1982 and 1986 confirmed a general deterioration in access and utilization measures for the poor and minorities relative to the nonpoor and Whites (see Fuchs 1993). Although national figures reflect a decline in hospital utilization by African Americans, in Harlem during the 1980s, relative to the New York City per capita averages, the rate of hospital admissions was 26 percent higher. The use of the emergency room was 73 percent higher, and the use of the hospital outpatient department was 134 percent higher (McCord & Freeman, 1990). The significantly reduced presence of primary-care physicians (74 percent less than the New York City average) in Harlem is doubtless related to this usage pattern; persons in Harlem seem to be substituting the use of hospital facilities for the use of physician services.

According to the review by the Council on Ethical and Judicial Affairs (1990), in 1986, African Americans were less likely than Whites to be satisfied with the care provided during their most recent hospitalization. This lesser satisfaction may be due to differences in hospital treatment of African Americans. For example, poor and African American patients enrolled in Medicare, the federal health insurance program for the elderly and disabled, were found to receive worse care at individual hospitals than other acutely ill Medicare patients. Only 47 percent of the African American and poor patients categorized as very sick upon admission were immediately put into intensive care, compared with 70 percent of all other patients in that condition. Further, doctors and nurses conducted less thorough interviews and physical examinations with these poor and African American Medicare patients (USDHHS, 1994b). In addition, African American patients hospitalized with pneumonia were found to receive treatments of lesser intensity than White patients.

At one point in the previous section, hospitals were characterized as operating to maximize the welfare of society (by serving as many as possible) subject to the constraint that their deficit cannot grow beyond given limits. Hospitals whose deficits become too great, perhaps due to services rendered for which they are not compensated, cease to operate. Serving as many people as possible raises the same issues noted above related to consumer heterogeneity. Having one "Grade A" standard of care may deprive persons willing, for example, to stay on a ward, because it is cheaper than other hospital accommodations, of the opportunity to do so. Is the welfare of society really being maximized when many consumers are deprived of choices in hospital services?

HEALTH REFORM

Recent discussions about reforming the system for financing and delivering health care in the U.S. have centered around two objectives — to slow the decades' long upward trend in health-care costs (and perhaps thereby reduce the deficit or balance the budget), and to provide guaranteed access to health care for all. These two objectives are mutually exclusive to the extent that guaranteeing access to care for all increases costs or impairs our ability to slow their growth. This tension partly explains our inability to achieve either of these goals. A brief discussion of the current system and an examination of recent proposals to reform the nation's health-care system by making it more competitive follow. Implications of these reform proposals for African Americans also are noted.

CURRENT U.S. HEALTH-CARE SYSTEM

The insurance-centered system for financing health care in the U.S. is complex and does not constitute a perfectly competitive market system. It combines elements of government insurance for the elderly and about half of the poor with employment-based insurance for most privately financed health care. Employment-based group plans cover 140 million people, slightly more than half of the population. Ten million retirees receive insurance coverage through a prior employer. Medicare and Medicaid cover another 60 million people, and 10 million receive military benefits. About 12 percent of the population (31 million) purchase insurance outside of any group plan, and 14 percent of the population lacks any form of health insurance (Aaron & Bosworth, 1994).

Part of the contribution of the federal health programs (Medicare and Medicaid) established during the 1960s was to complete the transformation of medical care from an ordinary market in which people's decisions are constrained by prices and incomes to one in which prices — at the point when important decisions about care are made — are zero or near-zero for most people due to third-party coverage (see Russell & Burke 1978). With decisions being made as though resources were free, the medical care sector has expanded rapidly. The structure of entitlements, payment policies, subsidies, and regulations has channeled innovation into directions culminating in today's costly health-care patterns (Sisk & Glied, 1994). Coverage, payment, and training policies have concentrated expenditures, and hence, innovative activity in hospitals rather than ambulatory sites. These policies also have promoted acute, curative care delivered by specialists and have slighted preventive and rehabilitative care delivered by primary-care clinicians.

Cost has become a paramount issue in the health-care system not only because of its rate of increase but also because of its growth as a share of Gross National Product (GNP). In 1990, national spending on health care was $696.3 billion, close to 13 percent of GNP. Estimated expenditures for 1994 are $1.06 trillion, nearly a 20 percent increase over the 1993 total of $884.2 billion (NCHS, 1995).

Alternative explanations for rising outlays emphasize technological advances such as organ transplants, bypass surgery, bone marrow transplants, and other major medical interventions that have become commonplace in the past few decades (Aaron & Bosworth, 1994). Noninvasive diagnostic tests, such as magnetic resonance imaging, have become routine. Although the cost per case is sometimes lower than the costs of the procedures they replaced (such as exploratory surgery), these techniques increase the total cost of care because they can be (and are) used in vastly more situations. In some ways, the issue of health care cost containment boils down to the degree to which society is willing to pay for the ever-increasing capabilities of medicine (see Newhouse 1994).

Radical changes in health care financing and organization were bound to come, but the timing of the revolution was determined primarily by the slow growth of the economy after 1973 (see Fuchs 1993). Slow growth in economic productivity, combined with a continuing escalation of health-care expenditures, jolted decision makers in both the public and private sectors to act. Their actions — emphasizing segmentation of insured populations, competition, and utilization review by payers — can be attributed partly to the antiegalitarian mood of the 1980s and partly to the loss of faith in federal regulation as an instrument of control. A more recent manifestation of change is the proliferation of managed care plans that vertically integrate insurance and the delivery of care, and have led to a decline in the role of price and an increase in the role of physicians and health plans in allocating services (Newhouse, 1994).

PROPOSALS FOR COMPETITIVE MARKET REFORMS

It is not surprising that economists would look at the lack of perfect competition in the markets for health-care services and consider that the way to achieve one or both of the two major objectives of health-care reform — cost containment and guaranteed access to services —would be to foster competition. Thus managed care was pushed to its frontiers to become "managed competition," and this latter concept is one of many that has been debated as a possible solution for the problems with the nation's health-care system.

Managed care integrates the financing and delivery of health-care services by using a network of physicians and other providers to care for enrollees in health-care plans. A primary- care physician provides basic health care to the patient and serves as a "gatekeeper," by deciding the appropriateness of referrals for specialty care and hospitalization. Managed care systems also establish financial risk sharing between the funding entity and the provider (s) of care; some plans require cost-sharing by enrollees as an additional means to contain overall expenditures (National Governors Association, 1993).

Health maintenance organizations (HMOs) provide the oldest and best known example of managed care. Although HMOs are touted for their ability to contain costs, Newhouse (1992) reported that the cost of medical care provided by HMOs increased at roughly the same rate as the cost for fee-for-service care. This was true even though HMOs are paid prospectively and, therefore, face strong incentives not to perform unnecessary or unproductive procedures on patients. In addition, Feldman et al. (1990) have found that HMOs do not make the markets for hospital services more competitive.

"Managed competition" expands the managed care concept along several dimensions. It would band together employers and individuals into large purchasing networks for which sponsors would acquire health insurance. Health-care providers would be required to compete on the bases of price and quality to win the business of these networks. The theory states that increasing the size of the networks of demanders for health care would help to equalize the market power of suppliers (of insurance and of physician and hospital services) and demanders, and, thereby, foster competition in the market for health care (Leigh, 1994b). Despite the inclusion of the word "competition" in the phrase, if implemented, managed competition would move the health-care markets toward bilateral monopoly, rather than toward pure competition.

Although on the surface it would appear that enhancing competition would always be good policy, the economic theory of second best states otherwise, and this theory seems to apply to the market for health-care services (Fielding & Rice, 1993). The theory of second best states that if a number of factors cause a market to deviate from the usual competitive conditions (i.e., large number of buyers and sellers, no one of whom is big enough to significantly influence market price; free and easy entry into the market for buyers and sellers; no governmentally imposed restraints on price and quantity; and reasonably good information about prices), then a second best optimum situation is achieved *only* by departing from all other optimum conditions (Lipsey & Lancaster, 1956–57).

As one application of this theory, consider whether managed competition would achieve a second best optimum. Managed competition would maintain market deviation from a number of the preconditions for perfect competition. It would increase and aim to equalize the power of groups of buyers and sellers in the health-care marketplace, but not increase the numbers of buyers or sellers, or facilitate their entry into the markets. However, some variants of managed competition would be without government restraints on prices, and all forms of it would provide an improved quantity and quality of information to consumers about prices. Thus, managed competition would not depart from all the competitive preconditions and, therefore, would not move the health-care markets toward a second best optimum.

In another example of the theory of second best, consider two of the noncompetitive features of the health-care services markets — there are few suppliers of insurance, physician services, and hospital services; and consumer information is poor. This theory finds that increasing the number of suppliers or improving the type and quality of information available will not bring us any closer to an optimal state and, in fact, may have the opposite effect (Fielding and Rice, 1993).

Specifically, in the market for health insurance, increasing the number of suppliers or insurance carriers could actually result in higher health-care costs and reduced access to care, according to Fielding and Rice (1993). As the number of health insurance plans increases from one to two in a given market, efficiency is enhanced because the ability of the single firm to set monopoly prices would be eliminated. However, as the number of health plans increases beyond two, each would have reduced advantage when bargaining with providers and, therefore, might confront higher prices than in the competitive situation. In addition, as the number of plans increased beyond one, the concern with adverse selection or the dominance of unfavorable risks among their enrollees would become an issue, and plans would then seek to avoid covering unhealthy persons, a step that would reduce access to care overall.

Increasing the number of suppliers in the market for physician services also would not lower prices and increase efficiency, or enhance the quality of care. Because most health-care consumers have insurance, which lowers their out-of-pocket costs, they are relatively insensitive to price. With physicians recommending the services received by consumers while, simultaneously, acting to protect their incomes, an increase in physician supply is likely to result in increased costs (Fielding & Rice, 1993). Quality of care also may be reduced as physician supply rises because the volume of any service provided by a given physician will fall. As this happens, the quality of care also would decline, especially for technically exacting procedures for which the success rate improves with practice.

Likewise, if increased information to consumers (one of the hallmarks of managed competition proposals) takes the form of insurers competing amongst themselves to offer more and more different kinds of benefits in their plans, efficiency in the market for health insurance may not be enhanced. The increased information could make it difficult for prospective purchasers to compare alternatives. Therefore, consumers may pay non-optimal prices for premiums — that is, higher prices than they would pay if they had clearer information and were able to choose the plan most compatible with their health-care needs (Fielding and Rice, 1993).

AFRICAN AMERICANS AND HEALTH REFORM

As noted above, reform proposals that aim to make the markets for health-care services more competitive may actually result in non-optimal allocations of resources and inefficient pricing. For African Americans, actions that would enable the markets for health-care services to satisfy the individual preconditions for perfect competition, could enhance their access to care, although these actions would not enable the markets to achieve a second best optimum.

For example, although increasing the number of providers in the market for physician services would not lead to optimal prices and quantities in this market, increasing the number of physicians in the inner cities and rural areas of this nation could improve access to care for Black Americans. Similarly, building hospitals in or near medically underserved areas could enhance the access of underserved populations (including many African Americans) to health-care services, and also provide employment for local residents. Being employed could ameliorate the standard of living for African Americans, a factor implicated by Blendon et al. (1989) in the health outcome disparities noted by race.

To make no effort to satisfy the currently unmet preconditions for perfect competition in the market for health-care services and, thereby, to achieve a second best optimum in these markets would be associated with decreasing the number of providers or demanders of services, or levying additional government restraints on price and quantity. However, as noted above, restricting the number of providers is likely to worsen the access to care among Black Americans. A more competitive market for health-care services, even if not optimal and not approaching second best optimality, seems as if it would do the most to help bridge the gap in health outcomes between Black and White Americans.

CONCLUSIONS

Looking at the need to provide more equitable access for African Americans to insurance and health- care services in an attempt to lessen racial disparities in health outcomes affords an alternative perspective from which to view reform proposals and the markets for health-care services. Although the markets for health-care services generally are non-competitive and the theory of second best tells us that actions to move these markets toward the competitive ideal (i.e., increasing the number of suppliers of services; increasing the information available) would be nonoptimal, many of these nonoptimal actions could benefit Black Americans. If appropriately targeted, an increase in the supply of physicians, for example, could lessen the inappropriate use of hospital emergency rooms by African Americans (as a substitute for physician office visits) and thereby not only save money but also improve health outcomes. Because targeting physicians by type and practice location is difficult and cannot be achieved instantly, even if steps are taken to achieve this, the results will not be seen in the near future. The fact that steps such as this would not render the market for physician services optimal becomes irrelevant, if one's primary objective is to lessen the racial disparities in health outcomes.

In another example, the simplistic assumption that all consumers have identical utility functions, which allows us to achieve Pareto optimality in the market for physician services, ignores the reality of heterogeneity of consumer preferences. Without acknowledging and providing services to accommodate this heterogeneity, equality in use, rather than improved outcomes and the attainment of an adequate level of care use (even if it may be lower and achieve a lower level of health and well-being than what the well-to-do achieve), remains our objective (Pauly, 1988).

This chapter has focused on differences in health outcomes among Black and White Americans and how changing the structures of the existing markets for health-care services to make them more competitive might influence the differentials noted. Attempts were made to explain the disparities in outcomes in the market for health insurance and in the markets for physician services and hospital services. Questions regarding what really happens to Black Americans in these markets are raised. The next challenge would be to systematically seek answers to these questions.

NOTES

* The author thanks Angela Stewart and Kaylan Walker for research assistance. This analysis is the author's own and should not be attributed to the Joint Center for Political and Economic Studies, its board of governors, or its sponsors.
1. This statement is true only for societies in which health care is produced as a separable commodity. It does not apply to societies in which physical and spiritual well-being are meshed in such a way that healing practices are not separable commodities.
2. Because of the great variability in the many factors that influence demand for hospital care, excess capacity results. For example, every case of pneumonia does not result in a hospitalization. The need for hospitalization with pneumonia depends on the nature of the disease (viral or bacterial), stage at which diagnosed, general health and age of the person with the disease, and availability of a suitable (and alternative) home care environment. Changes in decisionmaking practices of providers and insurers

which have reduced the number and length of hospital stays in recent years also have added to the un-predictability of demand for hospital services. Facilities built to accommodate peak demand for services as estimated two decades ago, for example, are likely to experience excess capacity today.

In spite of persisting excess capacity, charges and fees remain high in many medical care facilities, because prices are set both to cover capital costs and according to the "usual and customary" fees for which insurance companies will reimburse in a given market area. In addition, hospitals know that low-ering the costs for their services will not increase demand and thereby revenue, since this form of de-mand is influenced more by a genuine need for services than by availability and price, or the sense that a service is offered at a "bargain" price.

3. In 1993, although 36 percent of both the Black and White populations were high school graduates, higher percentages of Blacks (30 percent) than Whites (19 percent) had not completed high school. In addition, the share with a bachelor's degree was lower for Blacks (9 percent) than for Whites (15 percent) (see U.S. Bureau of the Census 1994).

4. In hypothetically perfect markets, the price of all services would be set so that the three forms of insurance would provide the same payment for each service. In actual markets, the three forms of insurance may pay differing amounts per service. Consider an appendectomy for which "usual and customary" physi-cian charges are $1,000 in a given market. Under the prepayment form of insurance, how much the phy-sician is paid for performing an appendectomy would be determined by the number of patients enrolled in the provider network for which the physician works (and for whom the network collects capitated, or per enrollee, payments) and the method for determining the salary that was negotiated at the beginning of the contract term. If few of the patients covered by this physician's network require services during a year and if the contract allows for salary augmentation based on the profits of the network, the physi-cian's salary may be increased by a bonus, unrelated in amount to the cost of the appendectomy.

If a physician were being reimbursed under an indemnity with a fixed schedule, because these schedules are often established to reimburse "usual and customary" charges for services in each market area, the physician would most likely receive $1,000. Had the appendix ruptured, had the physician been required to perform more than the standard appendectomy, and had the physician billed $1,200 for his services, he would only have been reimbursed $1,000. The physician would likely be able to appeal this decision by the insurer or seek the additional $200 from the patient, if the policy did not outlaw bal-ance billing. Similarly, a physician being reimbursed by an insurer for costs would be paid $1,000 for the appendectomy.

5. Only suggestive evidence exists about differences in assessing the loss associated with health events. Fried-man et al. (1989) speculate that the sense of loss and the experience of fighting HIV/AIDS, for example, are different for Whites than for most minorities and the poor. Because the majority of Whites with HIV/AIDS have both education and employment, their sense of outrage about the disease is greater, and this outrage motivates them to fight for what is being lost. Many Blacks and members of other minority groups, who may never have had these advantages, lack this sense of loss, the associated drive to fight against the loss, and the educational tools with which to wage the fight.

6. Quality of care from any physician is expected to fall as the supply of physicians increases and as the vol-ume of any service provided per physician falls, because of the presumption that "practice makes per-fect." Physicians who have performed any procedure 100 times, for example, are expected to be better at it than physicians who have performed it only 10 times. There is firm evidence of this with respect to certain surgical procedures for which the outcomes are more favorable at institutions whose staff per-form a greater number in any year (Jollis et al., 1994).

REFERENCES

Aaron, H.J., and Bosworth, B.P. 1994. "Economic Issues in Reform of Health Care Financing." In *Brookings Papers on Economic Activity*, M.N. Baily, P.C. Reiss, and C. Winston, eds., 249–286. Washington, DC: The Brookings Institution.

Arrow, K.J. 1963. "Uncertainty and the Welfare Economics of Medical Care." *American Economic Review* 53: 941–973.

Blendon, R.J., et al. 1989. "Access to Medical Care for Black and White Americans: A Matter of Continuing Concern." *Journal of the American Medical Association* 261 (January 13): 278–281.

Blomqvist, Å. 1991. "The Doctor as Double Agent: Information Asymmetry, Health Insurance, and Medical Care." *Journal of Health Economics* 10: 411–432.

Centers for Disease Control and Prevention. 1994. *HIV/AIDS Surveillance Report* 6 (no. 2). Atlanta: U.S. Public Health Service.

Council on Ethical and Judicial Affairs. 1990. "Black-White Disparities in Health Care." *Journal of the American Medical Association* 263 (May 2): 2344–2346.

Cutler, D.M. 1994a. "A Guide to Health Care Reform." *Journal of Economic Perspectives* 8 (Summer): 13–29.

Cutler, D.M. 1994b. "Comments and Discussion" on Aaron, H.J., and Bosworth, B.P., "Economic Issues in Reform of Health Care Financing." In *Brookings Papers on Economic Activity*, M.N. Baily, P.C. Reiss, and C. Winston, eds., 287–289. Washington, DC: The Brookings Institution.

Davis, K. 1972. "Economic Theories of Behavior in Nonprofit, Private Hospitals." *Economic and Business Bulletin* 24: 1–13.

Dula, A., Kurtz, S., and Samper, M. 1993. "Occupational and Environmental Reproductive Hazards Education and Resources for Communities of Color." *Environmental Health Perspectives Supplements* 101: 181–189.

Ellis, R.P., and McGuire, T.G. 1993. "Supply-Side and Demand-Side Cost Sharing in Health Care." *Journal of Economic Perspectives* 7 (Fall): 135–151.

Farley, P. 1986. "Theories of the Price and Quantity of Physician Services: A Synthesis and Critique." *Journal of Health Economics* 5: 315–333.

Feldman, R., et al. 1990. "Effects of HMOs on the Creation of Competitive Markets for Hospital Services." *Journal of Health Economics* 9: 207–222.

Feldman, R., and Dowd, B. 1986. "Is There A Competitive Market for Hospital Services?" *Journal of Health Economics* 5: 277–292.

Feldman, R., and Sloan, F. 1988. "Competition Among Physicians, Revisited." *Journal of Health Politics, Policy and Law* 13 (Summer): 239–261.

Fielding, J.E., and Rice, T. 1993. "Can Managed Competition Solve the Problems of Market Failure." *Health Affairs* 12: 216–228.

Frank, R., and Salkever, D. 1991. "The Supply of Charity Services by Nonprofit Hospitals: Motives and Market Structure." *RAND Journal of Economics* 22 (Autumn): 430–446.

Friedman, S.J., et al. 1989. "The AIDS Epidemic Among Blacks and Hispanics." In *Health Policies and Black Americans*, D.P. Willis, ed., 455–499. New Brunswick, NJ: Transaction Publishers.

Fuchs, V.R. 1993. *The Future of Health Policy*. Cambridge, MA: Harvard University Press.

Fuchs, V.R., and Zeckhauser, R. 1987. "Valuing Health — A 'Priceless' Commodity." *American Economic Association Papers and Proceedings* 77 (May): 263–268.

Hay, J.W. 1983. "The Impact of Public Health Care Financing Policies on Private-Sector Hospital Costs." *Journal of Health Politics, Policy and Law* 7 (Winter): 945–952.

Jollis, J.G., et al. 1994. "The Relation between the Volume of Coronary Angioplasty Procedures at Hospitals Treating Medicare Beneficiaries and Short-Term Mortality." *The New England Journal of Medicine* 331 (December 15): 1625–1629.

Leffall, L.D. 1990. "Health Status of Black Americans." In *The State of Black America 1990*, 121–142. New York: National Urban League, Inc., 1990.

Leigh, W.A. 1994a. "The Health Status of Women of Color." In *The American Woman 1994–95: Where We Stand—Women and Health*, C. Costello and A.J. Stone, eds., 154–196. New York: Norton.

Leigh, W.A. 1994b. "Implications of Health-Care Reform Proposals for Black Americans." *Journal of Health Care for the Poor and Underserved* 5: 17–32.

Lillie-Blanton, M., et al. 1992. "Rural and Urban Hospital Closures, 1985–1988: Operating and Environmental Characteristics that Affect Risk." *Inquiry* 29 (Fall): 332–344.

Lipsey, R.G., and Lancaster, K. 1956–57. "The General Theory of Second Best." *The Review of Economic Studies* 24: 11–32.

McCarthy, T.R. 1985. "The Competitive Nature of the Primary-Care Physician Services Market." *Journal of Health Economics* 4: 93–117.

McCord, C., and Freeman, H.P. 1990. "Excess Mortality in Harlem." *The New England Journal of Medicine* 322 (January 18): 173–177.

National Center for Health Statistics. n.d. *Excess Deaths and Other Mortality Measures for the Black Population: 1979–81 and 1991*. Hyattsville, MD: U.S. Public Health Service.

National Center for Health Statistics. 1995. *Health United States, 1994*. Hyattsville, MD: U.S. Public Health Service.

National Governors Association. 1993. *Backgrounder: Basic Elements of Managed Care*. Washington, DC: National Governors Association.

Newhouse, J.P. 1970. "Toward A Theory of Nonprofit Institutions: An Economic Model of a Hospital." *American Economic Review* 60: 64–75.

Newhouse, J.P. 1992. "Medical Care Costs: How Much Welfare Loss?" *Journal of Economic Perspectives* 6 (Summer): 3–21.

Newhouse, J.P. 1994. "Symposium on Health Care Reform." *Journal of Economic Perspectives* 8 (Summer): 3–11.

Nickens, H.W. 1991. "The Health Status of Minority Populations in the United States." *Western Journal of Medicine* 155: 27–32.

Noether, M. 1988. "Competition Among Hospitals." *Journal of Health Economics* 7: 259–284.

Pauly, M.V. 1986. "Taxation, Health Insurance, and Market Failure in the Medical Economy." *Journal of Economic Literature* 24: 629–675.

Pauly, M.V. 1988. "Is Medical Care Different? Old Questions, New Answers." *Journal of Health Politics, Policy and Law* 13 (Summer): 227–237.

Phelps, C.E. 1992. "Diffusion of Information in Medical Care." *Journal of Economic Perspectives* 6 (Summer): 23–42.

Rice, M.F., and Winn, M. 1991. "Black Health Care and the American Health Care System: A Political Perspective." In *Health Politics and Policy*, T.J. Litman and L.S. Robins, eds., 320–334. Albany, NY: Delmar Publishers.

Russell, L.B., and Burke, C.S. 1978. "The Political Economy of Federal Health Programs in the United States: An Historical Review." *International Journal of Health Services* 8: 55–77.

Sisk, J.E., and Glied, S.A. 1994. "Innovation Under Federal Health Care Reform." *Health Affairs* 13 (Summer): 82–97.

U.S. Bureau of the Census. 1994. *Statistical Abstract of the United States: 1994*. Washington, DC: U.S. Government Printing Office.

U.S. Department of Health and Human Services. 1993a. "Rates of Coronary Artery Bypass Surgery Differ by Race." *AHCPR Research Activities* 167 (August): 4. Rockville, MD: U.S. Department of Health and Human Services.

U.S. Department of Health and Human Services. 1993b. "Socioeconomic Factors Affect Rate of Hospital Admissions." *AHCPR Research Activities* 168 (September): 2. Rockville, MD: U.S. Department of Health and Human Services.

U.S. Department of Health and Human Services. 1994a. "Racial Differences Found in Access to Medication for HIV-Related Illnesses." *AHCPR Research Activities* 174 (May): 1–2. Rockville, MD: U.S. Department of Health and Human Services.

U.S. Department of Health and Human Services. 1994b. "Differences Found in Quality of Hospital Care for Some Medicare Patients." *AHCPR Research Activities* 176 (July): 1–2. Rockville, MD: U.S. Department of Health and Human Services.

Weisbrod, B.A. 1991. "The Health Care Quadrilemma: An Essay on Technological Change, Insurance, Quality of Care, and Cost Containment." *Journal of Economic Literature* 29: 523–552.

White-Means, S.I., and Thornton, M.C. 1989. "Nonemergency Visits to Hospital Emergency Rooms: A Comparison of Blacks and Whites." *The Milbank Quarterly* 67: 35–57.

Windom, R.E. 1989. "From the Assistant Secretary for Health." *Journal of the American Medical Association* 261 (January 13): 196.

5

THE CONTINUING SIGNIFICANCE OF RACE IN MEETING HEALTH CARE NEEDS OF AFRICAN AMERICAN ELDERLY

Shelley I. White-Means

INTRODUCTION

That older African Americans stand in unique relationship to various aspects of African American life is in part a reflection of the era in which they spent their formative years. In the 1940s and 1950s African Americans shared a sense of commonality and community based on their race, a bond that is less prevalent in the experiences of younger people (Smith and Thornton, 1993; Carprini, 1989). They grew up at time when separate but equal was the national credo, and there were two unequal societies, one white and one black. Those born before World War II encountered overt and systematic discrimination designed to impede if not fully circumvent social and economic progress for African Americans. Although the postwar period was characterized by a reduction of overt and systematic racism and expansion of political and economic power, and much progress has occurred, present data illustrate that African Americans generally and older African Americans in particular face continued subjugation and economic difficulties due to racial group membership (Hughes and Hertel, 1990). Some suggest that the changes brought about over the past 30 years by civil rights have done little to alter the day-to-day living related to human growth and development of African Americans (Gurin, Hatchett and Jackson, 1989; Jaynes and Williams, 1989), especially the African American elderly.

These earlier life circumstances are intimately related, perhaps more than for majority elderly, to later life opportunities (Gibson and Jackson, 1992; Jackson, Antonucci and Gibson, 1990). A general lack of opportunities and resources (i.e., good jobs, adequate housing, financial resources) at earlier periods in their lives is a source of many more problematic aspects of aging in the later years. Much of contemporary experience is related to past participation in a dual labor market where African Americans generally have more often been in the secondary sector. Thus limited educational opportunities, poor jobs, and low income during preadolescence and young adulthood will be reflected in poor job histories across the life span, which is again reflected in limited employment related benefits and lowered retirement options and resources in old age (Taylor and Chatters, 1988; Wilson-Ford, 1990; Riley, 1987).

Concomitant with increasing age are higher levels of disability and a greater need to use health care services than at any previous point in life. To meet these needs, older African Americans require access to a health care system that is generally inaccessible without some form of health care financing vehicle, insurance for most persons. However, African Americans are less likely to have private sources of financing and more likely to rely on government subsidized insurance programs such as medicare and medicaid.[1]

The central premise of this chapter is that if current health care reform does not recognize the unique circumstances of African American elderly, this population will face great difficulty in meeting its health care needs. Moreover, there are intergenerational policy implications for African American families which should not be ignored.

FINANCIAL AND HUMAN CAPITAL RESOURCES AND MEDICAL UTILIZATION AMONG AFRICAN AMERICAN ELDERLY

On many dimensions of life, we find African American elderly stand in a unique position of deprivation. Family human resources are sometimes pooled to counterbalance these conditions. However, these efforts may simply forge new difficulties for future generations of African American families.

---

[1] Medicaid is the federal and state financed health insurance program for low income persons and those with physical disabilities. Medicare is the health insurance program for elderly person, financed in part by social security contributions and federal tax receipts.

Health Status

Chronic disease patterns vary by race. African Americans have higher rates of hypertension, heart disease, diabetes, cerebral vascular disease, and renal disease compared to whites (Special Committee on Aging and Congressional Black Caucus Health Braintrust, 1991). The medical conditions of African American elderly (e.g., arthritis, diabetes) are more likely to require long term chronic care than the conditions of whites, who are more likely to require acute medical care.

Poverty, Age and Race

Poverty rates vary greatly among subgroups of the elderly. In 1992, elderly African Americans faced a 33 percent poverty rate and elderly whites faced an 11 percent rate (Bureau of Census, 1995). Thus African American older persons were three times more likely to live in poverty. From the Asset and Health Dynamics Among the Oldest Old (AHEAD) data, Couch and Daly (1995) find that African-Americans are more at risk of poverty than whites. Among African-Americans age 70 and older, 54 percent are near poverty, 31 percent are at the official poverty state, and 6.5 percent live in deep poverty. The corresponding percentages for whites are 27, 11, and 2.

Medicaid Dependency

Medicaid dependency increases with age. Using data from the 1987 National Medical Expenditure Survey, White-Means and Hammond (1993) find that 6.5 percent of those age 65–74 are dependent on Medicaid, 9.6 percent and 15 percent of those aged 75–84 and 85 and older, respectively, depend on medicaid. Racial disparities in the elderly persons' dependency on medicaid are more pronounced in the South than in any other region of the country. At age 65 and older, Southern African Americans are four times more likely than Southern whites to rely on Medicaid. While 57 percent of Southern African Americans who are age 85 and older rely on medicaid, only 14 percent of whites do so. In extreme old age (85 years and older), 83.4 percent of southern whites are insured by medicare and only 43 percent of African Americans.

It is important to note that poverty status in old age does not assure coverage by medicaid. Thus only 36 percent of non-institutionalized older persons have medicaid coverage (National Caucus and Center on Black Aged, 1987).

Service Use

Poverty status and no medicaid coverage imply less use of physician services and prescribed medicine (Kasper, 1986). Persons living at or near poverty have little if any extra money to meet medical expenses of copayments and deductibles, if they need covered health services. Even if their insurance (medicaid or a combination of medicaid and medicare) covers copayments and deductibles, there are other out-of-pocket costs. There is little extra money for a person who receives about $100 a week or less in income for such expenses as prescriptions, transportation, parking, bathroom adaptations, special foods, or housekeeping chores (National Caucus and Center on Black Aged, 1987), not to mention home maintenance, utilities, and telephone.

An essential feature for health care access among the poor and elderly is community health centers (Davis, 1991). Elderly who are most likely to use neighborhood health centers are African American, female, moderately disabled and insured by medicare with medicaid supplements.

Preliminary findings suggest that the emergency room (EMR) serves as an integral part of the custodial care systems of noninstitutionalized African American older persons. Not only is there a tradition in the African American community of using the EMR for primary care services (Satin and Duhl, 1972), there is also a tradition of EMR use for long-term care. Recent data also indicate that a disproportionate share of long-term care EMR visits are made by African Americans (Craig, 1991). While the emergency room is an inadequate substitute for formal and informal services provided to older persons in the community, some research suggests that it serves that role for some of them. Family members, primarily because of either the depletion of their emotional resources or the inconveniences of caring for older persons, resort to the emergency room as a caregiver's respite facility (American College of Emergency Physicians, 1992). A recent survey of emergency physicians reports that primarily older women between the ages of 75 and 85 have caregivers who require this respite and temporarily abandon them (American College of Emergency Physicians, 1992).

As physicians are seeing increasing numbers of older persons with nonemergent conditions, the EMR is also serving the role of a network for home health referrals, referrals for community meals programs, and prescription of new medications (Craig, 1991). Recent research indicates that many older persons who qualify for home health services are not enrolled in those programs. In a recent demonstration project that was implemented by the Hospital of the University of Pennsylvania, an inner-city teaching hospital, older persons who came to the EMR were screened to evaluate their community needs (Brookoof, 1991), a form of case management and geriatric assessment. During an eight month period, 450 older persons were referred for home care because of their geriatric assessment in the EMR. In the judgment of attending EMR physicians, access to home health obviated the need for EMR visits for 22% of these older persons. The primary diagnoses for these patients were arthritis (23%), infections/cellulitis (19%), organic brain syndrome resulting from a stroke (17%), diabetes (17%), and skin ulcer (15%). In many cases, access to home monitoring or technical services (e.g., intravenous infusions, respiratory therapy) were home health treatments that made EMR visits unnecessary.

Finally, the EMR serves as the backup system for home health agencies. Many home health nurses encourage older persons to visit the EMR, which can monitor health concerns when the home health aide is not providing direct patient care services. This positive association between use of home health services and use of the EMR has been verified through analysis of data from the National Medical Expenditure Survey (White-Means, 1995), where older persons with higher levels of home health visits also had higher levels of nonemergent EMR visits.

Human Capital Resources

Some researchers suggest that there is a cultural tradition within the African American community that compels family and fictive kin to assume the responsibility for aging family members (Mindel, Haberstein, and Wright, 1988; Cox and Monk, 1991). We know that a central part of African American older persons' medical care services is provided in the home by family and friends (informal caregivers). These social networks provide care, because of the strong familial traditions that develop in minority communities. These informal networks also develop as adaptations to being discriminated against and excluded from mainstream institutions.

Contrary to perceptions, these informal caregiving services are not free. There is an implicit cost to their use, such as the life satisfaction, physical wellbeing, and foregone earnings of caregivers. When compared to white ethnic caregivers (primarily German-, Irish-, and English-American ethnics), African-American caregivers provide more total hours of assistance, even controlling for the levels of functional impairment of older persons (White-Means and Thornton, 1990).

With these extensive time commitments, many African American caregivers quit their jobs in the labor market to engage in elder care. The National Channeling data indicate that spouses (36%), daughters (26%), sons (17%), siblings (20%), and other relatives (18%) quit their jobs due to caregiving responsibilities (White-Means, 1993).

As caregiving hours increase, life satisfaction declines and physical depreciation increases among caregivers for African American elderly (White-Means and Thornton, 1996). The burdens of caregiving (taking on tasks including lifting and moving and providing medical services that the caregiver is unequipped to give) are also positively associated with physical depreciation of the caregiver and negatively associated with levels of life satisfaction.

CONTINUING SIGNIFICANCE OF RACE IN HEALTH CARE FOR AFRICAN AMERICAN ELDERLY

There are pleas in the health services literature to ignore the variable race and emphasize instead the insurance status of medical patients to understand medical utilization patterns (Bagley, 1995). This is because insurance status defines the payment system that assures access to medical services. Insurance status is an easily measured and conceptualized term. Its inclusion in health services research models allows researchers to compare findings with those of international researchers whose populations are insured by national health insurance plans with varying levels of comprehensiveness and insured access.

On the other hand, race is an ambiguous concept (Bagley, 1995). It is usually operationalized by a grouping of populations in four categories: white, African American, Hispanic and Asian. And this grouping combines populations in categories where there is diversity of language, culture, norms and skin color. The suggestion is that since the categories are too broad, they should be ignored.

White-Means and Thornton (1995) show that when racial groups are not conceptualized, researchers risk misunderstanding medical utilization patterns. First, empirical results reflect the circumstances of the racial group that is most heavily represented in the sample. Second, empirical models may exclude variables that reflect the unique experiences of some of the populations that are studied. White-Means' (1995) conceptualization of race in a model of community-based elders' use of the emergency room indicated that the role of informal support varies by race. Moreover, cultural medicine traditions in African American older person's homes are associated with increased use of emergency rooms.

To ignore race in health care leads one to ignore evidence of racial barriers in post acute care services (Wallace, 1995). Due to heavy reliance on medicaid, African American elders have difficulty obtaining placement in nursing homes. Profit maximization strategies of for-profit nursing homes include selecting patients with less severe illnesses and greater comprehensiveness in insurance coverage, criteria least favorable for African American patients. Nursing home placement difficulties also may lead to longer hospitalizations, as African American elderly wait on beds, or to discharges of African American elderly to the home where families are inadequately equipped to provide for health care needs.

To ignore race in health care is to ignore differences in health status, according to race. Interracial differences in health status do occur because of differences in insurance status and by differences in health prevention behaviors. However, interracial differences in health status also occur because of interracial differences in targeting by cigarette and alcohol companies, the supply of fresh produce in supermarkets that are located in minority communities, and also the quality of housing, education and employment opportunities (Gamble, 1994 and Dymski, chapter 7 of this volume). Moreover, there are racial differences in exposure to community violence and environmental toxins, each associated with higher risks of depleted health status (Williams, Lavizzo-Mourey, and Warren, 1994). The experience of racism is associated with higher levels of hypertension and other physical and mental health conditions (Kreiger, 1990; Williams and Chung, 1995). In sum, racial disparities in health status are due to differences in vulnerability to behavioral, psychosocial, economic, and environmental risk factors and resources (Williams, Lavizzo-Mourey, and Warren, 1994). Disparities in health status are associated with higher levels of health needs and potential demand for medical services.

There is evidence that medical treatment varies by race, even after accounting for differences in income and insurance status (Gamble, 1994). African American patients are less likely to be treated for chest pain with coronary angiography, bypass surgery or angioplasty than white patients (Gamble, 1994). Similarly, after adjusting for insurance and clinical status, researchers have found that whites are more likely to receive chemodialysis, intensive care for pneumonia, and kidney transplants (Williams, Lavizzo-Mourey, and Warren, 1994). Whites are more likely to receive treatment using newer technologies and newer services (Escarce, et al., 1993). These racial differences in treatment are most pronounced in the rural South (Gamble, 1995). Racism in medical treatment (Secretary of Health and Human Services, Louis Sullivan, 1991) is a characteristic of the health care system that is not easily captured by standard empirical measures in research, such as socioeconomic status and insurance status.

Table 5.1 reports descriptive analysis from the National Medical Expenditure Survey (NMES), 1987.[2] It presents data on patterns of ambulatory medical visits, according to race. The central role of the clinic in ambulatory visits for African Americans is clear. Combining information on all types of clinic visits in Table 5.1, African American elderly have over 22 percent of their ambulatory visits in clinics. On the other hand, whites go to clinics for only 13 percent of their ambulatory visits.

Table 5.1. Places of Ambulatory Medical Visits According to Race (Weighted Frequencies).

Place	African American Patients	White Patients
Doctor's Office/group	73.2	78.8
Doctor's Clinic	11.4	7.4
Neighborhood/Family Clinic	3.6	1.8
Surgical Center		0.1
Company Clinic	0.1	0.1
School Clinic	—	0.1
Other Clinic	6.8	3.6
Home	—	—
Laboratory	0.8	1.9
Walk-In Urg Center	0.1	0.3
Hospital Clinic/Emergency		
Room	0.2	0.1
Telephone	—	—
Dental	—	—
Long Term Care	—	—
Home Health	—	—
Optical	0.1	0.1
Radiology	—	—
Amulance	—	—

[2] The 1987 wave of NMES is the most recent. It's a survey collected every ten years. This 19787 data base was the one used to generate many of the health expenditure predictions for Hilary Rodham Clinton.

Table 5.2 reports patterns of ambulatory expenditures according to payer and race. African American elderly average lower total expenditures than whites. This expenditure pattern contrasts with racial patterns of disease.

Table 5.2. Distribution of Ambulatory Expenditures, According to Payer and Race.

Payer	Average $		Average Share of Total	
	Afr. Amer.	White	Afr. Amer.	White
Self	113.74*	171.60	38.14*	45.12
Private Insurance	33.64*	67.53	4.11*	10.20
Medicare	118.97	201.97	31.96*	29.07
Medicaid	50.63*	9.80	15.86*	2.26
Other Federal	8.35	7.35	2.58*	1.42
Other State	4.54*	9.99	1.42	1.82
Workmen's Compensation	0.90	1.64	0.29	0.30
Other	10.01*	2.35	0.56	0.34
Free	0.14	1.31	0.04	0.13
All Payers	*340.92*	*473.54*	*100.00*	*100.00*

Statistically significant at .10 or better

Both African American and white elderly pay most of the charges for their ambulatory medical visits as an out-of-pocket expense (Self). African American elderly cover 38 percent of the bill and white elderly cover 45 percent.

The data in Table 5.2 also show the level of dependency of the elderly on government programs. African Americans are significantly more likely than white elderly to depend on federal and state health care programs to share the burden of charges for ambulatory visits (52 percent vs. 35 percent). Although elderly whites are more likely to have private health insurance, this payer only covers 10 percent of their ambulatory visit charges.

Examining the dollar magnitudes of average ambulatory visit expenditures in isolation does not provide a clear picture of the nature of the burden already faced by the elderly in paying their medical bills. We must examine expenditure data as it compares to the financial resources of the elderly.

Besides collecting data on medical expenditures and health, the NMES has data on income and poverty status of the elderly. Similar to the information reported by Couch and Daly (1995), based on the AHEAD data, there are distinct racial patterns in the poverty status of the elderly. For African American elderly, 44 percent live in poverty and an additional 26 percent have low income. The respective percentages for white elderly are 15 percent and 18 percent.

What percentage of an elderly person's income do expenditures on ambulatory care represent?[3] Are there differences in this financial burden according to race? Data from NMES are again useful in answering these questions. Total expenditures on ambulatory care represent 71 percent of monthly personal income for white elderly and 172 percent of monthly personal income for African American elderly. Out-of-pocket payments for ambulatory care represent 32 percent of monthly personal income for white elderly and 64 percent of monthly personal income for African American elderly. Ambulatory expenditures represent a significant financial burden, especially for African American elderly.

PUBLIC POLICY, RESEARCH, AND PLANS TO MEET THE HEALTH CARE NEEDS OF AFRICAN AMERICANS ELDERLY

Health care reform has been at the forefront of the policy agenda during the Clinton administration. After an unsuccessful attempt to set up a national health insurance plan, the secondary strategy is to reform health programs for particular groups, i.e., the poor and the aged, via reform of medicaid and medicare.

In September 1995, proponents of Medicaid reform suggested that it is possible to reduce the federal government financing obligations by $182 billion via reform of this program (Haveman, 1995). The changes suggested are to (1) give nursing homes more flexibility to discharge senior citizens without their consent from nursing homes, (2) allow states to require spouses of nursing home residents to sell their homes, cars and other assets to finance care, (3) require adult children to pay for the nursing home care of their parents, and (4) annual federal state block grants that replace the current system of open-ended federal matching and encourage states to come up with innovative ways of providing services for low income persons.

At the same time there are efforts to reform medicare. Dollar magnitudes such as $270 billion in savings over a seven year period is the guesstimate for medicare reform (Pianin, 1995). The proposed reforms consider a five prong strategy, including (1) mitigating the growth of reimbursements to medical providers, (2) increasing the premiums for physician insurance and increasing annual deductibles of medicare beneficiaries, (3) allowing insurees to switch to managed care plans, (4) increasing the age of eligibility from 65 to 67, and (5) income related premiums, with persons having incomes greater than $100,000 paying more.

In February, 1996, the medicaid policy compromise included giving states the ability to determine the scope, magnitude of reimbursement and duration of services provided to medicaid elderly (Haveman, 1996). The National Governor's Association's proposal is guided by four goals:

---

[3] The measure of income is family income divided by the number of persons in the household.

1. guaranteeing basic health care needs of the nation's vulnerable populations,

2. controlling the growth of health care expenditures,

3. flexibility in design and implementation of cost-effective care, and

4. federal protection from rising costs due to changes in the economy, demo-
    graphics or natural disasters (Thompson, et al., 1996).

Whatever the form of the final policy changes, one thing is clear. The elderly and
their families will face an increased financial burden in securing adequate health
care.

In the current health reform arena, policy changes and research have been
closely linked. Numerous policy simulations have been performed to predict the
impact of changes in health care financing. Long term care policy simulations regarding the elderly person's use of nursing and home health, as well as expenditures, are based on assumptions of race neutrality in policy. For example the well
known Brookings ICF Long Term Care Financing Model considers that the key
demographic factors affecting disability status, utilization and expenditures are independent of race.[4] The model assumes that annual disability rates vary by age,
marital status, and previous disability. It assumes that nursing home use probability
varies by the same factors, as well as previous nursing home use. Home health use
is predicted to vary according to disability and previous Medicare home health use.
This model has been used by DHHS, GAO, Pepper Commission, AARP, and
Merrril Lynch (Weiner, Illston, and Hanley, 1994).

Policy simulation models, with few exceptions (e.g., Buchanan et al. 1991) fail to
acknowledge the role of race/ethnicity in influencing medical utilization patterns.
Even when acknowledged, by including dummy variable measures for race in the
base model, these simulations predict the role of policy variables (e.g., changing
insurance coverage) and assume that there will be an equal impact on all populations. Some simulations never acknowledge the data limitations of inadequate sample sizes of African Americans or other minority groups.

DISCUSSION

In the Pauly, et al. (1991) treatise on criterion for national health reform, the
authors list two factors that are essential: (1) efficiency, and (2) equity. Equitable
access to care includes treating persons with different levels of income in different
ways. First, tax contributions should be progressive. Second, this implies that premiums, deductibles and copayments should vary with income. Proposed health re-

---

[4] The ICF Long Term Care Financing Model is an econometric simulation of the use and financing of
nursing home and home health care by a national representative sample of the elderly from 1986 through
2020.

form does not change the current system of income taxation and thus contributions remain progressive. However, proposed medicare and medicaid reform only partially address equity in out-of-pocket payments. They include income related premiums, yet exclude income related deductibles and copayments. As reform leads to higher deductibles and copayments and ignores the financial burdens that these payments already impose for the elderly, health reform may lead to exclusion of access to health care, particularly for African American elderly.

Public good aspects of health and medical care consumption suggest that society is willing to subsidize medical care of older persons. There is disutility from knowing that older persons suffer and die, while medical technology could limit these losses. Society's willingness to subsidize the care of the elderly is an inverse function of the income of older persons (Pauly, 1991); society has no desire to subsidize the medical consumption of wealthy elderly persons. From this theoretical perspective alone, we should observe public policy that assures equitable and adequate access by different rates of subsidization of medical care for older persons, according to income.

Research on racial patterns of medical utilization also indicate that alleviating financial inequity is insufficient to address potential racial inequity in health care for the elderly. Physical proximity to medical facilities and uniform standards of medical treatment are also needed.

Current medicare and medicaid policy changes have intergenerational effects that are ignored; human capital transfers are ignored. That is, losses of financial resources (wages, social security, retirement benefits) among family caregivers, as well as depletion of caregivers' physical health are ignored. These exclusions are particularly relevant for African American elderly and their families because they face larger burdens of this type than majority elderly and their families. These losses of subsistence-level financial and human capital resources contribute to multigenerational cycles of poverty. In contrast, much more prevalent in discussions are concerns raised about financing elder care via income, sales or value-added taxes because this would entail passing program financial cost to younger generations (Wolfe, 1993).

As we depend on research to guide public policy, it is important to acknowledge inherent biases in the research. Data sources seldom include large enough samples to adequately describe implications for minority populations. We risk implementing policy and reacting in surprise when populations are affected unequally.

Today's African American elderly comprise persons who have experienced the least opportunities for educational and economic advancement. These elderly were informed in the 1960's that the implementation of medicare and medicaid would assure that they faced limited constraints in access to medical care. Yet, at the last stages of their lives, they face significant burden and risk of unmet health care needs.

REFERENCES

American College of Emergency Physicians. 1992. "Abandonment of the Elderly in the Emergency Depart-
    ment: Results of a Survey by the American College of Emergency Physicians." *Frontlines* Fall.
Bagley, C. 1995. "A Plea for Ignoring Race and Including Insured Status in American Research Reports on
    Social Science and Medicine." *Social Science and Medicine* 40 (8): 1017–1019.
Buchanan, J., E. Keeler, J. Rolph, and M. Holmer. 1991. "Simulating Health Expenditures Under Alternative
    Insurance Plans." *Management Science* 37 (9):1067–1090.
Bureau of the Census. 1995. "Sixty-Five Plus in the United States." *Bureau of the Census Statistical Brief.*
    May, SB/95–8. US Department of Commerce, Economics and Statistics Administration: Washington,
    DC.
Couch, K. and M. Daly. 1995. "Poverty Among the Oldest Old: New Estimates from AHEAD," Annual
    Meeting of the Southern Economic Association (November).
Cox, C. and A. Monk. 1991. "Minority Caregivers of Dementia Victims: A Comparison of Black and His-
    panic Families." *The Journal of Applied Gerontology* 9 (3): 340–354.
Craig, B. 1991. "Reaching the Elderly Through Emergency Rooms." *Aging* 362: 29–36.
Davis, Karen. 1991. "Inequality and Access to Health Care." *Milbank Quarterly* 69 (2):253–273.
Delli Carprini, M. 1989. "Age and History: Generations and Sociopolitical Change." PP. 1–10. In R. Sigel
    (ed.), *Political Learning in Adulthood*. Chicago: University of Chicago Press.
Escarce, J., K. Epstein, D. Colby, and J. S. Schwartz. 1993. "Racial Differences in the Elderly's Use of Medi-
    cal Procedures and Diagnostic Tests." *American Journal of Public Health* 83 (7): 948–954.
Gamble, V. 1994. "The Politics of Health: Race Blindness in DC?" *Dissent* Spring:200–203.
Gibson, R. and J. Jackson. 1987. "The Health, Physical Functioning, and Informal Supports of the Black
    Elderly." *Milbank Quarterly* 65 (Suppl. 1): S421–S454.
Gurin, P., S. Hatchett and J. Jackson. 1989. *Hope and Independence: Blacks' response to Electoral and
    Party Politics*. New York: Russell Sage.
Haveman, J. 1996. "Governors' Reform Plan Ends Welfare Guarantee." *Washington Post*, February 7, 1996.
Hughes, M., and B. Hertel. 1990. "The Significance of Color Remains: A Study of Life Chances, Mate Se-
    lection and Ethnic Consciousness among Black Americans." *Social Forces* 68:1105–1120.
Jackson, J., T. Antunucci and R. Gibson. 1990. "Cultural, Racial and Ethnic Minority Influences on Aging."
    In *Handbook of the Psychology of Aging (3rd ed.)*, J. Birren and K. Schaie eds., 103–123. New York:
    Academic Press.
Jaynes, G. and R. Williams. (eds.) 1989. *A Common Destiny: Blacks and American Society*. Washington,
    D.C.: National Academy Press.
Kasper, J.D. 1986. "Health Status and Utilization: Differences by Medicaid Coverage and Income." *Health
    Care Financing Review* 7 (4):1–17.
Kreiger, N. 1990. "Racial and Gender Discrimination: Risk Factors for High Blood Pressure?" *Social Sci-
    ence and Medicine* 30:1273–1281.
Mindel, C., R. Haberstein and R. Wright. 1988. *Ethnic Families in America*. New York: Elsevier.
National Caucus and Center on Black Aged. 1987. *The status of black elderly in the United States*. A report
    for the U. S. House of Representatives Select Committee on Aging. Washington, D. C.: U. S. Govern-
    ment Printing Office.
Pauly, M., P. Danzon, P. Feldstein, and J. Hoff. 1991. "A Plan for Responsible National Health Insurance."
    Health Affairs 10:5–25.
Riley, M. 1987. "On the Significance of Age in Sociology." *American Sociological Review* 52: 1–14.
Satin, D. and F. Duhl. 1972. "Help? The Hospital Emergency Unit as a Community Physician." *Medical
    Care* 10 (3): 248–271.
Smith, R. & M. C. Thornton. 1993. "Racial Solidarity: Group Identification and Consciousness Among Older
    Black Americans." In *Aging in Black America*, J. Jackson, L. Chatters and R. Taylor, eds., 203–216.
    Newbury Park, CA: Sage.
Special Committee on Aging and Congressional Black Caucus Health Braintrust. 1991. "Profiles in Aging
    America: Meeting the Health Care Needs of the Nation's Black Elderly." Serial No. 101–29. Wash-
    ington, D.C.: US Government Printing Office.

Sullivan, L.W. 1991. "Effects of Discrimination and Racism on Access to Health Care." *Journal of the National Medical Association* 266:2674.

Taylor, R. and L. Chatters. 1988. "Patterns of Informal Support to Elderly Black Adults: Family, Friends and Church Members." *Social Work* 31: 432–438.

Thompson, T., B. Miller, L. Chiles, J. Engler, M. Leavitt, R. Romer. 1996. "Restructuring Medicaid: The Governor's Proposal." *Federal Information Systems Corporation, Federal News Service, February 21, 1996.*

Wallace, P.E. 1995. "Characteristics of Black Medical Elderly and Their Access to Postacute Care." *Journal of the National Medical Association* July 87 (7):467–72.

Weiner, J., L. Illston, and R. Hanley. 1994. *Sharing the Burden.* Brookings Institute: Washington, D.C.

White-Means, S. 1995. "Conceptualizing Race in Economic Models of Medical Utilization: A Case Study of Community-Based Elders and the Emergency Room," *Health Services Research* 30 (1): 207–223.

White-Means, S. and J. Hammond. 1993. "Health Insurance and Disability Levels of Older Black and White Women in the South." *Journal of Applied Gerontology* 12 (4):482–496.

White-Means, S. and M. Thornton. 1995. "What Cost Savings Could Be Realized By Shifting Patterns of Use from Hospital Emergency Rooms to Primary Care Sites?" *American Economic Review* 85 (2): 138–142.

White-Means, S. and M. Thornton. 1996. "Well-being Among Caregivers of Indigent Black Elderly." *Journal of Comparative Family Studies* 28 (1):109–128.

White-Means, S. and M. Thornton. 1990. "Ethnic Differences in the Production of Informal Home Health Care." *The Gerontologist* 30 (6): 758–768.

Williams, D.R. and A.M. Chung. 1995. "Racism and Health." In *Health in Black America* edited by R. Gibson and J. Jackson. Newbury Park, CA: Sage Publications.

Williams, D., R. Lavizzo-Mourey, ?? Warren. 1994. "The Concept of Race and Health Status in America." *Public Health Reports* 109 (1):26–41.

Wilson-Ford, V. 1990. "Poverty among Black Elderly Women." *Journal of Women and Aging* 2:5–20.

Wolfe, J. 1993. The Coming Health Crisis: Who Will Pay for Care for the Aged in the Twenty- first Century? *: Chicago: University of Chicago Press.*

Part IV

Race, Crime, and the Neighborhood

6

RACE AND CRIME: WHAT IS THE CONNECTION?

Kwabena Gymah-Brempong

INTRODUCTION

Crime and public policy towards crime has been a topic on the minds of the U.S. electorate in recent years. Indeed the last few Congressional and Presidential elections have revolved around the issue of who can, and how best to fight crime in the nation. This is fueled by the perception that the crime rate in the U.S. is rising. While the aggregate crime rate has not increased over the last two decades, crime seems to have turned increasingly violent. While victimization rates of household crimes and personal theft crimes decreased from 1973 to 1992, the victimization rate for violent crimes has been stable since 1973, making the average crime more violent.[1] As society has perceived crime as increasing, it has spent increasing amount of resources to fight it. In 1990, all levels of governments in the U.S. spent $74.2 billion to fight crime. Not only are large amounts of resources devoted to fight crime, these resources have been increasing at a very brisk pace. Between 1979 and 1990, total expenditure on the justice system by all levels of government increased by 185.3 percent.[2] This has heightened the debate over how best to decrease crime

---

[1] See U. S. Department of Justice, *Criminal Victimization in the United States: 1973–92 Trends*, (Washington DC: Bureau of Justice Statistics, 1995).
[2] See U. S. Department of Justice, *Sourcebook of Criminal Statistics—1993*, (Washington DC: Bureau of Justice Statistics, 1994), tables 1.1 — 1.3.

in the U.S.—whether to rely solely on punishment or to include some preventive measure in public policy.

An interesting characteristic of the profile of crime statistics in the U.S. is the over-representation of African Americans in the criminal population, both as victims and as perpetrators. Arrest rates among African Americans for property crimes is about five times that of whites and African Americans are four times as likely to be victims of a violent crime as their white counterparts.[3] The over representation of African Americans in crime statistics makes public policy discussions of crime and crime control policies in the U.S. invariably involve issues of race relations. Why are African Americans over-represented in the criminal justice system? Are African Americans inherently more criminal than non-African Americans or do poor socioeconomic conditions provide an explanation for their over-representation in the criminal justice system? Are African Americans discriminated against by the police and the criminal justice system or is it the case that the over representation of African Americans in the criminal justice system is due to the different way African Americans and whites perceive the probability of arrest and punishment? Does the observed positive correlation between crime rate and the proportion of the population that is black (RACE hereafter) stem from the way the explanatory variables in crime generating functions are calculated?

This chapter uses data from Florida counties to investigate the empirical relationship between RACE and crime rates. Specifically, it investigates whether the often found positive correlation between the property crime rate and RACE in studies of criminal behavior using macrodata is robust after adjusting for racial differences in economic opportunities. The question of whether RACE *per se* or lack of economic opportunities is the significant determinant of crime is at the center of the debate over what to do about crime. If lack of economic opportunities rather than RACE is the source of criminal behavior, then public policy toward crime should focus on improving the economic conditions of all economically disadvantage groups, racial minorities included. On the other hand, if RACE *per se* is the source of criminal behavior, then short of incarcerating or exterminating the race that is criminal in nature, public policy cannot affect the crime rate. Studies such as this one can shed some light on public policy to reduce crime in the United States.

Our approach to investigating the relationship between RACE and crime is to estimate a three equation supply of crime model using aggregate data but adjusting the socioeconomic variables to reflect the extra economic disadvantages African Americans face. We then test for the significance of the coefficient of RACE in the supply of crime equation and compare it to the estimates of the traditional model. The use of aggregate data to estimate the economic model of criminal behavior is fraught with problems, such as the identification of structural parameters and biased coefficient estimates (Fisher and Nagin, 1978). However, if different data sets and methodologies produce similar results, one can have some confidence in the estimated coefficients. This study contributes to that effort. We note that we are only interested in the sign and statistical significance of the coefficient on RACE rather than in its absolute magnitude.

---

[3] See *Sourcebook of Criminal Statistics—1993*, tables 4. 17, 4. 17 and 5.23.

The rest of the chapter is organized as follows: section two reviews and discusses the results of previous research on the relationship between RACE and crime; section three introduces the model used to investigate the relationship between RACE and crime and discusses the data used for the analysis. Section four presents and discusses the statistical results while section five concludes the chapter.

REVIEW OF PREVIOUS RESEARCH

Justice Department statistics indicate that African Americans are over represented in the U.S. criminal justice system relative to their share in the population. Arrest records indicate that a disproportionately more African Americans are arrested for crimes than their white counterparts. For example, in 1991 48.3 percent and 36.4 percent of all persons arrested for property and violent crimes respectively in U.S. cities were black. This compares to a 12 percent share in the U.S. population.[4] Crime rates among black youths far exceed those of their white counterparts—-the ratio being about three to one. African Americans are also over-represented in the U.S. prison population. For example, in Florida, African Americans constitute 58 percent of the state's prison population compared to their 13.9 percent share of the population in 1993. In addition to the over-representation of African Americans in criminal justice statistics, some empirical models of criminal behavior based on aggregate data include RACE as an explanatory variable and find it to be positively and significantly related to the crime rate regardless of the methodology used and the number of deterrence and other socioeconomic variables included in the crime generating equation (Ehrlich: 1973, 1975, Swimmer: 1974, Chapman: 1976, Mathur: 1978, Sjoquist: 1973, Avio and Clark: 1978, Holtman and Yap: 1978 and Cornwell and Trumbull: 1994).[5] On the other hand, Gyimah-Brempong (1986), using aggregate data shows that RACE *per se* has no effect on criminal behavior if one correctly controls for racial differences in socioeconomic factors that determine criminal behavior.

Few studies provide an explanation, theoretical or otherwise, for the positive relationship between RACE and crime. For economists, this lack of systematic explanation is surprising since the economic model of crime is based on differences in the *choices* made by potential criminals rather than on differences in the *characteristics* of the agents or a group of agents themselves. Mathur (1978) has argued that the positive relationship between RACE and crime reflects discrimination against African Americans in the legal labor market. Unemployment statistics seem to support this explanation. However the question to be asked is why the coefficient of RACE remains positive and significant after controlling for unemployment rates in studies using aggregate data. Swimmer (1974) argues that RACE is positively related to crime rates because it captures the effects of discrimination against African Americans (non-whites) by white law enforcement officers. The problem with

---

[4] See *Sourcebook of Criminal Statistics, 1993.*
[5] In this paper, we use crime supply and crime generating function interchangeably.

this interpretation is that it looks to the *motivation* of law enforcement officers to explain the overwhelming preponderance of African Americans in the criminal justice system. There is no way to prove the motivation of law enforcement officials. Besides, appealing to discrimination to explain the over-representation of African Americans in the criminal justice system may imply that the majority of African Americans incarcerated are falsely accused and convicted, a presumption that may be just as wrong and dangerous as the notion that "African Americans are inherently criminal." While one cannot deny the existence of racial discrimination among some law enforcement officers, can the RACE effect not be explained without recourse to guessing the intentions of law enforcement officers? Is it possible to explain this apparent racial effect using the available data without trying to second guess the motivation of law enforcement officers?

Sah (1994) provides an analysis that could, in principle, explain why the supply of offenses by African Americans is higher than that of the general population. In his analysis, differential participation in crime by different groups can be explained by differences in the *perception* of punishment probabilities. Perception of punishment probabilities is positively related to the proportion of criminals the group *observe* to be punished and negatively related to the number of criminals the group observes. If African Americans observe a lower proportion of criminals punished, then their *perceived* probability of punishment will be lower than that of the general population, hence they will commit more crimes, all other things equal; their perceived probability of punishment will be high if they observe a greater number of criminals punished hence they will commit fewer crimes. This argument implies that African Americans supply more offenses because they *perceive* a lower probability of punishment if they commit an offense. This is, however, inconsistent with the data. As indicated above, African Americans have higher arrest rates and higher incarceration rates than the general population, hence their *perceived* punishment probability should be higher. They should therefore have lower participation rates in criminal activities than the average for the population as a whole if this hypothesis is to hold for African Americans. That African Americans have higher participation rates in crime than other groups implies that all is not equal. It is also not clear why any particular group should have different perception of punishment probabilities from the average if that group is not given a differential treatment by the criminal justice system or is not faced with circumstances that are different from that of the general population.

While economists have not provided a rationale for the positive relationship often found between RACE and the crime rate, criminologists have had a long tradition of "explaining" the link between crime and RACE. Such explanations include racial differences in intelligence without regard to environmental factors (Wolfgang, Figlio, and Sellin, 1972; Herrnstein and Murray, 1994), breakdown of social organizations in the black community (Frazier, 1965), aggression to gain social acceptance (Gordon *et al.*, 1963), and differential processing of African Americans in the criminal justice system (Sellin, 1947). These studies have been discredited by modern criminological research.[6] However the criminology literature suggests that the positive correlation between crime and RACE found by studies using aggregate data is the result of covariation between RACE and other determinants of crime. It is, however, not clear why there should be a place for RACE in the crime generation equation after controlling for these other socioeconomic determinants of crime.

Studies that have used microdata to investigate the economic model of criminal behavior generally find no significant relationship between RACE and crime. Phillips and Votey (1987, 1975) and Votey and Phillips (1972) using a variety of data, find no significant correlation between RACE and crime once they control for labor market participation. Good and Pirog-Good (1987) find that black youths are less likely than white youths to engage in criminal activity when they have a job in the legal sector. Tauchen *et al* (1994), on the other hand, using microdata from Philadelphia finds a positive relationship between RACE and arrest after adjusting for socioeconomic characteristics of the youth. (One should note however that arrest rates are more likely to reflect discrimination on the part of law enforcement officers rather than actual participation in crime). In studies using prison releasees, researchers have found no significant correlation between RACE and recidivism once employment opportunities and incomes are considered (Myers: 1983a, Schmidt and Witte: 1984, and Witte and Schmidt: 1983). Myers (1983b) finds that black ex-prisoners are less likely than their white counterparts to recidivate given employment and income. There seems to be an agreement from a majority of these studies supporting the contention of Phillips and Votey that *"race is not a factor in determining whether an individual engages in crime ... There appears to be a labor market effect of RACE but not a criminal effect."*[7]

What is the source of the conflicting relationship between RACE and crime? The positive correlation between crime and RACE found in studies that use aggregate data may be due to the way the variables explaining criminal behavior are measured at the aggregate level. The economic approach to criminal behavior predicts that lack of economic opportunities increases the probability of criminal behavior. We refer to these lack of economic opportunities collectively as "criminal capital," for lack of a better term.[8] At the aggregate level, this criminal capital is proxied by variables such as the average unemployment rate, poverty incidence, and lack of education. However, these aggregate measures do not accurately reflect the lack of economic opportunities facing African Americans. There is no doubt that African Americans face higher unemployment rates, have higher incidence of poverty, and have lower levels of education on the average than their white counterparts and for the population as a whole. Table 6.1 shows that African Americans are three and half times as likely to be poor as whites, twice as likely to be unemployed, earn about 30 percent less than whites, and have lower levels of education than whites. In addition to high unemployment rates, African Americans also tend to have low-

---

[6] For a discussion of these theories and the criticisms thereof, see Georges-Abeyie D. (ed.), *The Criminal Justice System and Blacks* (New York: Clark Boardman, 1984).

[7] See Votey and Phillips (1987).

[8] We use the terms "criminal capital" and "socioeconomic deprivation" interchangeably.

paying unstable jobs and experience longer spells of unemployment than whites. It is interesting that while the education gap narrowed between 1980 and 1990, the other gaps did not narrow significantly.

Table 6.1. White and Black Criminal Capital.

	Unemployment Rate (%)	Median Family Income	% Family in Poverty	Less than High School	College or More
White	6.3	38,751	6.9	16.3	17.1
Black	14.3	21,161	27.8	27.5	8.4
Black/White	2.27	0.55	4.03	1.69	0.49
Ratio					
White	4.7	40,704	8.9	8.8	22.0
Black	11.3	22,866	30.9	12.3	11.3
Black/White	2.40	0.56	3.5	1.40	0.51
	Ratio				
	1980	1990			
% White Population:	85.9	84.10			
% Black Population:	11.8	12.3			

Source: US Bureau of the Census, Statistical Abstract of the United States, 1994, (114th Edition, Washington, DC, 1994).

What Table 6.1 indicates is that the aggregate criminal capital statistics used to represent a jurisdiction in studies of crime generation are not reflective of the characteristics of the economic deprivation facing African Americans in that jurisdiction. When one uses such aggregate characteristics to explain crime generation, there remains large residuals that are correlated with the proportion of the population that is black across jurisdictions. It is the effects of this residual criminal capital that RACE captures in empirical models. For example, the unemployment rate in a community is a weighted average of the unemployment rates of the various races with the weights equal to their respective shares in the population. Suppose the black unemployment rate is 20 percent and the white unemployment rate is 5 percent; suppose also that African Americans constitute 10 percent of the population while whites constitute 90 percent of the population. The average unemployment rate in this community is 6.5 percent, a figure that is closer to the white unemployment rate than the black unemployment rate and which seriously underestimates the black unemployment rate. This residual unemployment rate, above the average for the community, is likely to be correlated with RACE across space and through time.

If criminal capital is positively correlated with the supply of offenses, one would expect that groups with larger supplies of such criminal capital will supply more crime than those with smaller quantities of such criminal capital. The community wide averages will not reflect this racial differential in criminal capital. Failure to account for this residual criminal capital creates the false impression that RACE is a significant variable in explaining the supply of crime. One can reconcile the apparent conflicting results between studies of crime generating functions using micro data and those using macrodata if one adequately controls for the residual criminal capital that is correlated with RACE. Studies using microdata observe the economic disadvantage (unemployment, poverty, income, or education) of the individual directly and hence are able to distinguish between these characteristics among individuals without regard to race. Once these characteristics are accurately accounted for, RACE does not matter for criminal behavior. In studies using aggregate data, individual characteristics are not observable; only jurisdictional averages are observable. These averages tend to underestimate the disadvantages faced by African Americans. However, the resulting residual criminal characteristics are correlated with RACE across jurisdictions hence RACE picks up the effects of this criminal capital.

METHODOLOGY AND DATA

Methodology

The approach we use to investigate the effects of race on criminal behavior follows the traditional supply of crime model of Becker (1968). The crime generation equation we estimate includes RACE as one of the socioeconomic characteristics of the community. However, unlike other researchers, we adjust the other socioeconomic variables of the community to reflect the relatively higher amounts of "criminal capital" that African Americans have. We then compare the estimates of this model with a model that does not adjust for the extra socioeconomic deprivation of African Americans to judge the effects of RACE on crime rates. If after adjusting for the excess socioeconomic deprivation faced by African Americans, RACE still remains a significant factor, we conclude that race indeed has an independent influence on crime and that it should be included in crime generation functions. This approach is similar to the one adopted by Gyimah-Brempong (1986).

The economic model of criminal behavior postulates that the decision to engage in criminal activity is influenced by the probability of arrest and punishment, the severity of punishment, returns from criminal activity relative to those from legal activity, and other socioeconomic characteristics. Because arrest rates, probability of punishment given arrest, and police employment are endogenous, the model used here is a simultaneous equation model of crime generation (CRIM), the probability of arrest and punishment (ARR), and police employment (POL). As argued in the literature, the probability of arrest and punishment depend, in part, on the crime rate, police employment, and the socioeconomic characteristics of the community (X), while police employment is in turn dependent on the crime rate, police wage rate (PWAGE), and the socioeconomic characteristics of the community (Phillips and Votey, 1972; Ehrlich, 1973). Crime is in part determined by ARR, the probability of conviction given arrest (P_{cla}), the severity of punishment (S), and a host of underlying economic opportunity and socioeconomic variables (X). We estimate the following three equation simultaneous model of property crime:

$$CRIM = C_j(ARR, P_{cla}, S, \mathbf{X}, \mathbf{RSCC}),$$
$$ARR = AR(CRIM, POL, \mathbf{X}), \tag{1}$$
$$POL = POL(CRIM, PWAGE, \mathbf{X}).$$

where RSCC is a vector that includes RACE as well as residual criminal capital for African Americans. We note that not all elements of X enter each equation in (1) above. We limit the analysis to property crimes only for convenience. From the standard Becker model, we expect the coefficients of ARR, P_{cla} and S to be negative in the $CRIM$ equation while the coefficients of $CRIM$ and POL in the ARR equation are expected to be positive. If citizens respond to an increased crime rate by increasing police employment, we expect the coefficient of $CRIM$ in the POL equation to be positive.

If socioeconomic economic disadvantages are positively correlated with crime generation, then we expect the coefficients of the elements of RCSS other than RACE to be positive and significant in the crime equation. If RACE *per se* is a determinant of criminal behavior, then its coefficient will be significant in the crime equation after adjusting for the extra disadvantages faced by African Americans. On the other hand, if RACE is not an independent determinant of criminal behavior then its coefficient is expected to be insignificant in the crime equation after adjustment is made for the extra disadvantages facing African Americans. The traditional approach to estimating the economic model of criminal behavior ignores RCSS in the crime equation.

Depending on the specific element of X that enters an equation in the system, the coefficient could either be positive or negative. With the exception of RCSS, most of the variables in the model have been extensively used by researchers investigating the deterrence effects of punishment and are by now standard (Becker, 1968; Phillips and Votey, 1975; Gyimah-Brempong, 1986; Mathur, 1978; Ehrlich, 1973; Cornwell and Trumbull, 1994).

To estimate (1), one must provide specific functional forms and define variables in each equation. The economic model of criminal behavior suggests that the crime rate is influenced by deterrence, proxied here by ARR and P_{cla}, and the opportunities to earn income legally as proxied by the unemployment rate (UNEMP) and the wage rate (WAGE). We did not have data on S, hence it is not included in the empirical model we estimate below. Additional socioeconomic variables contained in the X vector include the proportion of the population that is young (YOUNG), income (INC), and an urban dummy variable (URB). These variables have been consistently used in the literature as explanatory variables in crime generation equation. We note that although percent poor (POOR) and average level of education (EDUC) indicate socioeconomic deprivation, they are highly collinear with UNEMP hence we retain only the latter variable in the crime equation. The element of RCSS vector included in the crime equation are RACE and the differential unemployment rate (UNEMPD).

We expect the coefficients of ARR and P_{cla} to be negative while the coefficients of YOUNG and UNEMP are expected to be positive. INC may have two opposing effects on the crime rate in a community. On the one hand, income may be a proxy for returns to crime since the "loot" is likely to be higher in high income jurisdictions than in low income ones and hence the coefficient is expected to be positive. On the other hand, higher income increases the opportunity cost of criminal activity, thus making income negatively correlated with criminal activity. The combined effects of these two opposing forces make the coefficient of INC indeterminate *a priori*. Also the coefficient on URB cannot be signed *a priori*.

ARR is an output of the police department hence *CRIM* and *POL* are inputs into this production function. In addition, Gyimah-Brempong (1989) has shown that socioeconomic characteristics of communities, such as INC, EDUC, and POOR should be included in the police production function as non-purchased inputs. However, these variables are highly correlated so the inclusion of all of them as explanatory variables would cause serious collinearity problems.[9] We therefore include INC as an argument in the *ARR* equation to capture the effects of these socioeconomic characteristics. Police productivity may also be influenced positively by population density (DENS), hence we include it as an additional explanatory variable. The coefficient of *POL* is expected to be positive while that of INC cannot be signed in advance. High crime rates (CRIM) imply a bigger pool of criminals for the police to arrest hence it will have a positive effect on the arrest rate. However, extremely high crime rates can swamp the police department, given capacity, hence decreasing the arrest rate. We therefore enter crime in the quadratic form by adding the square of crime (CRIM2) in the *ARR* equation.

The demand for police personnel depends on *CRIM*, the taste for police services as represented by INC and URB, the ability to pay proxied by the median value of single family homes (HOME), and the average wages of police personnel (PWAGE). However, there is a high degree of collinearity between INC and HOME so we include only HOME in the *POL* equation.[10] The coefficient of *CRIM* is expected to be positive. Communities with high property values and hence high revenues from property taxes can afford to employ more police. The coefficient of HOME is therefore expected to be positive in the *POL* equation. We expect the coefficient of PWAGE to be negative since an increase in the price of an input is expected to decrease the quantity purchased.

Neither economic theory nor the criminology literature provides any guidance as to the functional forms of these equations. For ease of interpretation of coefficients

---

[9] The Pearson correlation coefficients between INC and EDUC, INC and POOR and POOR and EDUC are .869, -.799, and .894 respectively.

[10] The Pearson correlation coefficient between INC and HOME is .914.

and following earlier research, we specify these equations in the double log form. The system of equations we estimate are presented in (2) below:

$$CRIM = \alpha_0 + \alpha_1 ARR + \alpha_2 RACE + \alpha_3 YOUNG + \alpha_4 WAGE$$
$$+ \alpha_5 UNEMP + \alpha_6 P_{cla} + \alpha_7 INC + \alpha_8 URB + \omega$$

$$ARR = \beta_0 + \beta_1 CRIM + \beta_2 DENS + \beta_3 INC + \beta_4 CRIM2 + \beta_5 POL + \xi \qquad (2)$$

$$POL = \gamma_0 + \gamma_1 CRIM + \gamma_2 PWAGE + \gamma_3 HOME + \gamma_4 URB + \omega$$

where α, β, and γ are coefficients to be estimated, while ω, ξ and μ are stochastic error terms.

The system of equations in (2) does not adjust for excess socioeconomic deprivation that African Americans face. This is the model that has been estimated by earlier researchers. We refer to this model as the "traditional" model. Our objective in this study is to investigate whether RACE has a significant effect on property crime rates after properly adjusting for excess socioeconomic disadvantage facing African Americans. To this end, we add a variable that proxies this excess socioeconomic deprivation—-excess unemployment faced by African Americans (UNEMPD)—-to the system of equations in (2). We refer to this new system of equations as the "expanded model." We compare the estimates of these two models to judge the effects of RACE on the crime rate.

Data

The endogenous variables in the model are property crime index *CRIM*, *ARR*, and *POL*. *CRIM* is measured as the FBI crime index for property crimes in a jurisdiction in a year while *ARR* is defined as the proportion of property crimes cleared by arrest. *POL* is measured as the full time equivalent of police department employment (both sworn officers and civilian) per 100,000 population in a jurisdiction in a year. The probability of conviction given arrest is generally measured as the proportion of convictions to charges filed. However, we could not obtain data to calculate this probability for most of the counties in our sample. Instead we had data on prison admissions for property crimes for each county for each year. We therefore proxy P_{cla} by the ratio of prison admissions for property crimes from each county to the number of arrests for property crimes in that county.[11] We refer to this variable as *PRISON*. The elements of X that proxy for labor market outcomes are the unemployment rate (UNEMP), the average wage rate in the county (WAGE), and police

---

[11] This may be a lower estimate of the probability of conviction given arrest since not all arrested for property crimes will be charged. It also does not consider those who are convicted but received other forms of punishment, such as fines or probation. While this may underestimate the probability of conviction given arrest, including this proxy in our model is far better than completely excluding the sanctions variable. Indeed the fit statistics are dramatically improved over a model that excluded the sanctions variable.

wage (PWAGE). PWAGE was measured as the average annual earnings of police personnel in each county. Other elements of the X vector representing socioeconomic characteristics of the community are median family income (INC), the proportion of the population that is between 14 and 24 years old (YOUNG), population density (DENSE), and the median value of a single family home in the jurisdiction (HOME). INC is measured as annual median household income in a jurisdiction while WAGE is hourly wage. All nominal variables were deflated to 1982 real values.

Variables contained in the RCSS vector are the proportion of African Americans in the jurisdiction's population (RACE) and the residual criminal capital facing African Americans (UNEMPD). The residual criminal capital variable is calculated as: UNEMPD = [UNEMP$_b$ – UNEMP]*w$_b$ where UNEMP$_b$ is the black unemployment rate, w$_b$ and is the share of African Americans in the population and all other variables are as defined above.[12] URBAN is a dummy variable that equals 1 if the county is an urban county, zero otherwise. The data are annual data for 1980 and 1990, collected from various sources. The sample consists of county level data for all the 67 counties for both years. The data for the calculation of the elements of X and RCSS were obtained from the Bureau of the Census, *Census of the United States*, 1980 and 1990. Data for the calculation of *CRIM, POL, ARR* and PWAGE were obtained from the tapes of the Florida Department of Law Enforcement (FDLE), *Crime in Florida*, (Tallahassee, FL: FDLE, 1981, 1991). Data for the calculation of PRISON were obtained from *Guidebook to Corrections in Florida: Annual Report*, 1981 and 1991, (Tallahassee, FL: Florida Department of Corrections). There were a total of 134 observations in our sample. Of these, we could not obtain complete information for two small counties for both years thus leaving us with 130 usable observations.

Summary statistics of the data are presented in Table 6.2. It is interesting to note that black unemployment and poverty rates are, on average, two and half times those of the community averages. The proportion of African Americans with less than high school education is 50 percent more than the average for the communities. These numbers are similar to those reported in Table 6.1 above and imply that the community averages of these variables seriously underestimate the economic deprivation of African Americans. If these variables are determinants of criminal behavior, then such community wide averages still leave a residual that will be picked up by RACE in a crime equation. It is interesting to note that the sample partial correlations between RACE and POORD, UNEMPD, and EDUCD are .625, .496, and .658 respectively.

---

[12] Note that this measurement implies that the analysis compares blacks to non-blacks rather than to whites.

Table 6.2. Summary Statistics Of Sample Data.

Variable	Mean	Standard Error
CRIM (per 100,000)	4,776.96	2,598.97
ARR (%)	28.06	10.99
POL (per 100,000)	180.81	50.26
POP	170,044.67	304,488.11
RACE (%)	14.41	10.37
YOUNG (%)	13.78	3.25
EDUC (%)	32.91	9.56
EDUCBLK (%)	55.53	11.09
UNEMP (%)	5.91	1.31
UNEMPBLK (%)	14.83	45.57
POOR (%)	14.70	5.59
POORBLK (%)	37.23	9.13
HOME (1982$)	38,311.22	13,486.11
INC (1982$)	14,247.65	2,912.29
URB	.6910	.4081
WAGE (82$)	5.59	.913
DENS	213.18	410.473
EDUCD	19.48	8.37
UNEMPD	7.96	42.84
POORD	19.44	7.04
PWAGE	19,178.71	1,834.72
PRISON (%)	*14.28*	*10.89*

N = 134

RESULTS

The data are for two years. It is possible that the structure of the relationships changed from one year to another. In that case, it may not be reasonable to pool the data. To test the appropriateness of pooling the data, we conducted a Chow test for structural homogeneity for the two years. With a calculated F statistic of 1.0084, we are unable to reject the null hypothesis of structural homogeneity of the equations in the two periods. We therefore pool the data for the two years. All equations in the system are over identified by both the rank and order conditions. We use the two stage least squares (2SLS) estimation procedure to estimate the system. We attempted to include county dummies to capture county fixed effects but we were only successful in the ARR equation.[13] 2SLS estimates of the traditional model are presented in Table 6.3. Column 2 presents the estimates for the *CRIM* equation, column 3 the *ARR* equation, while column 4 presents the estimates for the *POL* equation. From the regression statistics, the equations in Table 6.3 fits the data relatively well with relatively high adjusted R^2s. F statistics reject the null hypotheses that all coefficients in each of the three equations—-*CRIM, ARR, POL*—-are jointly equal to zero at α = .01 in each case.

In the *CRIM* equation, the sign of the *ARR* coefficient is negative, relatively large and significantly different from zero at α = .01. This is in accord with theoretical expectations. We note that the estimated elasticity here is larger in absolute value than has been estimated by some researchers (Ehrlich: 1975, Avio and Clark: 1978, Sjoquist: 1973, among others). The large absolute value of this coefficient may be due to the fact that we measure crime rate as the aggregate property crime rate. Earlier researchers have generally disaggregated crimes into various components and have also included several other deterrence variables. The coefficient of PRISON is negative, relatively large, and significantly different from zero at α = .01 or better. The negative and statistically significant coefficients on *ARR* and PRISON in the *CRIM* equation provides further empirical support for the deterrence hypothesis. The coefficient of YOUNG is insignificant while that of URB is positive and significant at α = .01 indicating that urban counties have higher crime rates than their non urban counterparts.

The coefficient of UNEMP is positive and significant indicating that economic deprivation as measured by higher unemployment rates increases the incidence of property crimes across counties in Florida. The coefficient of WAGE is negative and statistically significant at α = .01. The positive coefficient of WAGE combined with the negative coefficient of UNEMP confirms the idea that economic opportunities, or lack thereof, have significant effects on the decision to engage in criminal activity. The coefficient of INC is positive and significant in the *CRIM* equation indicating that income is acting as a proxy for opportunity for the criminal—-a finding that is consistent with the results of previous research. Consistent with the results of previous research that use aggregate data (Ehrlich: 1975, Cornwell and Trumbull: 1994, Avio and Clarke: 1978, among others), the coefficient of RACE is positive, relatively large, and highly significant, suggesting a strong positive relationship between the proportion a county's population that is black and property crime rates.

---

[13] I thank the editors of this volume for this suggestion.

Table 6.3. 2SLS Estimates of Crime Equation: Traditional Model.

VARIABLE	CRIM	Coefficient Estimates ARR	POL
Constant	−4.4387 (2.835)*	—	8.2704 (2.175)
CRIM	—	.1844 (3.626)	.2714 (2.160)
CRIM2	—	−.0721 (2.537)	—
ARR	−1.6047 (3.828)	—	—
POL	—	.1911 (2.446)	—
PWAGE	—	—	−.5499 (4.884)
WAGE	−.0863 (2.018)	—	—
RACE	.3036 (3.057)	—	—
YOUNG	−.2133 (0.752)	—	—
UNEMP	.2888 (1.996)	—	—
INC	.4381 (2.168)	.2074 (1.760)	—
URB	.7885 (4.917)	—	−1.2016 (4.780)
DENS	—	.0755 (2.579)	—
HOME	—	—	.8921 (2.512)
PRISON	−.4805 (1.948)		
N	130	130	130
F	15.810	233.160	41.800
R^2	.4710	.8971**	.6090

*absolute value of 't' statistics in parentheses
**Note that this statistic is adjusted for the absence of a constant term

In the *ARR* equation, *CRIM* has a positive and statistically significant coefficient, indicating that as the crime rate increases, production of the police department increases. However, the coefficient of CRIM2 is negative and significant at $\alpha = .01$, indicating that extremely high crime rate act as a capacity overloading variable as argued by Votey and Phillips (1972). As the crime rate increases, the marginal productivity of the police department decreases, given its personnel. The coefficient of *POL* is positive and statistically significant indicating that arrest rates are positively related to police employment per capita. This implies that current efforts to increase the number of police officers on the streets in the United States will increase arrest rates. The increased arrest rates will lead to a decrease in the crime rate, all things equal. The coefficient of DENS is positive and significant, indicating that the police are more effective in making arrest in densely populated areas than in sparsely populated areas. The coefficient of INC is positive and significant at conventional levels. The significant coefficient estimate of INC is consistent with the findings that socioeconomic characteristics of communities should be treated as non purchased inputs into police production functions (Gyimah-Brempong: 1989). The results here are also consistent with the finding of Walker (1992) who finds that arrest rates in Leeds, England are highly correlated with socioeconomic deprivation, such as poverty, unemployment, and overcrowding.

In the *POL* equation, the coefficient of *CRIM* is positive and significant indicating that communities with high crime rates employ more police personnel per capita. This result is not surprising given the current concern with "the rising crime rate" in the US. The coefficient of HOME is positive and significant at $\alpha = .01$ indicating that communities with higher value homes employ more police per capita than those with lower value homes. Communities with high value properties can generate more property tax revenues and hence *can afford* to employ more law enforcement personnel per capita than those with low property values. Consistent with the theory of input demand, the coefficient of PWAGE is negative and significantly different from zero at $\alpha = .01$, indicating that higher police wages decrease the number of police personnel demanded by counties. The coefficient of URB is negative and significant at $\alpha = .01$ or better. This implies that, all things equal, per capita police employment is lower in urban counties than in rural counties. This may be due to economies of scale in police production.

Table 6.3 indicates that there is a strong positive correlation between property crime rates and the proportion of the population that is black in Florida. Does this indicate that African Americans are inherently more criminal than their non-black counterparts? If the answer to this question is negative, then what explains the strong correlation between "blackness" and property crime rate after controlling for average socioeconomic deprivation? In this section, we present an explanation for this positive correlation between RACE and property crime rate. To do so, we estimate the expanded model and compare the estimates to those of the traditional model presented in Table 6.3 above.

Coefficient estimates of the expanded model are presented in Table 6.4. As in Table 6.3, column 2 presents the estimates for the *CRIM* equation, column 3 the *ARR* equation while column 4 presents the estimates for the *POL* equation. Regression statistics indicates that the model fits the data relatively well with F-statistics indicating a rejection of the null hypothesis that all coefficients are jointly equal to zero at $\alpha = .01$ or better for each of the three equations in the system. The coefficients are of the expected signs and therefore in accord with theoretical expectation.

In the CRIM equation, the coefficient of ARR is negative, relatively large and significantly different from zero at any reasonable confidence level. As in Table 6.3, the coefficient of PRISON is negative and significant at $\alpha = .01$. The negative and significant coefficients of ARR and PRISON implies that inclusion of UNEMPD in the crime equation does not affect the validity of the strong deterrence effect we find in this study. The coefficient of WAGE is negative and significant while that of UNEMP is positive and significant. The coefficient of YOUNG is negative but statistically insignificant at the usual confidence levels. As in Table 6.3, the coefficients of INC and URB in the crime equation are positive and statistically significant at conventional levels. The variable that measures excess socioeconomic deprivation of African Americans—-UNEMPD—-has a positive and statistically significant coefficient. The coefficient of UNEMPD is particularly large relative to that of UNEMP as estimated in both Tables 6.3 and 6.4. The positive and significant coefficients of UNEMP and UNEMPD imply that the excess socioeconomic deprivation that African Americans face has a positive effect on property crime rates that is independent of the effect that average unemployment rate has on crime. The coefficient of RACE in this expanded CRIM equation is positive and a little bit higher in absolute value than its counterpart in Table 6.3. However, it is statistically insignificant at any reasonable confidence level. This suggests that the proportion of the population that is black has no significant *independent effect* on property crime rates in Florida counties after properly adjusting for socioeconomic deprivation. This estimate is consistent with the arguments advanced in section two above as well as with the results of crime studies based on micro data.

In the ARR equation, the coefficient of CRIM is positive and significant as in Table 6.3. The coefficient of CRIM2 is also negative and significant. In accordance with theoretical expectation, the coefficient of POL is positive and significant. The coefficient of INC is positive and levels in this equation. The coefficient of DENS is positive and significant as in Table 6.3. In the POL equation, the coefficients of CRIM and DENS are positive and significant at 99 percent confidence level while that of URB is negative and significant. As in Table 6.3, the coefficient of HOME is positive, relatively large, and significantly different from zero at $\alpha = .01$ or better. Again, as expected, the coefficient of PWAGE is negative and statistically significant at any reasonable confidence level.

Does the proportion of the population that is black per se have any significant impact on crime rates in Florida counties? A comparison of the estimates in Tables 6.3 and 6.4 provides an insight into this question. Statistically, there is no difference in the explanatory power of the models in Tables 6.3 and 6.4. Indeed, an F test to test the equality of the two sets of equations produce an F statistic of 0.978, leading us not to reject the null hypothesis of equality of the two sets of equations.[14] With no

---

[14] Since our interest is in the relationship between race and crime, we concentrate on comparing the crime equations in the traditional model and the expanded model.

difference in the overall explanatory power of the two sets of equations, we compare the individual coefficient estimates in the two crime equations.

In looking at the crime equations, one observes that the signs and statistical significance of almost all the variables are the same in Tables 6.3 and 6.4. In particular the coefficients of WAGE, *ARR*, YOUNG, UNEMP, INC, and URB are virtually the same in Tables 6.3 and 6.4. The small differences in the absolute magnitudes in the coefficients are not statistically significant. Although the crime equations in Tables 6.3 and 6.4 are the same and almost all the coefficient estimates in the two sets of equations are equal, there is one striking difference between the estimates in Tables 6.3 and 6.4. The coefficient of RACE in Table 6.4, although positive and slightly larger, is not statistically significant while it is positive and highly significant in Table 6.3.

The coefficients of UNEMPD is positive and statistically significant in Table 6.4. The positive and significant coefficient on this variable combined with insignificance of RACE in the expanded equation suggests that once one controls for the extra socioeconomic deprivation faced by racial minorities, RACE *per se* has no significant impact on crime rates across communities. Apparently, RACE proxies for the excess socioeconomic deprivation in studies using aggregate data but do not adjust for this excess deprivation. Once we adjust for this excess deprivation, we are able to reconcile the contradictory findings of studies based on aggregate and micro data on the effects of RACE on crime.

To further check if our interpretation of the results is valid, we re-estimated the system of equations in Table 6.4 excluding RACE from the crime equation and compared the results to the estimates in Table 6.4.[15] The calculated F statistic to test the equality of the two crime equations is 0.9862. We are unable to reject the null hypothesis that the two crime equations—-with and without RACE but both adjusting for excess socioeconomic depravation—-are statistically the same at any confidence level. Besides the F-test, the coefficient estimates in the two crime equations are practically the same. Finally, we estimated a model in which we replaced UNEMPD by a race/unemployment interaction term in the *CRIM* equation.[16] The coefficient on this interaction term was positive, relatively large, and statistically significant as was that of UNEMP. The coefficient of RACE in this equation was again statistically insignificant. We also note that none of the other coefficients in the model changed significantly.

What can we conclude from the exercise above? The calculations in this paper show that once a researcher controls for the burden of extra unemployment, the proportion of the population that is black has no significant impact on the crime rate. The often found positive correlation between the proportion of the population that is black and crime rates across jurisdiction is the result of not adjusting for the excessive socioeconomic deprivation faced by African Americans. It is this excessive socioeconomic deprivation that RACE captures in research that does not con-

---

[15] Coefficient estimates are not presented here for space considerations. They are, however, available upon request from the author.

[16] The coefficient estimates of this model are not presented for space consideration. They are, however, available upon request from the author.

trol for such effects. This result is similar to the results obtained by Gyimah-Brempong (1986). The fact that two separate data sets have produced similar results should increase our confidence in the results that RACE has no significant impact on crime rates. Our results are consistent with the conclusion of Philips and Votey (1987) that race is not a factor in crime but that there is labor market effect of race. If our interpretation of the data is correct, why do researchers not control for this excess socioeconomic deprivation and exclude RACE from their regressions? The reason may be that using RACE is easy on the researcher since he/she does not have to worry about calculating all the excess socioeconomic burden that African Americans face.

It may be argued that RACE captures all the information contained in the excess socioeconomic deprivation faced by African Americans; so in the interest of parsimony, it should be used in place of such a variable. While no essential information may be lost by the use of RACE to proxy the true underlying causes of crime, such an approach will produce misleading results, at best, with disastrous consequences for public policy towards crime. For example if such an approach concludes that RACE has a significant effect on crime, then the only way to reduce crime will be to reduce the population of the race that has a high incidence of crime or to restrict that race's interaction with the general public and with each other. This obviously may lead to discrimination against that race in law enforcement and in the criminal justice system as a whole, at best. On the other hand if careful and diligent research effort that isolate the underlying causes of crime show that economic deprivation is a major cause of crime, that some races tend to face more deprivation than the average for all races and hence are associated with higher crime rates, then policy to reduce crime will involve concerted effort to reduce the excess socioeconomic deprivation facing these races. For a better understanding of the causes of crime as well as better policy formulation and implementation, it is necessary for researchers to account for the excess socioeconomic deprivation of minority groups instead of using RACE to proxy such deprivation.

How consistent are our results to those of previous research? As indicated above, the results obtained here are similar to results obtained by Gyimah-Brempong (1986). Our results are also consistent with those of studies that use micro-data and find no significant relationship between RACE and crime. The results are, however, different from those of researchers who find a positive relationship between crime and RACE. This is in large part because these researchers do not adequately control for the socioeconomic deprivation of African Americans. Sah (1994) has argued that racial differences in criminal behavior can be explained by differences in the perception of punishment probabilities. Unless one argues that differences in socioeconomic deprivation are negatively correlated with differences in the perception of arrest and punishment, our results are not reconcilable with his model. Besides these differences, our results focus on factors that can be influenced by policy towards crime while RACE cannot be so influenced.

Herrnstein and Murray (1994) argue that criminals, on average, have lower IQs than non-criminals, and that African Americans tend to be less intelligent than the U.S. population as a whole. They argue that socioeconomic factors have nothing to do with criminal behavior. Racial differences in intelligence, they contend, goes a long way to explain the disproportionate involvement of African Americans in crime. This argument is refuted by the statistics they cite. They present statistics showing that overall IQ scores have increased for all races and the white/black cognitive ability differential has narrowed since the 1960s. The statistics presented would imply that overall crime rate and the ratio of black crime rate to white crime rate should both decrease. However, they show that not only has the overall crime rate increased since the 1960s, but the ratio of black to white crime rates has been increasing as well. This outcome is contrary to their hypothesis that crime and intelligence are inversely related. They also show that even if one controls for intelligence, educational attainment, and socioeconomic status of parents, *there is a large black/white unemployment differential that persists*. The central results of this paper is that *racial differences in socioeconomic opportunities* explain the differences in crime rates among the races. It is this racial differences in unemployment rates not explained by Herrnstein and Murray's IQ differential, we contend, that explains the racial differences in criminal activity.

One of the most powerful arguments for the economic approach to the study of crime is that it does not depend on differences among individuals or among groups to explain crime rates. It explains criminal behavior by the choices people make, given the different *choice sets* they face. In this regard, it can explain why the same person obeys the law most of the time but may commit a crime under some circumstances. If we are to believe in Herrnstein and Murray's assertion that low intelligent people commit crimes while highly intelligent people on average do not, then we will be hard pressed to explain the rash of crimes committed by CEOs of large U.S. Corporations and Wall Street tycoons in recent years. Our explanation of the correlation between RACE and crime does not depend on inferior intelligence, breakdown of social institutions in the black community, aggression, or differential processing of African Americans by the criminal justice system as the criminal justice literature (Wolfgang *et al*: 1972, Frazier: 1965, Gordon: 1963, Selling: 1947, and Herrnstein and Murray) will have us believe. Rather, our explanation relies on differences in environmental factors that affect criminal behavior. Once these differences in environmental factors are properly controlled for, the positive and significant relationship between race and crime disappears.

The implications to be drawn from our results are different from those to be drawn from Herrnstein and Murray's analysis. From the point of view of understanding criminal behavior, Herrnstein and Murray's argument implies that since intelligence is genetic (they contend), criminal behavior is genetic in nature; one is born a criminal! Our results imply that criminal behavior is the result of *choices* people make given their environment. From a public policy point of view, Herrnstein and Murray's argument imply that short of extermination or the creation of concentration camps, public policy cannot affect the crime rate. Our results, on the other, hand imply that public policy can change criminal behavior by changing the potential criminal's choice set. To us, this is a more fruitful approach to reducing the crime rate than an appeal to racial differences in intelligence which, after all, are neither objectively measurable nor humanely changeable by public policy.

Table 6.4. 2SLS Estimates of Crime Equation: Expanded Model.

Coefficient Estimates VARIABLE	CRIM	ARR	POL
Constant	−9.8686 (2.586)*	—	19.166 (2.825)
CRIM	—	.3714 (3.298)	.2714 (1.719)
CRIM2	—	−.0721 (2.537)	—
ARR	−3.0120 (5.438)	—	—
POL	—	.3591 (2.642)	—
WAGE	−.1141 (2.207)	—	—
RACE	.3262 (1.239)	—	—
YOUNG	−.1775 (0.530)	—	—
UNEMP	.3664 (2.195)	—	—
UNEMPD	3.0852 (2.612)	—	—
PWAGE	—	—	.5494 (4.884)
INC	.4923 (1.600)	.5944 (2.053)	—
PRISON	−.4668 (1.935)	—	—
URB	.7619 (4.087)	—	−1.2047 (4.780)
DENS	—	.0751 (2.583)	—
HOME	—	—	.8921 (2.512)
N	130	130	130
F	15.810	233.160	41.800
R^2	.4710	.8971**	.6090

*absolute value of 't' statistics in parentheses
**statistic adjusted for no constant term

CONCLUSION

This paper used data from Florida and a simultaneous equation model to further investigate the often found positive relationship between RACE and crime in empirical research in crime. We find that race per se, or specifically the proportion of the population that is black, has no significant effect on crime rates in Florida counties, if one adjusts for the excess socioeconomic burden that face African Americans. Our result is more consistent with the economic model of crime than the approach that just include RACE as an explanatory variable in crime generating functions. This result is consistent with the conclusion of studies that use micro data, such as those by Philips and Votey, that finds that African Americans do not have a crime problem; rather, they have a labor market problem. It is, however, contrary to the results obtained by a majority of researchers who have estimated supply of crimes equations using aggregate data. We find that the reason most empirical studies of crime find a positive and significant relationship between RACE and crime is that they do not adjust for extra economic burden borne by racial minorities.

Our findings have both research and policy implications. On the research front, it implies that researchers should go beyond the use of RACE as proxy for socioeconomic variables that have impact on crime to better understand the determinants of crime. From policy perspective, our result imply that if crime rates among minorities, and for that matter all races, are to be reduced then a concerted effort should be made to reduce the factors that affect criminal behavior, such as providing opportunities to earn a "living" income legitimately. There is no race that is inherently more criminal than other races; only environmental variables—variables that can be changed by public policy—differ across races. Since our results imply that African Americans are not inherently more criminal than non African Americans, public policy to control and reduce crime should concentrate on changing the opportunities available to African Americans. After all, these factors can be changed by public policy while RACE cannot be so changed short of extermination!

A note of caution is in order. This result has been derived from data for counties in one state—-Florida. It could be that the data is flawed or the sample is not representative. Second, the results have been derived using a relatively simple methodology. A different methodology and data set may well not support our conclusions. The results should therefore be considered exploratory. There is therefore the need to continue the research with different data sets and different methodologies. It is, after all, through such efforts that theories are built or rejected and newer and better explanations developed.

REFERENCES

Avio, K. L. and C. S. Clark. 1978. "The Supply of property Offenses in Ontario: Evidence on the Deterrent Effect of Punishment." *Canadian Journal of Economics* 11 (1):1–19.

Becker, G. 1968. "Crime and Punishment: An Economic Approach." *Journal of Political Economy* 76 (2) (March/April):169–217.

Block, M. K. and J. M. Heineke 1975. "A Labor Theoretic Analysis of the Criminal Choice." *Journal of Legal Studies* 4 (1) (January):241–247.

Chapman J. I. 1976. "An Economic Model of Crime and Police: Some Empirical Results." *Journal of Research into Crime and Delinquency* (January):48–63.

Cornwell, C. and W. N. Trumbull. 1994. "Estimating the Economic Model of Crime With Panel Data." *Review of Economics and Statistics* 76 (2) (May):360–366.

Danzinger, S. and D. Wheeler 1975. "The Economics of Crime: Punishment or Income Distribution." *Review of Social Economy* 33 (2):113–131.

Ehrlich, I. 1973. "Participating in Illegitimate Activities: A Theoretical and Empirical Investigation." *Journal of Political Economy* 81 (May-June):521–565.

_____.1975. "The Deterrent Effect of Capital Punishment: A Question of Life and Death." *American Economic Review* 63 (2):397–417.

Eide, E. 1994. *Economics of Crime: Deterrence and the Rational Offender*. Amsterdam, The Netherlands: Elsevier Science.

Fisher, F. M. and D. Nagin. 1978. "On the Feasibility of Identifying the Crime Function in a Simultaneous Model of Crime Rates and Sanction Levels." In *Deterrence and Incapacitation; Estimating the Effects of Criminal Sanctions on Crime Rates*, Blumstein A., J. Cohen, and D. Nagin, eds., 638–653. Washington DC: National Academy of Sciences.

Frazier, E. F. 1965. *The Negro in the United States*. New York: McMillan.

Goldberger, A. and C. Mansky. 1995. "Review Article: The Bell Curve by Herrnstein and Murray." *Journal of Economic Literature* 33 (June):762–778.

Good, D. H and M. A. Pirog-Good. 1987. "The Simultaneous Probit Model of Crime and Employment for Black and White Teenagers." *Review of Black Political Economy* 16 (1,2) 109–128.

Gordon, R. A., J. Short, D. S. Cartwright, and F. L. Strodtbeck. 1963. "Values and Gang Delinquency: A Study of Street Corner Groups." *American Journal of Sociology* 69:109–128.

Grogger, J. 1992. "Arrest, Persistent Youth Joblessness, and Black/White Employment Differentials." *Review of Economics and Statistics* 74 (1):100–106.

Gyimah-Brempong, K. 1986. "Empirical Models of Criminal Behavior: How Significant a Factor is Race?" *Review of Black Political Economy* 15 (Summer):27–43.

_____.1989. "Production of Public Safety: Are Socioeconomic Characteristics of Local Communities Important Factors?" *Journal of Applied Econometrics* 4:57–71.

Heineke, J. M., ed. 1978. *Economic Models of Criminal Behavior*. Amsterdam, The Netherlands: Elservier Science.

Herrnstein, R. and C. Murray. 1994. *The Bell Curve: Intelligence and Class Structure in American Life*. New York: The Free Press.

Mathur, V. K. .1978. "Economics of Crime: An Investigation of the Deterrence Hypothesis for Urban Areas." *Review of Economics and Statistics* 60 (3):459–456.

Montmarquette, C. and M. Nerlove .1985. "Deterrence and Delinquency: An Analysis of Individual Data." *Journal of Quantitative Criminology* 1 (March):37–58.

Myers, Jr., S. L. 1987. "Introduction." *Review of Black Political Economy* 16 (1,2):1–15.

_____. 1983a. "Racial Differences in Post-Prison Employment." *Social Science Quarterly* 64 (3) (September):655–669.

_____. 1983b. "Estimating the Economic Model of Crime: Employment Versus Punishment Effects." *Quarterly Journal of Economics* 98 (September):157–166.

Phillips, L. and H. L. Votey. 1987. "Rational Choice Models of Crimes by Youth." *Review of Black Political Economy* 16 (1,2):129–187.

_____. 1975. "Crime Control in California." *Journal of Legal Studies* 4 (2):327–350.

Richards, P. and C. R. Title .1982. "Socioeconomic Status and Perceptions of Personal Arrest Probabilities." *Criminology* 20 (November):329–346.

Sah, R. K. 1994. "Social Osmosis and Patterns of Crime." *Journal of Political Economy* 99 (6): 1272–1295.

Schmidt, P and A. D. Witte .1980. *An Economic Analysis of Crime and Justice: Theory, Methods, and Applications*. New York: Academic Press.

Sellin T. 1928. "The Negro Criminal: A Statistical Note." *Annals of the American Academy of Political Social Sciences* 140:52–64.

Sjoquist, D. 1973. "Property Crime and Economic Behavior: Some Empirical Results." *American Economic Review* 63 (3):439–446.

Swimmer, E. E. 1974. "Measurement of the Effectiveness of Urban Law Enforcement: A Simultaneous Approach." *Southern Economic Journal* 40 (April):618–630.

Tauchen, H., A. D. Witte, and H. Griesinger. 1994. "Criminal Deterrence: Revisiting the Issue with a Birth Cohort." *Review of Economics and Statistics* 76 (3) (August):399–412.

Votey, H. and L. Phillips. 1972. "Police Effectiveness and the Production Function for Law Enforcement." *Journal of Legal Studies* 1:423–436.

Walker, M. 1992. "Arrest Rates and Ethnic Minorities: A Study in a Provincial City." *Journal of the Royal Statistical Society, Series A* 155 (2):259–279.

Witte, A. D. 1980. "Estimating the Economic Model of Crime With Individual Data." *Quarterly Journal of Economics* 95 (February):57–84.

Wolfgang, M., F. M. Figlio, and T. Sellin. 1972. *Delinquency in a Birth Cohort.* Chicago: University of Chicago Press.

7

WHY DOES RACE MATTER IN HOUSING AND CREDIT MARKETS? CURRENT RESEARCH AND FUTURE DIRECTIONS

Gary A. Dymski

> US experience suggests ... it is immensely difficult to confine the anti-discrimination principle to the individualist legal and political context from which it is proclaimed; and that the effort to protect individuals against discrimination leads with what seems like inevitability to arguments concerning collective rights of racial and other sub-groups.
>
> —Lance Liebman (1983: 12–13)

> Eventually, even the definition of discrimination comes to mean different things to blacks and whites.
>
> —Derrick Bell (1980: 658)

INTRODUCTION

For the past two decades, an academic and policy debate has raged over racial discrimination and redlining in US credit and housing markets. A substantial body of research has not resolved the core questions in this debate: Does race matter, how much does it matter, and what should public policy do about it? This paper summarizes the voluminous empirical evidence and the slimmer theoretical literature, and also considers why this debate has become so public and contentious at this historical moment.

We find disagreement about the causes and evidence of discrimination arises largely between two views, which we term the perpetrator approach and the structural approach. In effect, researchers using these approaches define discrimination differently and have different views about the need for compensatory government intervention. Consequently, work in this area will be contentious for the foreseeable future. We go on to suggest some directions for future research, and examine some policy questions related to the research considered here.[1]

RACIAL DISCRIMINATION AND REDLINING: DEFINITIONS AND CONTEXT

Discrimination occurs whenever agents who individually share some common characteristic can complete a market transaction only at a higher cost or more stringent terms than other agents; it also occurs when agents sharing this characteristic are less likely to succeed in an uncertain market transaction (such as applying for a loan), or have less access to resources.[2]

"Redlining," in turn, occurs when a given market transaction costs more or is less likely to be approved in a geographic area with a high minority population (or in an inner-city location) than in a low minority (or suburban) area, even when differences in these areas' economic characteristics are considered. So discrimination disadvantages an agent independent of her location; redlining disadvantages agents in a location independent of their individual characteristics.

Why do researchers and policy-makers care so much in the mid-1990s about racial discrimination and redlining in housing and credit markets? Two immediate reasons are that housing and credit have been included in civil rights legislation, and that data on residential mortgage flows are readily available. Section 5 discusses some deeper causes: the withdrawal of government efforts to revitalize the inner city; and the 20–year-long attack on efforts at redressing racial inequality.

Race is a protected category under the "equal protection" doctrine and the "due process" rights included in the U.S. Constitution and its amendments. The Civil Rights Act of 1964 and its subsequent amendments clarified and extended this protection. So the Fair Housing Act of 1968 provides, in section 3605 (a):

It shall be unlawful for any person or other entity whose business includes engaging in residential real estate-related transactions to discriminate against any person in making

---

[1.] The literatures on credit and housing-market discrimination are vast and rapidly growing. This paper does not fully cover them; it refers to some of the more important papers, and refers to papers that provide additional references. Attention is largely restricted to research done by economists.

[2.] Some would substitute the phrase "other agents with identical economic characteristics" for the phrase "other agents" in this sentence.

available such a transaction, or in the terms or conditions of such a transaction, because of race. (42 U.S.C., sec. 3601–3631 (1988))

Similarly, the Equal Credit Opportunity Act (ECOA) of 1974 makes racial discrimination against loan applicants unlawful.

These civil-rights acts were among the fruit of the civil rights movement. In the early 1970's, a related movement of community-based inner-city groups was largely responsible for two laws. The Home Mortgage Disclosure Act (HMDA) of 1975 requires lenders to report the number and dollar volume of residential loans by census tract. The Community Reinvestment Act of 1977 (CRA) requires banks to meet credit needs in their entire market area.[3] When the thrift bail-out bill passed in 1989, the HMDA was amended to require more detailed reporting. As of 1990, banks must report every mortgage loan application, including the applicant's race and income and the disposition of the application.

Numerous court cases and Congressional fine-tuning have clarified the legal meaning of discrimination. In March 1994, the federal agencies responsible for punishing credit-market discrimination issued a unified policy statement incorporating these clarifications. Three types of discrimination are identified (Marsden 1994):

overt discrimination — refusing to initiate a transaction with a person of color;

disparate treatment — screening minorities more harshly than whites in application processes, or subjecting minority applications to different application processes;

disparate impact — conducting commercial practices that disproportionately harm a racial minority without being justified by a legitimate business need.

The first two elements of this list emphasize discrimination as intentional behavior. The third element refers, by contrast, to situations in which procedures that are racially neutral on their face lead to ex-post racial disparities unrelated to economic fundamentals.

These three legal categories of discrimination are generated by market processes. A market process may be termed discriminatory when it widens racial differences in access to or control of economic resources. Discriminatory economic processes fall into three categories:

1. Personal discrimination (bigotry): racially differential outcomes that are due to racial preferences unrelated to economic factors.

---

[3] The language of the Act states that lenders "have a continuing and affirmative obligation to help meet the credit needs of the local communities in which they are chartered" (para. 802(a)(3), 12 USC 1901; Title VII of Public Law 95–128, 91 Stat. 1147, Oct. 12, 1977). Squires (1992) provides an overview of the US community reinvestment movement. Fishbein (1992) discusses the purposes of the CRA thoroughly, documents the subsequent evolution of reporting requirements under HMDA, and discusses the use of HMDA data by activist community organizations.

2. Rational discrimination: racially differential outcomes which arise when agents use race or characteristics correlated with race to make valid statistical inferences about the distinct market prospects of different racial groups.

3. Structural discrimination: racially differential outcomes that arise because of identifiable economic factors associated with the agents or property involved.

Category (2) refers to outcomes based on anticipated disparities, and category (3) to those based on existing disparities. An example may clarify the difference between these two categories. Suppose whites and minorities are members of a loan pool for a limited number of loans; and suppose credit will be allocated on the basis of their current levels of wealth and their prospective levels of earned income. Minorities are subject to structural discrimination if they have lower average wealth levels than whites and are chosen less often for loans on this basis; if minority and white wealth levels are the same, minorities are subject to rational discrimination if loans are based on prospective income and minorities' average prospective incomes are lower than whites.

EMPIRICAL STUDIES OF REDLINING AND DISCRIMINATION IN THE MORTGAGE MARKET

For years, community activists have argued that banks have violated the CRA and ECOA and contributed to inner-city decline by leaving good credit risks there unfunded. Banks' defenders have responded that banks cannot afford uneconomic loans in the competitive post-deregulation era; and anyway, the market abhors a vacuum — so non-bank lenders attuned to neglected neighborhoods will keep financial markets efficient by meeting any financial needs banks no longer serve.

HMDA data have served both sides in this debate, which has had two phases, corresponding to the two levels of bank reporting since HMDA became law in 1975.

The Redlining Model

Prior to 1990, researchers could use HMDA data to construct redlining models of the form:

$$\text{Detrended mortgage flows in a given area} = f\left(\begin{array}{c}\text{Area economic variables, area} \\ \text{social variables [including race]}\end{array}\right) \quad (1)$$

Area economic variables might legitimately affect housing value, and hence mortgage flows; but if mortgage decisions are based solely on economic fundamentals, then area social variables, including neighborhood racial composition, should be insignificant. Redlining arises when area race affects loan flows, even when controlling for economic fundamentals.[4]

Three approaches have been used to establish redlining. One approach is to estimate equation (1) by census tract; in this event, redlining is inferred if higher-minority population is a negative determinant of loan flows. The first published studies of redlining using HMDA data (Ahlbrandt,1977; Hutchinson et al, 1977; and Schafer, 1978) took this approach.[5] But this is a flawed test of *neighborhood* redlining: census tracts are too small to qualify as distinct "neighborhoods," and larger communities are ignored.

A second approach corrects this problem by separating data into geographic subsets corresponding to community boundaries. Bradbury, Case, and Dunham (1989) grouped Boston's census tracts into 60 "neighborhood" areas; Shlay (1988) divided Chicago tracts into suburban, gentrified, and "neighborhood" areas. These (and many similar) studies have found that loan flows vary negatively with minority population, so minority and inner-city neighborhoods are not receiving what Shlay terms their "fair share" of mortgage credit. This approach, while it improves on the first, is susceptible to the criticism of pre-selection bias.[6]

A third approach to redlining remedies the pre-selection bias problem by using a neutral method for sorting census tracts. The well-known Atlanta study (Dedman, 1988) divided tracts into five tiers based on median income, and three distinct tiers based on minority population. A subsequent study of Los Angeles (Dymski, Veitch, and White, 1991) divided that city's census tracts into quintiles based on median income and on minority population. Both studies evaluated the sensitivity of loan flows to racial composition for each income tier separately. Both studies found dramatically lower loan flows in high-minority tracts.[7] This third method has the same flaw as the first, on a different scale: its tier groupings map spatially contiguous communities only imperfectly.

Numerous criticisms of all these models of redlining have been made. These studies do not control for whether lower loan flows in minority areas are due to lower loan demand there (Benston, 1981). Further, areas that are apparently redlined may have greater lending risks, due to greater residential turnover and a higher proportion of renters (Canner, 1981) or to market failure (Guttentag and Wachter, 1981, discussed below).[8] In effect, skeptics have viewed redlining as a

---

[4.] Mortgage flows must be detrended to remove scale effects. This is normally done in one of two ways: raw loan flows in every tract may be divided by the single-family housing stock located there; or the logarithms of loan flows can be used if the list of regressors includes single-family structures.

[5.] Early redlining studies are discussed Bradford *et al.* (1977, Part II).

[6.] Pre-selection bias arises because the suspicion that a certain geographic area is subject to redlining is not independent of the statistical test for whether it is. For example, a researcher could accuse a bank of unfairly treating neighborhood X, on the basis of data concerning loan-flow gaps in X. A variety of bank policies could generate gaps of the sort observed; finding X gaps is not sufficient to demonstrate the bank uses X as an operational variable in its decision-making process.

[7.] Both studies also supplemented HMDA data with transactions data to examine the impact of the non-bank mortgage lenders, especially mortgage companies, not covered under HMDA. In both cases, non-bank lenders did not close the lending-disparity gaps left by HMDA-reporting lenders.

[8.] Galster (1992) provides a comprehensive survey of studies that criticize the redlining model. Market failure occurs when markets fail to give the right resources to the right agents at the right prices due to one

spurious statistical result, and argued that only more complete data could determine whether what appears to be bank redlining behavior is dictated by economic factors. As Canner puts it:

> Far from being arbitrary or irrational lender behavior, redlining is the competitive market outcome of utility-maximizing households and profit-maximizing mortgage lenders. Conventional mortgage redlining is only slightly different in form from the more traditional price rationing that characterizes all competitive free markets (Canner 1981: 68).

The Mortgage Discrimination Model

Several studies in the 1970's and 1980's, including the Atlanta study cited above, obtained non-HMDA data about individual mortgage applicants and found stronger evidence of discrimination. And as of 1990, HMDA reporting requirements have required lenders to collect data on applicants. These data allow researchers to estimate reduced-form discrimination equations that incorporate more elements of demand and supply, of the form:

$$
\begin{matrix} \text{Probability of loan} \\ \text{denial for a given} \\ \text{application pool} \end{matrix} = f \begin{pmatrix} \textit{Individual} & \text{Individual} & \text{Area} & \text{Area} \\ \text{economic} & \text{social} & \text{economic} & \text{social} \\ \text{variables,} & \text{variables,} & \text{variables,} & \text{variables} \end{pmatrix}. \qquad (2)
$$

The first study of the 1990 HMDA data (Canner and Smith 1991) found that the denial rate for black applicants for conventional mortgage loans was 26.3%, the Hispanic rate 18.4%, and the white rate 12.1%. High-income blacks were approved less frequently than low-income whites. This result was controversial (see Fishbein, 1992), since it was consistent with, but did not conclusively prove, discrimination against minority loan applicants.

Subsequently, a study by the Federal Reserve Bank of Boston (Munnell et al., 1992) set new standards of rigor. Boston bank lenders provided researchers with complete access to their case files on 1990 home-mortgage applicants, allowing a full accounting of applicant creditworthiness based on the information available to banks. These authors found that African-American applicants had a 60% greater chance of loan denial than equally creditworthy whites. For many analysts and policy-makers, this result was the statistical "smoking gun" showing that banks do discriminate by race.

However, numerous critics have subsequently challenged the study's conclusions. These critiques have followed two lines of attack. First, they have pointed up methodological flaws such as coding errors, sensitivity to outlying data points, and the exclusion of factors important in bank decision-making.

---

or more impediments. For example, market-failure redlining could occur if lenders fail to make loans in an area because they believe other lenders may avoid it too.

Second, some critics have challenged the adequacy of equation (2) itself. Rachlis and Yezer (1993), following Maddala and Trost (1982), argue that a single reduced-form equation misspecifies mortgage-market behavior. Several decisions are made in a chronological sequence by applicants and lenders: the applicant selects a lender; the applicant or lender selects a specific mortgage product, the lender approves or denies the application, and then an approved applicant decides whether to accept; and after funding occurs, the borrower decides over the life of the mortgage whether to repay or default.[9] In these authors' view, only a simultaneous-equation approach can accurately depict this process. One-equation models are likely to overestimate the significance of discrimination due to partial-observability bias. No single-equation model such as (2) is adequately identified if the market processes in which it is embedded might differentially affect the comparison groups (minorities and whites). Further, discrimination may occur at any of the distinct stages of the mortgage process, not only at the application processing stage highlighted in equation (2).

Some critics (for example, Brimelow and Spenser, 1993) have argued that equation (2) is irrelevant, because rational banks make loan decisions based on expected default rates. The empirical evidence on mortgage default rates and race is ambiguous; some studies find no significant differences, while others find minority default rates to be higher.[10] If lenders practiced personal discrimination in mortgage markets, they must be forgoing good risks, and minority mortgagees should have lower default rates than white mortgagees. Since the empirical evidence does not support this conclusion, it follows, lenders are not discriminating.

Both lines of criticism have been answered. Carr and Megolugbe (1993) and Browne and Tootell (1995) counter the methodological criticisms of the Boston study point-by-point, and demonstrate that this study's central conclusion is robust.[11] Galster (1993) counters the default-rate critique; he argues if lenders do not discriminate, and if at the same time minorities face discrimination in markets other than the credit market, then minorities' ex post default rate on mortgages *should* be higher than whites'.[12] Galster assumes that "rational discrimination" is illegal; but as the discussion in Section 6 suggests, this assumption is not universally shared.

[9.]Carr and Megolugbe (1993) list the other stages in the mortgage process: market area delineation, advertising and marketing, prescreening, product steering, loan servicing and securitization.

[10.]Quercia and Stegman (1992) review this literature. One recent study which finds higher minority default rates is Berkovec et al. (1993).

[11.]Similarly, Glennon and Stengel (1994) experiment with different regression specifications, and find that this study's empirical conclusions are robust.

[12.]Berkovec et al. also test for differences in default rates by neighborhood racial composition, and find no evidence that mortgages in minority neighborhoods have higher default rates. These authors, like Galster, regard the use of higher minority default rates, when unsupported by observable borrower economic characteristics, as illegal. Ferguson and Peters (1995) use a simple model of bank lending to show that *if* minority applicants are less creditworthy on average than white applicants, then it cannot simultaneously be true that minorities both have higher default rates and higher loan denial rates -- that is, the conceptual arguments behind the two empirical attacks on the Boston study are inconsistent (given the premise of lower minority creditworthiness).

Audit Studies

The Boston Fed study sets a high standard for empirical models based on equation (2); researchers without that study's access to bank files will be hard-put to avoid the charge of omitted-variable bias. And as this discussion shows, for some economists, even well-designed regression studies showing that race affects loan decisions cannot *prove* that lenders use applicants' race in their decision-making.

Audit studies of bank behavior, by contrast, *can* demonstrate bankers' racial bias to these skeptics' satisfaction.[13] Audit studies are suited to detecting personal discrimination because they provide direct evidence and thus avoid the objection that observed racial differences are due to unobserved, unmeasured causes. No audit study completed to date has examined banks' actual loan decision processes for racial discrimination. However, pilot studies of Louisville, Chicago, and New York have examined the pre-application stage and found subtle differences in the treatment of black and white testers. Lending officers were more likely to steer, switch, or discourage minority applicants. Minorities were not given "helpful hints," as were whites; and their financial ratios, when marginal, were interpreted negatively (unlike whites').

RACIAL DISCRIMINATION IN HOUSING

Housing-market research has relied much more than credit-market research on the direct evidence of audit studies to test for overt discrimination and disparate treatment (Fishbein, 1992). The Department of Housing and Urban Development has sponsored two definitive audit studies of housing market practices, the Housing Market Practices Survey (HMPS) of 1977 and the Housing Discrimination Study (HDS) of 1989. The HMPS used paired black and white testers in 40 cities, and established audit studies as a viable research methodology; however, the HDS, which encompassed 3800 audits in 25 cities, has provided information of unprecedented depth.

Overall the HDS concluded that 53% of black renters and 59% of black homebuyers (as well as 46% of Latino renters and 56% of Latino homebuyers) experience discrimination by rental and sales agents: they are not shown available units, are shown fewer units, or are provided with less information and assistance. Further, just over 20% of both blacks and Latinos are "steered" away from white areas, higher-income areas, and higher-home-value areas. Rental and sales agents were disproportionately located in white neighborhoods, and are much more likely to recommend units in neighborhoods with higher concentrations of minority residents than the metropolitan average. Further, black- and Latino-owned units are less likely to be advertised or to be offered for open house than are white units. The

---

[13.] In an "audit" study, white and minority subjects pose as housing- and/or credit-market applicants, and then carefully record their experiences. The testers' contacts must be randomized and their experiences standardized to allow data collection. Cloud and Galster (1993) review audit studies.

comprehensive nature of the HDS, and the size of its samples, make these audit results authoritative. Clearly, many real estate agents are racially biased both in shunning minority clients and in treating the absence of black or brown residents as a locational advantage.[14]

Some indirect evidence on trends over time supplements this direct point-in-time evidence of housing discrimination. Leigh (1992) reviews housing trends from 1940 to the present. She finds that blacks' relative overexposure to unsafe or overcrowded housing conditions has fallen, and racial disparities in rent levels and in the probability of home ownership have been steadily reduced. Nonetheless, serious racial gaps in housing persist. For example, the percentage of black home owners has risen substantially; at the same time, the gap between the proportion of white and black homeowners has remained constant at approximately 20% since 1940. As Leigh notes, blacks caught up with whites' 1940 home ownership rate — in 1987 (!). Supplementing these results, Stone (1991) finds that blacks are more likely to be in unaffordable or crowded housing than are whites.

One immediate consequence of discrimination in housing markets is deepening racial segregation. Turner and Weink (1991) show that US residential segregation is higher than affordability considerations or individual preferences alone would predict; they suggest this "extra" segregation is due to discrimination in housing allocation processes.

However, what sort of discrimination may be at work is difficult to establish. For one thing, the effects of behavioral and structural factors overlap. The disparate treatment of minorities documented in the HDS reduces minority demand for housing in white areas, and decrease the minority-owned housing supply offered to whites. Overt discrimination by real-estate agents and residents increases white demand in white areas, and reduces it in mixed areas. At the same time, structural discrimination leads to fewer minorities being able to afford homes. The correlation of minority status with lower incomes, and of minority neighborhoods with lower levels of public investment — what Galster and Keeney (1991) call the "nexus of urban racial phenomena" — encourages housing-market bias against minority areas.

Leigh (1992) documents the persistence and even growth of racial segregation and isolation: despite black gains in suburbanization, the elimination of racial covenants, and the presence of fair-housing laws, racial segregation and isolation has remained stable or even deepened over time.[15] Massey and Denton (1993) argue that racial segregation, in turn, deepens structural discrimination independent of any other economic dynamics:

[14.] It should be emphasized that the HDS findings do not suggest that every white real estate agent overtly dislikes or hates minorities, or is consciously promulgating racial inequities or segregation. More subtle biases could generate the HDS results -- for example, any given real estate agent's perception of what a "good neighborhood" is may well be racially coded even if that agent does not intend to disadvantage minorities. In any event, real estate agents might counter charges they are racially biased by noting that whites have very low tolerance for integration in neighborhoods (see Massey and Denton 1993: 92–96).

[15.] The shift of some minorities to suburbs has often led to segregated suburbs, not to integrated ones; indeed, by numerous measures, minorities' geographical isolation has increased (Abramson et al. 1995).

With or without class segregation, residential segregation between blacks and whites
builds concentrated poverty into the residential structure of the black community and
guarantees that poor blacks experience a markedly less advantaged social environment
than do poor whites (1993: 125).

THE NEGLECTED HISTORICAL CONTEXT OF
REDLINING AND DISCRIMINATION ANALYSIS

The evidence reviewed in sections 3 and 4, is asymmetric. For while audit studies of
housing processes have been extensive and thorough, only fragmentary audit studies
have been conducted in credit markets. Investigations of inequities in credit markets
has rested on indirect evidence — statistical studies making use of HMDA and Census data. No such comprehensive data are collected on housing-market transactions — nor are real-estate agents bound by any equivalent of the CRA.

And what does the indirect credit-market evidence mean? Redlining studies
demonstrate disparate racial impact, which in turn suggests either overt discrimination, disparate treatment based on race, or disparate treatment based on place. In
principle (see Bell 1980), such findings should shift the burden of proof to lenders
to prove a "business necessity" for these racial gaps in credit flows. Indeed, two
mid-1970s cases found redlining to be illegal under the Fair Housing Act; and the
first class-action lawsuit was filed under ECOA and the Fair Housing Act in 1992
(Cloud and Galster 1993). Nonetheless, redlining studies have fallen out of favor.
Attention now centers on whether discrimination against individuals — not neighborhoods — occurs.

This shift in attention corresponds with the shift from the redlining model
(equation (1)) to the discrimination model (equation (2)) in empirical testing using
HMDA data. Economists engaged in this research have come to two divergent conclusions about the usefulness of equation (2). The "optimistic" view views equation
(2) as useful if it is interpreted modestly. For example, Galster (1992) praises the
(1992) Boston study as thorough, and argues that it uncovers disparate-treatment
discrimination. But Galster tempers his praise, warning that equation- (2) studies
conducted without access to bank loan files cannot detect discrimination. Omitted-
variable bias is a "fatal shortcoming," since "crucial control variables such as credit
and employment histories, indebtedness, and assets and characteristics of the property" (1992: 650) are missing.[16]

Stengel and Glennon (1995) also cautiously affirm equation- (2) studies. These
authors used four anonymous banks' loan files to construct "Boston-style" equations; they then compared this indirect evidence of disparate treatment discrimination with confidential case-file audits conducted by the Comptroller of the Currency.
They find that while differences in bank structure make it impossible to draw pre-

---

[16.]The complaints discussed above about using one-equation models to characterize the multi-market
processes implicated in discrimination are very similar to Galster's cautionary statement here.

cise conclusions from indirect evidence, regression evidence is a useful diagnostic tool for deciding when to conduct deeper inquiries into discriminatory practices.

But in a second, "pessimistic" view, equation (2) is useless for investigating discrimination into credit markets. In the most complete statement of this viewpoint, Ronald Weink (1992: 222–223) contrasts the civil rights laws that pertain, respectively, to housing and to credit:

> ... The Fair Housing Act addressed not only access to housing but consumption of housing. It is not clear that equal credit opportunity [as per the Equal Credit Opportunity Act of 1974] implies dual objectives similar to those of the Fair Housing Act. If equal credit opportunity means equality in the use (consumption) of credit, fair lending will be attained only when everyone of similar financial means ... is equally in debt. Indeed, whereas racial integration was specifically identified as a major social objective of the Fair Housing Act, credit allocation was specifically identified as *not* being a major objective of laws whose primary purpose was to ensure equal credit opportunity either to individuals (e.g., the ECOA) or to neighborhoods.

Weink concludes that regulators should use audit studies of bank procedures and bankers to detect discrimination in credit markets, because assessments based on HMDA data will have them "looking [for discrimination] in the wrong places" (227).[17] Weink (and other critics such as Lacker (1995)) find it unfair that banks must not only desist from discriminating against individuals, but also take on a social burden: making loans in impacted areas that put their profits at risk. This injunction, Weink argues, crosses the line from governmental assurance of equal opportunity to inappropriate public interference in the use of privately-owned wealth.

Weink's interpretation errs on two points, and is debatable on two other points. First, the errors: the fair housing act has *not* been used to insure racially-equal housing; and the federal law aimed at credit-market discrimination (the ECOA) differs in intent and substance from the federal law aimed at spurring reinvestment in underserved neighborhoods (the CRA).[18]

The two points on which Weink's viewpoint can be challenged are as follows. First, the notion that government should intervene in markets only to discourage or punish discrimination assumes that outcomes in these markets are (otherwise) efficient; we develop a criticism of this assumption in sections 6 and 7 below. Second, Weink assumes that all unjust race effects, redlining and discrimination included, can be traced back to intentionally racist acts committed by specific banks. Weink's view invokes what Freeman (1978) calls the "perpetrator" perspective: all racial inequalities stem from biased perpetrators; hence, if perpetrators are deterred, dis-

---

[17.] In this same paper, Weink admits he "could never quite define 'fair lending' or 'equal credit opportunity' " while serving as President Reagan's special assistant for fair lending in the office of the Comptroller of the Currency.

[18.] Weink is not the only one to confuse the two federal statutes. Lacker's article on neighborhoods and banking, for example, asserts that the CRA "was inspired by the critics' view that banks discriminate against low-income communities" (1995: 13). Indeed, Avery *et al.* (1994) point out that federal regulators of both laws have increasingly focused on detecting discrimination, not identifying "fair share" lending inequities.

crimination will disappear. The "perpetrator" perspective finds indirect evidence unsatisfactory because only direct behavioral evidence is capable of uncovering specifically discriminatory intent. In this view, the third legal category of discrimination, disparate impact, is no longer important: for if discrimination always involves an illegal act, then rigorous enforcement of overt discrimination and disparate treatment should, in principle, eliminate disparate racial impact.[19]

We now subject the perpetrator perspective to closer scrutiny. While well-suited for uncovering personal discrimination, it is poorly suited for attacking *other* types of legal and economic discrimination — disparate impact, and rational and structural discrimination, respectively.

The Historical Context

The centrality of the perpetrator perspective in current analyses is due to two factors: first, inattention to the historical and political context within which fair-housing and community reinvestment law has developed; second, the absence of an adequate theory of race effects in housing and credit markets. This section addresses the first factor; Section 6, the second.

Since the 1930s, the federal government has intervened directly in shaping urban space and in creating housing and housing-credit markets. Indeed, "market forces" in the housing and banking industries were literally created by social legislation. The federal government built public housing and freeways, and established the thrift industry to finance housing purchases. The federal visible hand was hardly benign: the Federal Housing Administration, which underwrote most single-family mortgages in the early post-war years, would not approve loans in minority or integrated areas; and most public housing built in the post-war years reinforced racial segregation.[20]

In the 1970s, President Nixon consolidated most federal urban programs into "block grants" under joint local and federal control. The Reagan Revolution took this a step further: the federal government largely withdrew from its role of bolstering housing supply by building public housing units and subsidizing new low/moderate-income units. The Reagan Administration preferred to let market forces dictate how much housing would be built at which income levels, and instead implemented a demand-side policy: low-income households were provided with vouchers they could use, in principle, to bid competitively for units in the mainstream housing market.[21]

---

[19] This perspective underlies the recent comment that "current definitions of discrimination in law and regulation are far too simplistic and vague to deal with the complex econometric issues that would be encountered should serious litigation . be focused on the problem of . testing for differential treatment" (Rachlis and Yezer 1993: 332).

[20] Further, the tax deductibility of mortgage interest has not only been the largest federal housing subsidy; but given the small numbers of Black households that own homes (64% versus 43.5% for all races in 1987, according to Leigh 1992: 17), it has disproportionately benefited white households.

[21] This demand-side approach has not, in practice, allowed lower-income households access to the mainstream housing market. Nonetheless, it has remained in place during the two subsequent presidencies. The

In this new approach, government policy must adjust to market forces: global financial integration has forced governments to dismantle regulatory barriers and subsidies which once provided excessive — and inefficient — levels of social housing and credit. Deregulation and reduced public expenditures for subsidized housing and social programs merely give free scope to market forces that cannot be resisted.[22]

So the federal government has shifted from a supply-side strategy aimed at overcoming deficiencies in market outcomes to a demand-side approach premised on the idea that markets are efficient. Public policy still aims at achieving fairness in light of Constitutional protections. But for many, fairness in the 1990's means something different from what it did in the 1960's. In the 1960's, achieving fairness meant eliminating inequitable conditions for minority individuals and neighborhoods; in the 1990's, achieving fairness means insuring that the market forces allocating capital and shelter select winners and losers in a racially neutral manner, *given* the pre-existing pattern of racial inequality in resources.

Shifting political forces have also affected the implementation of ECOA and the CRA over time. The ECOA is being interpreted by the conservative Reagan/Bush/Clinton Supreme Court. The CRA, whose passage in 1977 can be attributed to a community-based movement which emphasized the social responsibility of banks, has been implemented by regulatory authorities for whom market forces take precedence over corporate social responsibility. A 1982 Federal Reserve study by Canner argues that in passing the CRA, the Congress did not intend banks to change their patterns of credit allocation or compromise their safety and soundness — the implication being that the former leads to the latter.

But can we be so certain that market outcomes are efficient? And on what basis is it supposed that lending in inner-city areas might compromise bank profits? Economists normally use theoretical models to answer questions of this sort. We turn to theoretical models of race next, but find the conceptual cupboard embarrassingly bare.

THEORETICAL MODELS OF RACE EFFECTS IN HOUSING AND CREDIT MARKETS

Next to the wealth of empirical work summarized above, theoretical aspects of race effects have received surprisingly little attention. Most studies use as their starting point some version of Becker's (1971) model, which traces race effects in housing and labor markets to individual agents' racial bigotry. This model supposes that

---

1986 tax-reform act restored a supply-side housing program in the guise of a tax-credit program -- developers seeking to build lower-income units can partially finance them by selling tax credits to corporations.
[22] We should note, however, that government involvement remains crucial in the housing market, even in the "anti-government" era. While lower-income housing subsidies have been cut, over half of all "unsubsidized" housing transactions now are underwritten by the federally-chartered Federal National Mortgage Association (Fannie Mae).

some whites so dislike minorities that they will pay a premium or accept lower wages or profits to avoid dealing with minorities in home or business settings. Becker goes on to argue that discriminators themselves bear the costs of discrimination, given free entry into these markets. So discrimination will die a natural death as discriminators tire of its price; no policy intervention is needed to overcome it, just free entry into markets.

For many economists, this is a doubly satisfactory theory. First, in a simple market setting it links discrimination to perpetrators, and perpetrators' behavior to racial preferences. Second, it concludes that little or no interference in the market is needed to address this evidently "social" problem. But this story is deceptively simple: its conclusion follows only given a particular specification of preferences and markets. The effects of racial preferences depend on the relative numbers of minority and white agents, on how many are bigoted, on the freedom of market entry, and on whether market participants face transaction and/or information costs.[23]

Consider the housing market. If only *some* real-estate agents in a given area are bigoted, minority home-seekers should be able to turn to unbigoted agents for assistance, paying no penalty apart from shoe-leather costs. But if *all* real-estate agents are equally bigoted and entry into their business is costly, minorities may pay a premium for lower-quality homes. If white residents alone are bigoted, whites may pay a premium to live in areas with few minorities (Becker's case); but if racial covenants or other means of legal exclusion force all minority residents into restricted housing quarters, rents in minority areas will command a premium over those elsewhere.

Several authors have extended Becker's model to the credit market. Dymski (1995) shows that racially-neutral bankers might offer stricter credit terms to borrowers in white than in minority communities if enough whites are bigoted; but if some minorities prefer white communities, "rational" (racially neutral) bankers might protect their profits by practicing personal discrimination against *these* prospective borrowers. Hunter and Walker (1995) argue that if lenders have "cultural affinity" with white borrower applicants, but not with minority borrower applicants, their information costs with whites will be much less that with minorities, and they will make many more loans to whites than to equally creditworthy minorities.[24]

These results suggest that when market entry isn't free, when minorities as well as whites have racial preferences, or when information costs exist, discrimination costs may not be borne by bigots, and hence racial differences may not lessen over time. Further deviations from the simple market-transaction case breaks the connection between perpetrator and discriminatory outcome altogether.

---

[23] Arrow's (1971) general-equilibrium model of discrimination is much clearer than Becker's original model in exposing Becker's fundamental logic. Mason (1992) demonstrates that Becker's conclusions are inconsistent with the empirical literature when labor is fully mobil. Recently, scholars such as the editors of this volume have begun to investigate an alternative possibility -- discrimination may occur because it is profitable, even in competitive market settings (Mason 1996, 1995 and 1993; Darity 1989; Darity and Williams 1985; Williams 1991 and 1987; Williams and Kenison 1996).

[24] Strictly speaking, these authors model cultural affinity between white lenders and white borrowers, not racial antipathy between whites and minorities. However, this comes to the same thing as Becker's racial preferences, especially because cultural-affinity ties arise exogenously.

Beyond Becker's Model: The Credit Market

Informational problems can lead to redlining even when no agents are Becker-type bigots. Stiglitz and Weiss (1991) show that the asymmetric distribution of information about creditworthiness between banks and potential borrowers in white and minority communities can lead to redlining. If banks cannot distinguish good from bad individual borrowers, but know that projects in the minority community are riskier than those in the white community, they may redline the minority community to avoid excess exposure to risk.

Why will loans in the minority community be riskier? Two theoretical explanations have been proposed. The first argument, originally suggested by Guttentag and Wachter (1981), and then refined by Lang and Nakamura (1993), explains redlining as due to neighborhood externalities and information costs. The argument goes that in any community, the return on lending (or the variability of this return) depends on the total volume of lending there. Given this, lenders concentrate their lending where other lenders are making loans. The second argument, also made by Guttentag and Wachter, argues that if it is costly to gather information on individual borrowers, and if borrowers' race and economic fundamentals are correlated, lenders can "rationally" use neighborhood racial composition as a low-cost substitute for costly information-gathering.[25]

These models raise more questions than they answer: why is so little known about redlined neighborhoods, and why is the cost of collecting information there so high? What neighborhood spillovers does lending volume generate? Where do the poorer economic fundamentals of redlined neighborhoods come from? These theories leave these questions unanswered, and fail to confront the historical legacy of inequality summarized in Section 5. They offer circular explanations instead: because redlining existed before, less is known about redlined areas and returns there are more variable, so redlining exists today.

Dymski (1995) suggests some ideas about neighborhood spillovers that might cause coordination failures among lenders: refurbishment effects, wherein home sales lead to refurbishment by their new owners, enhancing the value of all homes in the neighborhood; liquidity effects, wherein home sales enhance all neighborhood homes' values by increasing these homes' liquidity; and branch spillover effects, wherein bank branches function as pure public goods in their local neighborhoods.[26] He also demonstrates the importance of intermarket linkages: given racial discrimination in the labor market (see Turner, Fix, and Struyk 1991), banks might "rationally" discriminate against minority loan applicants who are as qualified as whites, due to minority applicants' lower or more variable future earned-income levels. Discrimination could take the form of either disparate treatment of individual minority applicants or the redlining of minority neighborhoods.

[25.] This last idea is an application of the "statistical" theory of discrimination, which Arrow (1971) and others developed to explain racial screening in the labor market.

[26.] The term "coordination failure" refers to any occasion on which market processes fail to achieve outcomes that yield the highest achievable level of social welfare.

Feedback effects from the credit market to the markets for earned income, of course, are also possible, though these are not explored in this paper.

Beyond Becker's Model: The Housing Market

Economists have recently developed far more models of credit-market discrimination than of housing-market discrimination. This relative neglect is perhaps due to the emphasis on credit-market research over the past 15 years due to the debate spurred by the HMDA and the CRA, for which no direct corollaries exist.

Nonetheless, some theoretical models of housing-market discrimination were developed in the 1970's; these models continue to inform contemporary empirical housing-market audit tests. These models examine what happens when housing search is costly and white agents or residents may be racial bigots. (see Masson, 1973; Lee and Warren, 1977; Courant, 1978; and Cronin, 1982). Interestingly, these models uniformly suggest that Becker's perpetrator-pays perspective does not work in the housing market. In particular, white prejudice makes housing search costlier for minority home-seekers than for white home-seekers; thus minorities will search less, pay more, and be less satisfied, *ceteris paribus*. Yinger's (1975) model of the rental market shows that racially-neutral landlords with bigoted white residents might discriminate against minority tenants in choosing tenants — again, passing discrimination costs along to minorities.

Summary

The simple Becker model only partially describes the circumstances of discrimination in credit and housing markets. Subsequent work has shown that even the meaning of discrimination becomes very murky in the presence of intermarket linkages, complex patterns of preference, or search costs. Racial perpetrators may not pay the costs of their discrimination, whereas in Becker's model they do; in consequence, Becker's conclusion that discrimination outcomes are unstable seems unwarranted.[27]

We have also shown that non-neutral racial preferences need not be present to generate discrimination. "Rational" discrimination can arise for several reasons, taking the form of either discrimination against individuals or redlining. Debate rages over whether rational discrimination is illegal. Some authors (such as Guttentag and Wachter 1981 and, more recently, Calomiris *et al.* 1994) argue that it is not. But, in a contest between due process and economic rationality, should it be the protection against disparate treatment that gives way? We return to this question in section 10 on anti-discrimination policy. This question is of central importance there, for once we set aside the idea that all discrimination derives from non-neutral

---

[27.]We also mention in this context Schelling's game-theoretic model of racial tipping 1971 shows how static equilibria of the sort Becker theorizes can be dynamically unstable.

racial preferences, eliminating discrimination involves much more than identifying and punishing racial perpetrators.

THE PERPETRATOR PERSPECTIVE, THE STRUCTURAL PERSPECTIVE, AND DISCRIMINATION RESEARCH

The previous sections have suggested tension between two different approaches. We have identified, on one hand, the "perpetrator" approach, which defines discrimination as action, and implicitly set opposite it a structural approach, which defines discrimination as both action and circumstance. These two approaches suggest different directions for future research.

We begin with the perpetrator view. In the past there was a mismatch between theoretical models of discrimination, which centered on racial preferences (and hence racial perpetrators), and empirical studies, which were necessarily structural due to data limitations. The new HMDA data and the increasing use of audit tools have made it possible to implement empirical studies which aim more directly at identifying racial perpetrators. Four provisional conclusions about future research directions follow:

- First, the theoretical basis of discrimination has been solidly established by the preference-based models of Becker and others, and by the missing-information models of Stiglitz and Weiss and others. These models demonstrate that lending institutions are the wrong targets in studies of discrimination; the right targets are individual perpetrators of intentionally racist acts. If redlining exists, it is consistent with lender profit maximization, and more importantly it is victimless.[28]

- Second, the audit methodology used so successfully in housing-market studies should be applied extensively to the credit market, and not just to the application-evaluation stage emphasized in HMDA-based studies.

- Third, redlining (equation- (1)) studies have been rendered redundant or even misleading by discrimination (equation- (2)) studies.

- Fourth, equation- (2) studies are useful — *if* they can be conducted on the same informational basis as the recent Boston Fed study.

[28.]This conclusion will surprise no one who searches the beaches of contemporary economic theory in search of pearls of insight. The present fashion is to imagine that institutions such as banks or firms are called into being by individual agents as optimal responses to circumstances such as costly transactions, missing information and incentive incompatibility, and so on. The idea of an institution being at once an optimal and an oppressive device is too much for most theoretical edifices to contemplate; so the latter possibility is jettisoned. Only the optimal survive in theory.

Point three is fundamental for those pursuing the perpetrator approach. To see this, note that most studies conducted with the new HMDA data ignore geographic variations in lending flows, or view them as justified due to local variations in risk correlated with racial residential patterns. For example, Carr and Megolugbe characterize the "locational risk characteristic of the underlying collateral" as one of the "legitimate risk factors" in the lender's decision (1993: 280). Several studies have tried to show that the correlation between area racial composition and lending flows disappears when more variables accounting for risk and economic fundamentals are included. Perle, Lynch, and Horner (1993) use 1982 Detroit data to show while lending flows appear sensitive to area racial composition in an equation- (1) model with four variables, they no longer are in a more fully specified (11–variable) model. Schill and Wachter (1993) take this approach one step further; they use an equation-2 model with 1990 (application-level) HMDA data to study race effects in Philadelphia and Boston. They find that individual race is a consistently significant determinant of loan denial; but while neighborhood racial composition significantly determines loan denial rates in the absence of neighborhood "quality" variables, it becomes insignificant when seven neighborhood "quality" variables (including the percentage of residents on welfare) are added.

As discussed above, point four is controversial among those committed to the perpetrator perspective. For some, HMDA-based studies are so replete with estimation and model-specification problems that they are effectively useless. For example, Rachlis and Yezer write that:

> the inability to use HMDA or other mortgage flow data in single-equation reduced-form models to test for discrimination in mortgage models are well known. Unfortunately, time and effort are still devoted to such seriously flawed analysis (1993: 324)

This extremely pessimistic view is opposed by Glennon and Stengel (1994), who argue that since the controversial Boston study "represents only one study, in one city, at one point in time," it should be replicated elsewhere. But this qualified call for more Boston-type studies is itself problematic. Glennon and Stengel themselves observe that "the intense publicity and controversy generated by the release of the Boston Fed study" make it "virtually certain that such a follow-up effort will never take place" (Glennon and Stengel 1994: 36). Lenders are unlikely to cooperate as they did in Boston. It is true that researchers employed by the Federal Reserve, FNMA, and the Comptroller have access to more data on lending and bank condition than is available to the general public; but even their privileged data are not sufficiently powerful to replicate the Boston study. So to call for more HMDA-based studies — *if* they can be conducted as was the Boston study — is to suggest that the HMDA-based studies that *can* be implemented are of little value, except as diagnostic tests (as per Stengel and Glennon 1995, cited above).

A Structural Response to the Perpetrator View

These conclusions are not acceptable for scholars pursuing a "structural" approach. Point two is uncontroversial, but point one does *not* follow if the structural approach is used in lieu of the perpetrator approach; see section 8 below.

However, points three and four will not be accepted by researchers pursuing structural approaches. For one thing, the utility of redlining analysis does not depend on how well it measures personal discrimination. The idea of structural analysis is that personal and structural forms of discrimination intertwine, and all of the effects of racial disparity cannot be attributed to the former.[29]

We have already noted the oft-repeated mistake of treating redlining analysis as a crude form of disparate-treatment analysis, and the CRA as merely a restatement of ECOA. The CRA aims at assuring geographic equity in access to capital and at increasing banks' responsiveness to communities; and redlining analysis offers one measure of banks' success in achieving these goals. Neither the CRA nor redlining analysis aim at the success or failure rate of individuals, except insofar as these are treated in the aggregate. Contrary to the comments often made by researchers committed to the perpetrator view, this shared aim does not make either the CRA or redlining analysis wrong. Studies might reasonably deploy redlining analyses for some purposes, just as they might use discrimination analyses for others.

Redlining analysis is one indicator of structural discrimination, which may occur even if all parties concerned try to behave in a racially "neutral" manner. When resources and capital are not distributed in a racially neutral way, loan flows too will not be. But these resource disparities *demonstrate* the existence of structural discrimination even while they reduce the likelihood that racial differentials in loan flows are due to personal discrimination. But simply because loan differentials between racially-different geographic areas are "explained" by these areas' differing distributions of resources does not demonstrate that race is irrelevant in economic analysis. To the contrary: it points up the importance of structural racial disparities in these market dynamics. But to take the next step — to understand the generation of the structural racial disparities that "justify" racially disparate housing and lending flows — requires new models that move beyond the *ceteris paribus* assumptions deployed in most contemporary models of discriminatory behavior.

NEW DIRECTIONS FOR RESEARCH
ON RACE EFFECTS: THEORY

Economists committed to the perpetrator perspective have tried to characterize discrimination as a specific set of behaviors which can be modeled simply and isolated

---

[29.]The arguments in this section emphasize credit-market evidence. In a parallel argument to the one developed here, Clark (1993) argues that racial disparities in housing-market outcomes must be attributed to direct and indirect evidence -- that is, to personal discrimination and to racial differences in the control over resources, which we term structural discrimination.

empirically in the right circumstances with the right tools. So discrimination is a virus which causes the market mechanism to malfunction — and regulatory chemotherapy can knock it out. In the structural approach, by contrast, discrimination is understood as a multi-faceted phenomenon that resists isolation. Indeed, discrimination permeates factor markets, and some consumer markets, and influences their dynamic trajectories. Consequently, it may be closer to the truth to view race effects as fundamentally important in the very constitution of these markets. Eliminating the effects of discrimination may thus mean, in at least some cases, rebuilding some markets from the ground up. This section considers possible future directions for theoretical and empirical research based on a structural approach to discrimination.

New structural models of race effects in the credit and housing markets will proceed by replacing one or more of the simplifying assumptions used in the perpetrator and asymmetric-information models discussed above. As suggested in section 6, complex patterns of preference might be incorporated, as might search costs, richer assumptions about the character and cost of information, intermarket linkages, and explicit attention to market dynamics (as opposed to statics). So many alternative assumptions are possible that some guiding principles must be found to select the most *promising* or *interesting* combinations.

One tried-and-true principle for constructing new models of the credit or housing market is to borrow judiciously. An obvious theoretical step is to apply the idea of racial differences in search costs, worked out for the housing market, to the credit-market context. Further, insights into housing and credit-market processes may be sharpened by the adaptation of models from the development literature on market interlinkage, from the labor-market literature on discrimination, and from the emerging literature linking the psychology of perception with market outcomes under uncertainty.

We have already hinted at the importance of intermarket linkages for discriminatory outcomes: racial bias in any one interlinked market will be readily transmitted to the other, and a path-dependent trajectory launched which widens initial racial differences. Several labor-market ideas might also be fruitfully applied to credit-market settings: Black's recent work (1995) on racial differences in borrowers' return from searches for lenders; racial differences in communication styles (Lang 1986); and factor- and consumption-market segmentation (Darity 1989, discussed in Dymski 1995). It might also be useful to investigate the link between racial bias and perception. On the one hand, racial bias may generate cognitive dissonance and other perceptual biases in economic transactions; on the other, agents who are not consciously bigoted may adopt racially-biased perception as an heuristic (a coping strategy) when they are faced with excessively uncertain or complex decision environments. [30] As Arrow has suggested, there is much to be gained

---

[30.] There is a growing literature on perception and judgment in decision-making; see, for example, Arkes and Hammond (1986). The idea is that rationality in the classical sense is not possible, so agents develop a variety of coping strategies. Economists, at least, have not yet explored the literature in this area for insights into the character and implications of racial bias.

by considering further "the interaction between reality and the perceptions of it" (1971: 31).[31]

Realism

Another guiding principle for building structural models might be to use a modeling framework that is more descriptively realistic. The central theoretical models proposed for race effects treat time, information, and lending risk in very one-dimensional terms. In real-world credit markets, time, information, and lending risk are far more complex. It should not be taken on faith that the simpler treatment of these key elements does not affect the conclusions reached; this should be determined through the construction and comparison of models.

A distinguishing feature of credit and housing market transactions is the lengthy time commitment they entail, relative to other market transactions. Thus, these transactions create special problems of illiquidity and uncertainty about return. However, both the Becker and the Stiglitz-Weiss models ignore these issues, in favor of a descriptively unrealistic "one-period" framework. Further, these models assume that all information about the return distribution on lending is knowable, and that it is known by lenders. This is the assumption that makes redlining optimal in the Stiglitz-Weiss model. But is it useful and realistic to imagine that lenders know this much? After all, a 30–year mortgage taken out in 1963 on a home in, say, Baldwin Hills in Los Angeles would have matured only after two major civil uprisings, five recessions, and two major earthquakes, not to mention substantial demographic neighborhood change. Further, given that lenders' cumulative loan decisions over the years shape the kind of investment made in any neighborhood, and the change in property values and hence in owners' equity, it would seem that at least for some purposes it would be descriptively inaccurate to treat loan risk as exogenous.

Models are, of course, always purposefully unrealistic; but when unrealistic models allow the real-world conclusion that (say) redlining and/or discrimination are optimal, analytical tractability alone is not a sufficient excuse for allowing the use of any given set of assumptions. Would a different characterization of (say) lending risk alter the Stiglitz-Weiss conclusion that redlining is an optimal lender response to a risky environment? If so, then the characterization of risk that *is* chosen should be considered very carefully indeed.[32]

---

[31] While borrowing ideas to better understand race effects in credit and housing markets may be useful, the structural peculiarities of these markets necessitates some caution. For example, in transplanting the "statistical" model of discrimination to the credit or housing market we must keep in mind that whereas contract renewal is important in the labor market, it is not in the mortgage market; and debtor "effort" involves an intermarket linkage, but laborer effort does not.

[32] We should note, apropos this discussion, that asymmetric information in the well-defined sense of Stiglitz and Weiss is not strictly necessary to generate redlining. If information is incomplete (but not asymmetric) -- because, say, future outcomes are fundamentally unknowable -- then lenders may use rules of thumb and opinion which lead to the conclusion that loans in the minority community are a "worse" risk than those elsewhere. Spillover effects could validate these prejudices. The key difference from the

Micro/Macro Links

Another suggested principle for building structural models of race effects is to build
in explicit links between macroeconomic conditions and microeconomic outcomes.
Historically, minority communities have been disproportionately sensitive to the
state of the business cycle, due to the "last-hired, first-fired" nature of many jobs
held by minority workers; at the same time, deindustrialization and industrial
downsizing have reduced this sensitivity. It is thus important to understand the
transmission mechanisms that link the macro and micro levels in minority communities. It is also important to build models that incorporate more aspects of labor
processes, social infrastructure, household dynamics, and migration processes. Not
only do these factors, and more, underlay the race effects observed in credit and
housing markets; but they have been in flux, possibly with important implications
for the character and extent of discrimination in the markets of interest here. Simple
representative-agent, partial-equilibrium frameworks like those of Becker and
Stiglitz/Weiss must be augmented to allow for shifts in these conditions.[33]

Space and Race

A final suggested principle for modeling race effects is to pay considerably more
attention to their spatial dimension. The unique influence of place in the dynamic
trajectory of agents locked into specific communities has been recognized in two
literatures developed largely by sociologists and geographers. One of these is the
huge social-theoretic literature linking discrimination and housing segregation; see,
for example, Wilson (1987), Massey and Denton (1993), and Kain (1992). This
literature goes beyond the perpetrator perspective in that it investigates how racial
segregation and isolation per se reproduce and deepen economic and social inequality.[34]

The second literature emphasizing the spatial aspects of credit and housing market dynamics is the writing on "financial exclusion" (see, for example, Leyshon and
Thrift 1995 and Dymski and Veitch 1992). This line of research, still in its infancy,
emphasizes the interactions among financial intermediary market strategies, credit
flows, and race in patterns of uneven urban development. The focus here shifts from
personal or rational discrimination as a residual effect of structure, to the problem
of how the structures that comprise structural discrimination are constructed and
reproduced over time.

---

asymmetric information case is that whereas Stiglitz and Weiss' lenders redline as an optimal outcome,
lenders' redlining in the unknowable future case cannot be called "optimal" in any normative sense.
[33] This is not to say that a general-equilibrium framework should be adopted in lieu of the partial-
equilibrium models discussed above. The solution of any model requires analytical compromise. What
compromise is best in any situation depends jointly on the tools and problems at hand.
[34] Preliminary work by economists on spatial aspects of race effects has focused largely on patterns of
neighborhood change per se. Kasarda (1993) documents that inner-city neighborhoods' degree of poverty
and segregation has deepened. Galster and Mincy (1993) show that racial composition significantly affected the "changing fortunes" of urban neighborhoods.

Economists have begun to propose models that emphasize the importance of spatial spillover effects in economic relations characterized by increasing returns. Thus far, formal increasing-returns models have *not* been used to analyze the effects of racial inequality or bigotry. However, these models have the potential to powerfully demonstrate the impact of race effects on individual and community welfare. As Benabou has written, "even minor differences in education technologies, preferences, or wealth, as well as minor imperfections in capital markets, can lead to a high degree of stratification [which] makes inequality in education and income more persistent across generations" (1994: 825).

NEW DIRECTIONS FOR RESEARCH ON RACE EFFECTS: EMPIRICAL STUDIES

The power of direct (audit) evidence in discerning racial bias is not in dispute. But as sections 3 and 7 have shown, the power of tests using indirect evidence to prove the existence of discrimination has been challenged. Even pristine equation- (2) tests of discrimination have been cited for imperfections by skeptics; these criticisms have subsequently led researchers and policy-makers to set standards so high that they may be impossible to implement. So indirect evidence may be at best a diagnostic tool for uncovering discrimination, as noted above. But this is hardly an indictment. Indeed, this section will argue that the creative use of indirect evidence, and especially of HMDA data on residential lending flows, can shed light on aspects of discrimination that get overlooked in equation- (2) studies.

Uncovering the Footprints of Racial Bias

Economists who have questioned the utility of indirect evidence to establish discrimination in the application-evaluation stage have usually argued that more attention should be paid to other aspects of the loan process; see especially Galster 1992 and Cloud and Galster 1993. These proponents of the perpetrator approach then suggest that more audit studies be done of these stages: the housing search process; the appraisal process; the applicant's decision on where to apply for credit; the decision on whether to complete the application, or withdraw it; and so on.

Expanding the range of inquiry to more than the bank's reject/accept decision (captured in equation (2)) is laudatory; however, there is no reason to restrict inquiries of this sort to audit studies alone. Because the expanded HMDA data encompasses all applications and their disposition, these data can shed some light on these other stages in the loan process. For one thing, the pattern of applications itself can be examined, independent of the pattern of loan flows. In effect, a redlining-type equation like equation (1) above can be constructed, with the loan-flow dependent variable replaced by a loan-application dependent variable. It would be most instructive to compare the relative effects of economic and racial factors on the flows of applications and loans.

The power of descriptive statistics per se should not be discounted. In an interesting comparative study of this sort, Avery *et al.* (1994) find that most black-white variation in mortgage originations results from differential black-white application rates, not from differential black-white approval rates: by implication, racial differences in the denial probabilities for those who do apply may not be as statistically significant, at least in some cities, as racial differences in the probability of applying for loans at different lending institutions.[35]

Descriptive statistics can also be developed and analyzed for minority/white differences in loan withdrawal rates and in the proportion of incomplete applications. Examinations of data for Los Angeles and Riverside reveal that minority applicants are much more likely to withdraw, or to have incomplete applications. So the "gross" minority/white difference between the number of loan applications and number of loan originations is much larger than the "net" difference. This gap appears to be robust; a challenge for future research is to understand more about why it arises. Here, indeed, audit evidence might shed light on indirect evidence (and not just vice versa).

HMDA data is also useful for developing comparative analyses of loan denial and loan origination rates for individual lenders. Within a size grouping of lenders, which institutions perform better, and which worse, in handling whites' and minorities' loan applications? Which lenders, considered against a panel of their peer institutions, perform worst with respect to white/minority denial rates? Analyses of this sort may provide clues as to where audit studies are warranted.

Finally, HMDA evidence can be used to examine the geographic pattern of residential loan applications, loan withdrawals, and loan flows for white and minority borrowers. Since different geographic areas have different racial compositions, matching the racial patterns of applications and approvals with the racial pattern of prior settlements may indicate whether racial "channeling" is occurring. Preliminary evaluations of Riverside and of Los Angeles reveal that there are large racial differences in the geographic pattern of applications, and further that the pattern of loan denials is not uniform among geographic areas within any racial grouping. A probit study (Dymski and Veitch 1994) for Los Angeles on 1990–92 data indicates that both area race and individual race are significant determinants of loan flows.

[35.]We might also mention a recent study by Schill and Wachter (1995a) which uses area race creatively. These authors use 1990 Boston data to estimate an equation-(2) model. They find that lower-income borrowers are more likely to be rejected, *ceteris paribus,* when they apply for home-purchase loans in middle- and upper-income areas. They give a curious interpretation to this result -- they argue that it provides evidence against the CRA, on the following grounds: the CRA, they argue, has induced lenders to make more loans in lower-income (high-minority) neighborhoods than previously; so lenders are more likely than before to channel lower-income borrowers into loans in such neighborhoods; thus concentrating poverty and locking these borrowers into neighborhoods they might otherwise escape. As Galster (1995) notes, this interpretation forgets that the Boston data were originally used to demonstrate lenders' *unwillingness* to make loans to such borrowers. Despite the implausibility of these authors' claims, their study does indicate some of the potential for merging area and individual race effects in unified studies of questions other than whether personal discrimination occurs in the application-evaluation stage of the loan process.

The interaction of area and individual race in application processing warrants further study.

And what about other cities: are there substantially fewer minority applications for home purchase in some areas than in others, relative to the proportions of white applicants? are there particular lenders with surprisingly few minority loan applicants in particular areas, relative to the number of whites in those areas? do minority applicants have lower probabilities of loan approval in white areas, compared with minority areas? This sort of evidence does not produce the murderer in the act of committing acts of personal discrimination; but it does show the footprints of the suspects.

The Shape of Structural Discrimination

And apart from their uses in unearthing personal discrimination, indirect evidence (especially HMDA data) are well-suited for understanding structural discrimination itself — the interrelations between residence patterns, credit flows, economic activity and wealth. More insights into these interrelations may be had by more fully exploiting dicennial Census data on neighborhood housing characteristics and on the employed workforce in analyses of HMDA data. For example, the Census reports a statistic for each census tract on the number of homeowner units that have been occupied in the past few years. This statistic could be used as a measure of housing demand; HMDA data from post-1990 years could then be examined, to see how well lenders of different sorts are meeting this demand.

It will be especially useful to examine trends in Census and HMDA data over time for different neighborhood areas. HMDA data have been collected in computer-readable form since 1981; and while the population of reporting lenders has expanded over time, it may be possible to assemble time series for institutions that have consistently reported HMDA data over the period 1981–present. Two uses of time-series HMDA data come immediately to mind. First, if the arguments made above about spillovers and coordination failure in credit markets are right, lending patterns should be characterized by path dependence. And following Benabou, small differences between loan flows to areas with different racial and income characteristics should widen, over time, into large differences. In effect, much of the observed pattern of redlining may be due to complex processes of uneven development. Second, it might be possible to examine the impact of macroeconomic conditions (interest rates, recession/expansion, and so on) on the relative levels of lending flows in white and minority areas. Here again, a preliminary analysis of Los Angeles data has indicated that mortgage flows vary positively with GNP growth, and inversely with interest rate and unemployment levels.

In sum, using indirect evidence to unearth patterns of racial difference in available data is especially important, because structural discrimination would continue to generate racial difference even if personal discrimination were somehow suddenly and precipitously to end.[36]

Lending Discrimination and the Industrial Organization of the Banking System

An important new stream of research incorporates aspects of the industrial organization of banking into investigations of discrimination and/or of redlining. In an equation- (2) case study, Kim and Squires (1995) find that the approval rate for black applicants increases with the lender's percentage of minority employees, ceteris paribus. These authors suggest adding other lender characteristics as determinant variables, including branch locations, counseling availability, and bank marketing practices.

The fundamental reorganization of banking practices and the banking industry that is currently underway bears special attention. On the one hand, an ongoing merger and consolidation wave has seized the industry, as savings and loan associations have failed, merged, or been bought out by banks, and as smaller banks have been swallowed by larger competitors. This trend has been driven by intensified competition, which has also led banks to segment their customer markets: instead of offering uniform services to all depositors, banks are increasingly catering to "upmarket" deposit and loan customers, while either shedding lower-balance customers or forcing them to pay high marginal rates. Further, banks are systematically closing branches, especially in lower-income neighborhoods. Since minority communities and individuals are disproportionately found in the markets that banks are shedding, these shifts increase structural discrimination.

Another shift involves the increasing prominence of secondary markets; some lenders will only originate mortgage loans they can sell off. Secondary-market criteria may have a systematically disparate racial impact, since the wealth ratios and cash-flow measures they stress are lower for minorities than for whites.

A few studies have begun to scratch the surface of these issues. Nesiba (1995), in a study of an Indiana county, has found that mergers significantly affected credit flows and the extent of redlining in the 1985–93 period. In two studies of Los Angeles, Pollard (1996) and Dymski and Veitch (1996) find that the reorganization of bank functions and bank mergers have significantly affected credit flows and bank branch locations. And Dymski and Veitch (1994) find that area and individual race coefficients are larger (that is, indicate a higher probability of discrimination) for loans sold off to the secondary market than for other loans, in a study of 1990–92 data for Los Angeles.

[36.] That structure matters was demonstrated in an Urban Institute simulation of the effects of eliminating personal discrimination (Struyk and Turner 1986): what happened varied widely in different cities, and depended on local market conditions. That is, structure mattered, independent of preferences.

CONCLUSION AND POLICY DIRECTIONS

We have drawn a contrast between two approaches to racial discrimination in the credit and housing markets. One approach uses a narrow definition of discrimination, according to which market discrimination can be tracked down to behaviors by bigoted individuals which change with the race of the transactor. We have challenged the sufficiency of this perpetrator approach in the above sections. To reiterate: this approach ignores structural discrimination and the significance of redlining independent of personal discrimination; and it does not address the fact that personal discrimination in one period is continually converted into structural discrimination in future periods.

Here, we might suggest a more general problem concerning the internal consistency of the perpetrator approach. This view attributes racial bigotry to preferences; that is, it interprets bigotry as innate, intentional and willed. The other possibility allowed for in theory is racially neutral preferences. But many more possibilities than these might arise. For example, bigotry might be learned socially, not innate. It might be unintentional — that is, due to ignorance of others. And bigotry may *not* be willed consciously — it may arise as an unconscious, even involuntary reaction. The "some of my best friends are ..." syndrome comes immediately to mind. These cases are, however, very troublesome in terms of this view's search for wrong-doers. Who should be punished? Only those who desire to hurt others? Or those who are responsible? And how can those assigned to make these rules assure that *their own* criteria are racially neutral? In sum, many rich questions lurk beneath the surface of the seemingly simple idea of bigotry. Needless to say, the questions supplied to these questions must be applied to very complex, involved decision and search processes, involving standardized information as well as personalized contacts.

The structural approach offers an essential analytical complement to the perpetrator approach, given these limitations in the perpetrator approach. It allows an investigation of inequalities between individuals of different races and between areas with different racial compositions, even when the existence of racially bigoted motives cannot be clearly established. It also allows for the investigation of market interlinkages and of complex dynamic trajectories in which factors linked to individual and area, and to personal and structural discrimination, intertwine.

It should be emphasized that the endorsement here of the structural approach does not constitute a rejection of the perpetrator approach. In principle, the structural approach encompasses the perpetrator approach and allows for additional analytical and empirical investigations. However, adopting the structural approach is not a way of avoiding controversy. This paper has, if anything, demonstrated the truth of the comment by Bell which appears above — discrimination *does* mean different things to different people, perhaps most especially to most whites and to most minorities. This division of views is clearly seen in the tangle over policy.

Policy Debate

Given the success of the audit method, it should be possible to minimize overt discrimination and disparate treatment by aggressive enforcement, including frequent inspections and hefty penalties for violators. The key is to raise the cost to discriminators of the disparate treatment of minority customers. However, even well-intentioned, independent regulators may find it difficult to close the door on discrimination of this sort. One problem has been discussed in this section — the fuzziness in establishing just what constitutes discriminatory intent. Another problem is that disparate treatment can be motivated either by personal *or* rational discrimination, and telling the difference between the two can be difficult at best. To determine whether "rational discrimination" is illegal in a given case, as Stengel and Glennon (1995) suggest, requires regulators to make an exceedingly fine distinction: (illegal) behavior involves the differential treatment of racial groups or areas; while (legal) behavior applies a "racially neutral" standard (backed by some "business necessity"), which coincidentally generates racially non-neutral results.

Reducing structural discrimination, in turn, requires far more than the aggressive enforcement of procedural fairness. It requires nothing less than reducing racial resource differentials — through the redistribution of wealth, measures to reduce labor-market discrimination, or the redress of skill and education differentials. And if, in turn, spillovers are significant in these markets, special efforts to address the resulting coordination failure will also be required: the creation of new lending institutions for channeling loanable funds into underserved neighborhoods; coordinated efforts to concentrate lending in redlined neighborhoods; efforts to improve branch networks and make them more flexible; and experiments at bank/community cooperation.

Many researchers today agree that while the assault on personal discrimination is laudatory, any attack on structural discrimination falls beyond the pale of possibility. Certainly, catching racial perpetrators in the act — or making them afraid to act out — will reduce the scale of discrimination. But such efforts are not sufficient. As we have discussed, personal discrimination in one period turns into structural discrimination in the next period; and interactions among markets amplify discrimination in any one market into others as well. Galster (1992) describes this amplification well. He views housing and mortgage markets as a deviation-amplifying feedback system: white stereotypes and minorities' perceptions of markets feed housing-market discrimination, which feeds neighborhood and individual disparities, leading to segregation, which feeds stereotypes (and so on). Housing-market discrimination affects the mortgage market through lower appraisals; while mortgage discrimination increases residential segregation and economic inequality. In sum,

> Intentional discrimination in one market makes it unnecessary to discriminate in another by helping to promulgate objective conditions of minority inferiority that permit otherwise race-neutral rules and institutional practices to have disparate racial impacts. (1992: 641)

Of course, this "web" of intersecting effects is precisely what prompted the 1960's War on Poverty. But for the 1990's, with that war lost, the question is, what handles are there today for reversing these perverse, intertwined dynamics?

Policy advice today tends to err on the side of caution. Even in describing structural problems, some research tend to cling to the perpetrator perspective. Schill and Wachter (1995b), for example, describe intertwined neighborhood development, and then attribute it primarily to racial preferences and to government restrictions in the housing market (such as zoning laws). In effect, for some economists, structural discrimination — which is a sort of differential endowment — is not the concern of economic analysis.

The current Administration has challenged this passive view. In October 1994, new federal regulations took effect which call for bank regulators to use HMDA data in evaluating CRA and ECOA compliance.[37] This marks a major shift in regulatory policy, since CRA enforcement had previously emphasized procedural (efforts-based) over substantive (results-based) compliance. It also indicates the willingness of regulators to look at credit flows and denial probabilities per se, without ironclad evidence of personal discrimination.[38] In January 1995, President Clinton went further, by authorizing more aggressive housing compliance examinations under fair housing laws, and creating an interagency task force on fair housing issues (see *CQ Researcher,* 5 (8), February 24, 1995, pp. 171–88).

However, these policy initiatives have drawn hostile responses from conservatives in Congress and from regulators, who have urged minimal interference with "market forces" and a narrow interpretation of fair housing and fair lending laws. The use of federal powers to attack structural discrimination and the CRA itself are viewed with great hostility. Overby (1995) summarizes this antipathy presents representative arguments. In his view, the idea of "community" reinvestment is legally indefensible, as is results-based regulation; the CRA can be salvaged only by interpreting it as an instrument for insuring equality of opportunity and access, and then only when these goals do not jeopardize lenders' safety soundness. In effect, he argues that regulators have, by confusing the intent of the CRA and of fair housing/fair lending law, gotten it right all along.[39]

In sum, at this writing, the question of what constitutes discrimination in the housing and credit markets is unsettled, as is the appropriate policy framework for attacking discrimination. The last chapter on these issues will never be written, so long as civil rights law extends to the credit and housing markets. In effect, the sub-

---

[37] "Community Reinvestment Act Regulations," Federal Register, October 7, 1994, 59 FR 51232.

[38] Avery, *et al.* (1994) suggest, for example, that racial mortgage-application ratios should be used by regulators as well as racial mortgage-denial ratios in deciding what grades to assign banks, or which banks to examine more closely.

[39] The tension between safety-and-soundness regulatory criteria and civil rights to fair housing and lending has been increasing. Especially notable is the recent Department of Justice suit against the Chevy Chase Bank under civil rights law, on the grounds that this institution's branch locations unlawfully denied equal access to credit because of their racial bias. A $140 million settlement was reached before the issues could be fully argued in the court of law. However, bank regulators were clearly concerned that the Department of Justice action threatened to supersede the safety and soundness principle they use to delimit the scope of CRA enforcement.

stantive and policy debates about discrimination in the housing and credit markets are among the forums in which the character of economic opportunity in the US is being molded. This makes it all the more crucial that researchers produce models and empirical evidence elaborating more deeply the relationships among discriminatory acts, structural inequality, banking industry transformation, and outcomes in the housing and credit markets.

REFERENCES

Abramson, A. J., M. S. Tobin, and M.. VanderGoot. 1995. "The changing geography of metropolitan opportunity: the segregation of the poor in US metropolitan areas." *Housing Policy Debate* 6 (1): 45–72.

Ahlbrandt, Jr., R. S. 1977. "Exploratory research on the redlining phenomenon." *Journal of the American Real Estate and Urban Economics Association*, Winter.

Arkes, H. R. and K. R. Hammond, eds. 1986. *Judgment and decision making: an interdisciplinary reader.* Cambridge: Cambridge University Press.

Arrow, K. 1971. "The theory of discrimination." In *Discrimination in labor markets,* O. Ashenfelter and A. Rees, eds., 3–33. Princeton: Princeton University Press.

Avery, Beeson, and Sniderman. 1994. *Economic Review* of the Federal Reserve Bank of Cleveland.

Becker, G. S. 1971. *The economics of discrimination, 2nd ed.* Chicago: University of Chicago Press.

Bell, D. 1980. *Race, racism, and American law.* Boston: Little, Brown and Company.

Benabou, R. 1994. "Human capital, inequality, and growth: a local perspective." *European Economic Review* 38: 817–26.

Benston, G. 1981. "Mortgage redlining research: a review and critical analysis." *Journal of Bank Research* 12: 8–23.

Berkovec, J., G. Canner, S. Gabriel, and T. Hannan. 1994. "Race, redlining, and residential mortgage loan performance." Working Paper 94–1, Department of Finance and Business Economics, School of Business Administration, University of Southern California, January.

Black, D. A. 1995. "Discrimination in an equilibrium search model." *Journal of Labor Economics* 13 (2): 309–34.

Bradbury, K. L., K. E. Case, and C. R. Dunham. 1989. "Geographic patterns of mortgage lending in Boston, 1982–87,'' *New England Economic Review* (September/October): 3–30.

Bradford, C., and the Urban-Suburban Investment Study Group. 1977 "Redlining and disinvestment as a discriminatory practice in residential mortgage loans,'' Center for Urban Studies, University of Illinois. Washington, DC: Department of Housing and Urban Development, Office of the Assistant Secretary for Fair Housing and Equal Opportunity.

Brimelow, P. and L. Spenser. 1993. "The hidden clue." *Forbes* January 4.

Browne, L. E., and G. M. B. Tootell, 1995. "Mortgage lending in Boston — a response to the critics." *New England Economic Review* (September/October): 53–78.

Calomiris, C. W., C. M. Kahn, and S. D. Longhofer. 1994. "Housing-finance intervention and private incentives: helping minorities and the poor." *Journal of Money, Credit, and Banking* 26 (3, Part 2) (August): 634–74.

Canner, G. 1981. "Redlining and mortgage lending patterns,'' *Research in Urban Economics,* 1: 67–101.

Canner, G. 1982. "The Community Reinvestment Act and credit allocation." *Staff Studies* 117 (June). Washington, DC: Board of Governors of the Federal Reserve System.

Canner, G., and D. Smith. 1991. "Home Mortgage Disclosure Act: expanded data on residential lending." Federal Reserve Bulletin 77 (November): 863–864.

Carr, J. H., and I. F. Megbolugbe. 1993. "The Federal Reserve Bank of Boston study on mortgage lending revisited." *Journal of Housing Research* 4 (2): 277–314.

Clark, W. A.V. 1993. "Measuring racial discrimination in the housing market: direct and indirect evidence." *Urban Affairs Quarterly,* 28 (4) (June).

Cloud, C., and G. Galster. 1993. "What do we know about racial discrimination in mortgage markets?" *Review of Black Political Economy* 22 (1) (Summer): 101–120.

Courant, P. 1978. "Racial prejudice in a model of the urban housing market." *Journal of Urban Economics* 5: 329–45.

Cronin, F. J. 1982. "Racial differences in the search for housing." In *Modeling housing market search*, William A.V. Clark, ed., 81–105. New York: St. Martin's Press.

Darity, Jr., W. 1989. "What's left of the economic theory of discrimination?" In *The question of discrimination: racial inequality in the US labor market*, S. Shulman and W. Darity, Jr., eds., 335–74. Middletown, CT: Wesleyan University Press.

_____ and R. Williams. 1985. "Peddlers Forever?: Culture, Competition, and Discrimination." *Papers and Proceedings of the American Economic Review* 75 (2) (May):256–261.

Dedman, B. 1988. "The color of money." *Atlanta Constitution* May 1–4.

Dowdle, M. 1991. "The descent of antidiscrimination: on the intellectual origins of the current equal protection jurisprudence." *New York University Law Review* 66: 1165–1232.

Dymski, G. A. 1995. "The theory of credit-market redlining and discrimination: an exploration." *Review of Black Political Economy,* (Winter):37–74.

Dymski, G. A., and J. M. Veitch. 1992. "Race and the financial dynamics of urban growth: L.A. as Fay Wray." In *City of angels*, G. Riposa and C. Dersch, eds., 131–58. Kendall/Hunt Press.

Dymski, G. A., and J. M. Veitch. 1994. "Taking it to the bank: credit, race, and income in Los Angeles." In *Residential segregation: the American legacy,* R. D. Bullard, C. Lee, and J. E. Grigsby, III, eds., 150–179. Los Angeles: Center for Afro-American Studies.

Dymski, G. A., and J. M. Veitch. 1994. "Another day in the neighborhood: individual and neighborhood race effects in Los Angeles mortgage lending." unpublished, University of San Francisco.

Dymski, G. A. and J. M. Veitch. 1996. "Financial transformation and the metropolis: booms, busts, and banking in Los Angeles." *Environment and Planning A.*

Ferguson, M. F., and S. R. Peters. 1995. "What constitutes evidence of discrimination in lending?" *Journal of Finance* 50 (2) (June): 739–48.

Fishbein, A. J. 1992. "The ongoing experiment with 'regulation from below': expanded reporting requirements for HMDA and CRA." Housing Policy Debate 3 (2): 601–636.

Freeman, A. 1978. "Legitimating racial discrimination through antidiscrimination law: a critical review of Supreme Court doctrine." *Minnesota Law Review*, 62.

Galster, G. C. 1992. "Research on discrimination in housing and mortgage markets: assessment and future directions." Housing Policy Debate 3 (2): 637–683.

Galster, G. C. 1993. "The facts of lending discrimination cannot be argued away by examining default rates." *Housing Policy Debate* 4 (1): 141–6.

Galster, G. C. 1995. "A response to Schill and Wachter's 'The spatial bias of federal housing law and policy'." *University of Pennsylvania Law Review* 143 (5) (May): 1343–44.

Galster, G. C., and W. M. Keeney. 1988. "Race, residence, discrimination, and economic opportunity: modeling the nexus of urban racial phenomena." *Urban Affairs Quarterly* 24 (1): 87–117.

Galster, G. C., and S. P. Killen. 1995. "The geography of metropolitan opportunity: a reconnaissance and conceptual framework." *Housing Policy Debate* 6 (1): 7–44.

Galster, G. C., and R. B. Mincy. 1993. "Understanding the changing fortunes of metropolitan neighborhoods: 1980 to 1990." *Housing Policy Debate* 4 (3): 303–352.

Glennon, D. and M. Stengel. 1994. "An evaluation of the Federal Reserve Bank of Boston's study of racial discrimination in mortgage lending." Economic and Policy Analysis Working Paper 94–2. Washington, DC: Comptroller of the Currency, April.

Guttentag, J. M. and S. L. Wachter. 1980. "Redlining and public policy," *Monograph Series on Finance and Economics* 1. New York: Solomon Brothers Center for the Study of Financial Institutions.

Hemeryck, S., C. Butts, L. Jehl, A. Koch, and M. Sloan. 1990. "Comment: reconstruction, deconstruction and legislative response: The 1988 Supreme Court term and the Civil Rights Act of 1990." *Harvard Civil Rights-Civil Liberties Law Review*, 25: 475–590.

Hunter, W. C., and M. B. Walker, 1995. "The cultural affinity hypothesis and mortgage lending decisions." *Working Papers Series: Issues in Financial Regulation.* Research Department, Federal Reserve Bank of Chicago, July.

Hutchinson, P. M., J. R. Ostas, and J. D. Reed. 1977. "A survey and comparison of redlining influences in urban mortgage lending markets." *Journal of the American Real Estate and Urban Economics Association*, Winter.

Kain, J. F. 1992. "The spatial mismatch hypothesis: three decades later." *Housing Policy Debate* 3 (2): 333–70.

Kasarda, J. D. 1993. "Inner-city concentrated poverty and neighborhood distress: 1970 to 1990." *Housing Policy Debate* 4 (3): 253–302.

Kim, S., and G. D. Squires. 1995. "Lender characteristics and racial disparities in mortgage lending." *Journal of Housing Research* 6 (1).

Lacker, J. 1995. "Neighborhoods and banking." Federal Reserve Bank of Richmond *Economic Quarterly*, 81 (2) (Spring): 13–38.

Lang, K. 1986. "A language theory of discrimination." *Quarterly Journal of Economics* 101 (May): 363–81.

Lang, W. W. and L. I. Nakamura. 1993. "A model of redlining." *Journal of Urban Economics* 33: 223–234.

Lee, C. H. and E. H. Warren. 1977. "Rationing by seller's preference and racial price discrimination." *Economic Inquiry* 14: 36–44.

Liebman, L. 1983. "Anti-discrimination law: groups and the modern state." In *Ethnic pluralism and public policy*, N. Glazer and K. Young, eds., 11–31. Lexington Books, D.C. Heath and Company, Lexington, MA.

Leigh, W. A. 1992. "Civil rights legislation and the housing status of black Americans: an overview." In *The housing status of black Americans,* W. A. Leigh and J. B. Stewart, eds., 5–28. New Brunswick, NJ: Transaction Publishers.

Leyshon, A. and N. Thrift. 1995. "Geographies of financial exclusion: financial abandonment in Britain and the United States." *Transactions of the Institute of British Geographers*, 20: 1–31.

Maddala, G. S., and R. P. Trost. 1982. "On measuring discrimination in loan markets." *Housing Finance Review*, 1 (3): 245–266.

Marsden, M. 1994. "Board issues fair lending policy statement." *Financial Update*, Federal Reserve Bank of Atlanta, 7 (1–2) (January-June): 1–3.

Mason, P. L. 1996. "Race and Egalitarian Democracy: The Distributional Consequences of Racial Conflict." In *The Impact of Racism on White Americans*, Benjamin Bowser, ed., 68–87. Newbury Park, CA: Sage Publications, Inc.

_____. 1995. "Race, Competition and Differential Wages." *Cambridge Journal of Economics*, 19 (4) (August): 545–568.

_____. 1993. "Accumulation, The Segmentation of Labor, and Racial Discrimination in Employment." *Review of Radical Political Economics*, 25 (2) (June): 1–25.

_____. 1992. "The divide-and-conquer and employer/employee models of discrimination: Neoclassical competition as a familial effect." *Review of Black Political Economy*, 20 (4) (Spring)73–89.

Massey, D. S. and N. A. Denton. 1993. *American apartheid: segregation and the making of the underclass.* Cambridge: Harvard University Press.

Masson, R. 1973. "Costs of search and racial price discrimination." *Economic Inquiry*, 167–86.

Munnell, A. H., L. E. Browne, J. McEneaney, and G. Tootell. 1992. *Mortgage lending in Boston: interpreting HMDA Data.* Working Paper No. 92–7. Boston: Federal Reserve Bank of Boston.

Nesiba, R. F. 1995. *Deregulation and discrimination: an evaluation of the impact of bank mergers on residential mortgage lending patterns in St. Joseph County Indiana 1985–93.* Ph.D. dissertation, Department of Economics, University of Notre Dame.

Overby, A. B. 1995. "The Community Reinvestment Act reconsidered." *University of Pennsylvania Law Review* 143 (5) (May): 1431–1532.

Perle, E. D., K. Lynch, and J. Horner. 1993. "Model specification and local mortgage market behavior." *Journal of Housing Research* 4 (2): 225–244.

Pollard, J. 1995. "Financial exclusion in Los Angeles." *Environment and Planning A*.

Quercia, R. G. and M. A. Stegman. 1992. "Residential mortgage default: a review of the literature." *Journal of Housing Research* 3 (2).

Rachlis, M. B., and A. M. J. Yezer. 1993. "Serious flaws in statistical tests for discrimination in mortgage markets." *Journal of Housing Research* 4 (2): 315–336.

Reed, V. M. 1992. "Civil rights legislation and the housing status of black Americans: evidence from fair housing audits and segregation indices." In *The housing status of black Americans,* W. A. Leigh and J. B. Stewart, eds., 29–42. New Brunswick, NJ: Transaction Publishers.

Schafer, R. 1978. *Mortgage lending decisions, criteria and constraints.* Cambridge: Joint Center for Urban Studies, MIT and Harvard, December.

Schelling, T. 1971. "Dynamic models of segregation." *Journal of Mathematical Sociology* 1: 143–86.

Schill, M. H., and S. M. Wachter. 1993. "A tale of two cities: racial and ethnic geographic disparities in home mortgage lending in Boston and Philadelphia." *Journal of Housing Research* 4 (2): 245–276.

Schill, M. H., and S. M. Wachter. 1995a. "The spatial bias of federal housing law and policy: concentrated poverty in urban America." *University of Pennsylvania Law Review,* 143 (5) (May) 1285–1343.

Schill, M. H., and S. M. Wachter. 1995b. "Housing market constraints and spatial stratification by income and race." *Housing Policy Debate* 6 (1): 141–67.

Shlay, A. 1989. "Financing community: methods for assessing residential credit disparities, market barriers, and institutional reinvestment performance in the metropolis." *Journal of Urban Affairs* 11 (3): 201–23.

Squires, G. 1992. "Community reinvestment: an emerging social movement." In *From redlining to reinvestment*, Gregory Squires, ed., 1–37. Philadelphia: Temple University Press.

Stengel, M. and D. Glennon. 1995. "Evaluating statistical models of mortgage-lending discrimination: a bank-specific analysis." Economic and Policy Analysis Working Paper 95–3. Washington, DC: Comptroller of the Currency, May.

Stiglitz, J. E., and A. Weiss. 1991. "Credit ationing in arkets with mperfect nformation." In *New Keynesian conomics, Vol. II*, Gregory Mankiw and David Romer, eds., 247–276. Cambridge: MIT Press.

Stone, M. 1991. *One third of the nation.* Washington, DC: Economic Policy Institute.

Struyk, R. J., and M. A. Turner. 1986. "Exploring the effects of racial preferences on urban housing markets." *Journal of Urban Economics* 19: 131–47.

Turner, M. A., M. Fix, and R. J. Struyk. 1991. *Opportunities denied, opportunities diminished.* Urban Institute Report 91–9. Washington, DC: Urban Institute Press.

Turner, M. A., R. J. Struyk, and J. Yinger. 1991. *Housing discrimination study: synthesis.* Washington, DC: U.S. Department of Housing and Urban Development.

Turner, M. A., and R. Weink. 1991. "The persistence of segregation: contributing causes." mimeo. Washington, DC: Urban Institute.

Weink, R. 1992. "Discrimination in urban credit markets: what we don't know and why we don't know it." *Housing Policy Debate* 3 (2): 217–240.

Williams, R. 1991. "Competition, Discrimination and Differential Wage Rates: On the Continued Relevance of Marxian Theory to the Analysis of Earnings and Employment Inequality." In *New Approaches to the Economic and Social Analysis of Discrimination*, R. Cornwall and P. Wunnava, eds., 65–92. New York: Praeger.

———. 1987. "Capital, Competition, and Discrimination: A Reconsideration of Racial Earnings Inequality." *Review of Radical Political Economics.* 19 (2):1–15.

——— and R. E. Kenison. 1996. "The Way We Were?: Discrimination, Competition, and Inter-Industry Wage Differentials in 1970." *Review of Radical Political Economics* 28 (2) (June):1–32.

Wilson, W. J. 1987. *The truly disadvantaged: the inner city, the underclass, and public policy.* Chicago: University of Chicago Press.

Yinger, J. 1975. "A model of discrimination by landlords." Working Paper 259–75, Institute for Research on Poverty, University of Wisconsin - Madison, February

INDEX

Date Due

McK DUE	JUN 0 7 2004		
MCK RTD	SEP 1 6 2004		